The Student's Guide
to Successful
Project Teams

The Student's Guide to Successful Project Teams

William A. Kahn

Routledge
Taylor & Francis Group
New York   London

Psychology Press
Taylor & Francis Group
270 Madison Avenue
New York, NY 10016

Psychology Press
Taylor & Francis Group
27 Church Road
Hove, East Sussex BN3 2FA

© 2009 by Taylor & Francis Group, LLC

Printed in the United States of America on acid-free paper
10 9 8 7 6 5 4 3 2 1

International Standard Book Number-13: 978-0-8058-6184-6 (Softcover) 978-1-84169-893-9 (Hardcover)

Library of Congress Cataloging-in-Publication Data

Kahn, William A., 1959-
　　The student's guide to successful project teams / William A. Kahn.
　　　　p. cm.
　　ISBN 978-0-8058-6184-6 (pbk. : alk. paper) -- ISBN 978-1-84169-893-9 (hardback : alk. paper) 1. Group work in education—Juvenile literature. 2. Project method in teaching--Juvenile literature. I. Title.

LB1032.K26 2009
371.3'6--dc22
　　　　　　　　　　　　　　　　　　　　　　　　　　　　　　　　　　　　　　2008019690

Visit the Taylor & Francis Web site at
http://www.taylorandfrancis.com

and the Psychology Press Web site at
http://www.psypress.com

For the Team:
Dana, Noam, Eliana, Zachary (and Conga)

Contents

About the Author ix

Preface.. xi

Acknowledgments xvii

1   Dimensions of the Student Project Team 1

2   The Learning Team 23

3   Team Formation 43

4   Team Roles and Responsibilities 63

5   Influence and Decision Making 91

6   Process Improvements 115

7   Useful Conflict 137

8   Full Engagement 167

9   Final Examinations 189

Project Team Development Exercises.................................... 209

References 233

Subject Index.. 235

Author Index.. 237

About the Author

William A. Kahn is Professor of Organizational Behavior at Boston University's School of Management, where he has taught since earning his PhD in psychology from Yale University in 1987. He teaches courses on effective group dynamics, team learning, negotiations, and managing organizational change. His research focuses on relationships at work, which includes hierarchical, peer, group, and inter-group relations. He has published articles in a wide variety of academic journals, authored several books, and serves on the Editorial Board of the Journal of Management Education. For the last decade he has coordinated the Team Learning component of the School of Management's Executive MBA Program. He has received the Broderick Prize for Teaching and, twice, the General Electric Team Learning Award from Boston University's School of Management.

Preface

The student project team can be a surreal experience. Students of all ages and levels of experience—undergraduates, graduate students in professional schools and doctoral programs, executive MBAs—are summarily placed in teams and asked to complete some sort of project for their coursework. The projects might be brief, lasting a week or two, or span the length of the course itself. They might include research reports, experiments, presentations, simulated exercises, and the like. Students are asked to create reasonably well-functioning teams. They are expected to think together and create together. They are expected to discuss ideas and perspectives that might differ quite radically from one another and, in working out those differences, arrive at sophisticated understandings of different types of problems and discover creative solutions to those problems. They are expected to produce, even while they hardly know one another's skills and abilities, interests and motives, or temperaments and styles.

Most student project teams are left to their own devices. Course instructors in most disciplines are often not trained to help teams. Nor do they have the time (even if they have the inclination) to spend with students, given the amount of material they wish to cover in their classes. They assume that students will work it out as best they can. And students mostly do. Some have much more success and fun than others. They are the lucky ones, who manage to land on a team with like-minded others whose styles, motives, and personalities do not clash too much. Others are not so fortunate. They find themselves on teams that are, by turns, apathetic or split into subgroups or marked by too much conflict. This is not much fun. It also undermines greatly students' abilities to learn the material that they are meant to learn.

I wrote *The Student's Guide to Successful Project Teams* to help students make their project team experiences not just manageable, but successful. Student project teams go on journeys, and those journeys can be more or less successful. People need help when they go on journeys. They will face obstacles, as a matter of course. They can surmount these as long as they understand them for what they are and have the tools by which to navigate through or around them. That is not to say that the journey is easy. Student project teams are complicated. They have no formal structure. There is no hierarchy, no job descriptions, and no clear delineation of roles and responsibilities. Students must figure out how to make decisions, divide up work, integrate their efforts on behalf of collective products, and evaluate their work. Without clear authority structures they must figure out ways to hold one another accountable. The internal worlds of these teams are thus marked by negotiation and persuasion, shifting expectations, and difficult conversations had and avoided. Project teams can be helped, however, through prevention and intervention.

When students know something about the various phases and stages of project team development, the obstacles that they are sure to face, and ways in which to successfully overcome those obstacles, they are far more likely to avoid the more dangerous pitfalls or to rescue themselves if they stumble into them. Knowledge, in the form of concepts and stories, helps normalize the project team experience as well. When students come up against difficult moments in their project teams—and they surely will, and should—they are more likely to handle those moments effectively if they realize that they are normal rather than abnormal, and need to be clearly confronted rather than avoided out of embarrassment and anxiety. Knowledge about the nature and dynamics of project teams offers the avenue toward insight. Students can look clearly at their teams and, on the basis of knowing about the processes by which such teams get stuck and can get moving again, develop insights that lead to useful actions. This book is meant to help them gain those insights, and the tools for applying them.

This book is meant for students whose instructors use project teams as a way to enhance learning in meaningful ways. Project teams offer a way for students to apply—and thus learn more deeply—course concepts through real-world research, problem solving, strategic planning, and idea generation. The project might run through much of the course. It might occur more intensively in one section of the course, or it might be a series of smaller projects, spread throughout the course. The types of courses vary. Management courses—organizational behavior, marketing, accounting, finance, economics, operations, strategy—each offer an opportunity for such projects. Social science courses in sociology, psychology, anthropology, political science, and geography offer settings in which students can learn course concepts more deeply by applying them in meaningful ways. So, too, do basic science courses—in chemistry, biology, and physics—in which students become immersed together in deeply exploring scientific phenomena.

This book is appropriate for various courses to the extent that the project team is in some ways significant to instructors and students alike. I have discovered over the course of working with many different project teams that students will go to the trouble of trying to build a strong team when they believe that it really matters to do so. If they are asked to undertake what look to be journeys of some significance—a long sail across a wide expanse, a briefer passage across an intense stretch, or a series of challenging rapids—they are more likely to try hard to build the best ship that they can. They understand that they will need to depend on one another, and are more likely to invest in creating a strong team. If they are asked instead to just get across a small pond, they will not be so particular about the craft, paying only enough attention to its capability as they need to for a passage of little consequence. This book, then, is more useful for students who need and want their teams to be as shipshape as possible, given the journeys on which their instructors have set them.

This book is structured according to the evolution of a project team, from its formation to its dissolution. The first chapter, "Dimensions of the Student Project Team," introduces the nature of the student project team and the various ways in which students might define the success of their teams. The chapter focuses on the ways in which teams evolve, and how that evolution is driven by students' learning about how their teams work. The second chapter, "The Learning Team," focuses in some depth on how that learning process might occur. The chapter focuses on what it means to create a learning team, through processes of experimenting with ways to work more effectively together. The chapter suggests the ways in which the existence of grades can complicate such learning. It also highlights the importance of members' abilities to create trusting, open communications that allow for ongoing feedback and learning. These two initial chapters provide the foundation for the rest of the book, which charts and follows the course of a successful team from its formation to its conclusion.

The third chapter, "Team Formation," focuses on how students shift from groups of individuals into teams. It emphasizes the importance of students developing a common mission and useful structures for their team—and the difficulty of doing so in the face of potentially significant differences in agendas, needs, and commitments. The fourth chapter, "Team Roles and Responsibilities," focuses on how students organize themselves to enable their project work to be performed fairly and equitably. The issue of workload equity is a crucial puzzle for students to solve. It is made easier by having specific roles, clarified in this chapter, by which project labor is divided and meetings are facilitated. This chapter also emphasizes the nature and practice of giving feedback to help sustain effective role performances.

The fifth chapter, "Influence and Decision Making," looks directly at how students influence one another on their project teams. The chapter offers insights about how team members can assume appropriate authority over one another in ways that allow for shared responsibility—even in the face of inevitable differences in need for power and influence. The chapter also describes the various types of team decision-making processes, and the conditions under which they are most useful. The sixth chapter, "Process Improvements," addresses the ways in which project teams fall into certain patterns of work and interaction, some of which are healthy and useful, and others of which are not. Identifying these patterns—which inevitably show up in team meetings—gives students the opportunity to make choices about which patterns to keep and which to jettison or alter. The seventh chapter, "Useful Conflict," looks in some depth at the nature of conflict in project teams. The chapter focuses on how students can effectively acknowledge, respect, integrate, and learn from their differences by engaging in difficult conversations, even in the face of the anxiety and defensiveness that such differences often trigger.

The eighth chapter, "Full Engagement," addresses the issue of how truly, how fully, students are engaged in the life and work of their teams. The chapter focuses on identifying and altering patterns of team interaction that keep members from saying what they think and feel, and thereby improving the team and their own enjoyment of it. The ninth and concluding chapter, "Final Examinations," focuses on the ways in which students can end their team journey with as much learning and as much closure as possible, even in the face of their desires to avoid the difficult conversations and emotions related to endings. The chapter also offers several final lessons about the nature of project teams, insofar as they are relevant to students as they leave this course and venture into other teams in a variety of settings.

The chapters follow much the same structure. In each chapter I identify the primary issues that students are likely to experience as their project teams work together over time. Although teams vary in terms of the speed and ease with which they navigate their journeys, the issues that they are likely to face are much the same. Students should therefore read the chapters sequentially. There will, inevitably, be matters of influence and divisions of labor to settle, just as there will be unwritten rules to develop about how to manage differences and make decisions. These are the givens. In each chapter I note the various "tolls" that teams have to pay to continue along their way. The payments are made in the form of students looking carefully at the processes by which they are working together, and making the changes necessary to become more effective as a team. In each chapter I also describe the obstacles that make it difficult to pay those tolls. I offer tools useful for overcoming those obstacles. I also offer various conceptual perspectives from other writers and researchers whose work can be usefully applied. These perspectives appear in resource boxes scattered throughout the book's chapters.

Each chapter contains stories of real student project teams. Over the last 15 years I have taught project team learning programs for undergraduate, MBA, and Executive MBA students. During that time I have worked with countless student project teams. I have recorded a number of their stories in this book (with the names changed to protect confidentiality). I owe a great debt to these students; they have taught me as much as I have taught them, and the material in this book reflects their efforts.

My former students were particularly helpful in the refinement of the nine team project development exercises at the end of the book. These exercises provide structure for the conversations that students need to have at different points along their project team journeys. At the end of each chapter in the book I suggest an exercise or two that would be most helpful at that point in the team's journey. Each exercise enables students to temporarily suspend their task-related activities and reflect on their processes; the focus is not on *what* the students are doing on their projects, but on *how* they are going about that work. Every project team will have process-related issues. The exercises offer structured ways for students to resolve these issues, become clear about how they are and how they need to work together, and move into more effective work on their tasks. It is in these structured conversations that their team's journey—whatever it might look or feel like—might become normalized, made familiar and manageable. When students are able to talk about how they are working and relating, they give themselves the opportunity to learn not only the course material but about themselves, as revealed through the prism of their team journeys.

Acknowledgments

In writing this book it became clear to me the various debts I owe to those who contributed to my understanding of student project teams and what enables them to be most effective. There are, of course, the legions of students—undergraduate and graduate students, and more recently, Executive MBA students—with whom I have had the pleasure to work over the last twenty years. They have taught me a great deal about what happens at the intersection of theory and practice, and have made significant contributions to both without always being aware of doing so. My work with student teams would also most likely not have occurred outside the context of the Boston University School of Management, whose mission is very much focused on supporting teamwork. Dean Louis Lataif has been deeply committed to team learning, to the point that he helped create the School of Management's Center for Team Learning, whose directors (Jeffrey Miller, and later, Sandra Deacon) helped develop some of the ideas that made their way into this book. Senior Associate Dean Michael Lawson had the wisdom to integrate Team Learning as a central component of the EMBA program, and was foolish enough to ask me to create and lead that component, for which I am in his debt. Finally, I owe a great deal to my own teachers, for what they have taught about the nature and dynamics of groups and teams: Clay Alderfer, David Berg, and Richard Hackman.

Chapter 1

Dimensions of the Student Project Team

Congratulations. You've just joined a project team. It looks simple enough. You chose several classmates—or they were chosen for you—and have a certain amount of time during the semester to work on projects, complete them reasonably well, and give presentations or hand in reports that will result, sooner or later, in a course grade, one that you hope is pretty high. Yet, as students who have worked in such teams know, there is much that moves beneath the surface. These teams can get complicated. They have no formal structure. There is no hierarchy, no supervisory structure, and no clear delineation of roles and responsibilities. You have to figure out how to divide up work and then piece the different parts together such that it comes off as coherent and smart. You have to make decisions about the quality of the work. You have to work with people whose styles and efforts might be quite different than your own. You have to figure out ways to hold one another accountable, even though you have no real authority over one another. Beneath the surface, there is the world of negotiation and persuasion, shifting expectations, and difficult conversations had and avoided. Welcome to the project team trip.

These teams are thus wonderful opportunities for learning, not simply about course material but about the *process* by which high-functioning teams are created and maintained. Knowing how to make project teams work really well is a crucial skill. Much of what occurs in organizational life revolves around teams—people working together, within and across departments and functions, to do what they cannot do by themselves. Like student project teams,

teams in organizations—whether they are temporary task forces, long-standing committees, or ongoing research and development teams—are responsible for developing and implementing ideas. People must know something about how to participate effectively, and have the skills necessary to make real contributions to teams of which they are members. Student project teams are the vehicles by which such knowledge and skills are acquired.

Too often, however, these teams break down, and students learn very little of use in terms of how to make truly successful teams work. Creating high-performing teams from a collection of individuals who vary widely in their motivations, capabilities, perspectives, and backgrounds is a complicated, difficult process. Teams break down in varying ways: Sharp disagreements about equity of participation and workload split members into warring factions; individuals are isolated and blamed; members settle for unsatisfactory results rather than discuss different expectations and provide feedback; struggles for control and leadership leave members arguing or simply withdrawing altogether; and members disengage, leaving one or two team members to do all the work. Too many students have had such experiences, and not surprisingly, they are not particularly eager for more project team experiences.

When teams break down or do not form properly to begin with, much gets lost: clear thinking about tasks and problems, the simple division of labor and integration of ideas, useful communication, the exploration of different perspectives that yield creative solutions, synthesis, and integration. Students turn away from one another. They turn away from the work of the team, and from the course material itself. When teams fail, the costs—to learning, to performance, and to students' course experiences—are quite high. Students lose out in several ways. First, they simply do not learn as much about course content. The theory of teams—any teams, whether in the classroom or the boardroom—is that people working together have better ideas, create better products, and implement better programs than any one person could by himself or herself. When project teams work badly, students simply do not learn as much or do as well as they otherwise might. Second, students lose out in terms of what they might learn about team process. Course instructors assign work to teams partly in the hopes that students might learn something about how to work well with others. When project teams break down irreparably, the learning suffers.

It does not have to be so. Your team does not have to be an awful experience. Prevention is possible, and so is intervention. This is partly a matter of knowledge. If you know something about the various phases and stages of project team development, the obstacles that you are sure to face, and ways in which you can overcome those obstacles, you are far more likely to avoid the pitfalls of project teams or to rescue your team if you happen to stumble. Knowledge helps normalize the project team experience. When you come up against difficult moments in your teams, you are more likely to handle those moments effectively if you realize that they are normal rather than abnormal, and simply need to be dealt with directly rather than avoided out of embarrassment and anxiety. You can then look clearly at your teams and, on the basis of knowing about the processes by which such teams get stuck and can get moving again, take useful action.

The aim of this book is to provide you with the kind of knowledge that can help you develop insights about how to make your teams more successful. Such knowledge comes in several forms. In this book I offer various concepts that make clear what happens in project teams throughout the various stages and phases of their development. I discuss the obstacles that, like hurdles, need to be cleared along the way, beginning with the formation of the team and ending with the termination of the team. I also describe exercises that help you surface, talk through, and overcome those obstacles. My aim is to offer various tools and strategies that, if used correctly, can create positive project team experiences in situations that might otherwise be painful and unsuccessful.

Throughout the book I describe several actual student project teams. We learn a great deal through the stories of others. We learn about the paths that different teams take and what happens to them along their journeys. We learn how team members think and feel. Mostly, we learn about the choices that they make, and how those choices influence their experiences and performances. You will be faced with many choices during the team experience. You will have to choose how much to engage in the team—how much effort to put into team projects and into building relationships with other team members. You will choose how open you are, in terms of saying what you really think and feel. You will choose how much to listen to or ignore other members' feedback, and how much to try and change how you act. You will choose how much you care about the quality and outcomes of the work itself, and how much you care about other members. You will choose what types of roles you play on your team, and how much those roles help or hinder that team.

You will make such choices, over and over during the life of the team, and not always be aware of doing so. These choices matter a lot, both for how much you learn and how well your teams perform. The success of student project teams is directly shaped by the choices that their members make about how they will be on their teams. This belief in the power of student choice serves as a foundation of this book. So, too, is the insistence that students are themselves each ultimately responsible for the nature of the teams that they create. Student project teams succeed and fail not because of the flexibility of the professor, or the clarity or difficulty of the assignment, or the extent to which team members are smart or nice. They succeed or fail as a result of the accumulated choices that each team member makes about the nature of his or her participation. Throughout this book I emphasize the range of such choices and their implications. Choices and consequences, followed by more choices and consequences—such is the way that our lives develop, and the nature of the teams we create.

Where Are You Going?

Scenario 1

You are a member of a team that has a semester-long project. The project has several deliverables—two short papers and a final presentation. The team has five members, and you feel fortunate that two of your teammates are particularly smart in the subject and want to do really well in the course. The remaining members, including you, care as well and are no dummies, but it's clear that these other two are going to really push the team to do well. Indeed, that is exactly what happens. The two become the team leaders, although they are not always on the same page; they argue a great deal about what the team should do and how it should do its work. Getting the first paper done is stressful. The team is up late the night before the paper is due, making changes and arguing. One of the leaders finally tells the others to go home, and she finishes it by herself, staying up almost the whole night to do so. The paper receives the highest grade in the class. The process is repeated for the second paper, except for the fact that one team member does not contribute much. You work pretty hard on the paper, but are disappointed that much of what you did is tossed out by one of the leaders during the final revision. That paper also receives a high grade. By the time of the final presentation, the team has become several subgroups—the two leaders, who struggle for power; the other two members, who contribute little and miss meetings; and you, frustrated but trying to keep the team together. The process of putting together the presentation is pretty bad, with team members angry at one another. The two leaders argue with one another. One of them finally stalks away, so the remaining one takes control of the presentation and does most of it. The professor gives the presentation a high grade.

Scenario 2

You feel lucky to be on a team with some of the people you really like in the class. The project is hard, with lots of different pieces that have to be done throughout the course, but working on it has as least been fun. Your meetings are not too long, thankfully, and most of the team ends up having dinner or going out for drinks afterwards. You are really glad that there are not a lot of strong personalities on the team. You've heard about the problems that other teams in the class are having, with people fighting with one another and trying to take control. You haven't experienced anything like that on your team. People are really nice to one another, and polite. They agree with one another a lot, and there is none of the conflict that you have seen on other teams. You and the others laugh a lot. The team does a pretty good job of figuring out what direction to take on the various assignments, and the leadership just seems to be naturally shared among most of the members, except for the shy person. You are thus a bit surprised when the first and second team assignments receive relatively low, below-average grades. The other members are frustrated as well. The team blames the professor for not being clear on the assignments, and for not having understood the ideas that the team had developed. You are not quite as sure—you wonder whether the team had really worked to come up with the best arguments and analysis. The team process continues to go really well as the end of the semester approaches and members begin to work on the final presentation. The team comes up with a good plan, members agree to it quickly, and they get their work done and submitted to the member who agreed to edit and give the presentation. The final grade is, again, disappointing.

Scenario 3

You are on a project team whose members have agreed that it would be good to try things in which they are not expert to get better at them. The project involves many dimensions—PowerPoint slides, presentations, analyzing numbers, facilitating team meetings, managing the project, editing, and interviews. The team members decided at their initial meeting that this was a good chance to get some practice with some of these aspects, as they were about to graduate and wanted to improve. You are impressed with this attitude, because most of the other student project teams that you've been on focused much more on just getting the work done as fast as possible—which meant that people who could do certain things quickly did them, and others did not learn what they did not already know. You are not particularly good at PowerPoint, so you volunteer to put together the slides for the two presentations. Another team member who seems a bit shy agrees to facilitate meetings. Another member who professes to be pretty disorganized decides to try project management. The team starts off slowly. The facilitator cannot really control the meetings, which neither start nor end on time and are filled with lots of tangential conversations. The project manager is, indeed, rather disorganized, and seems unable to put together a simple flow chart that lays out roles, responsibilities, timelines, and the like. You struggle with the PowerPoint slides for the first presentation, staying up all night by yourself to get the slides done. You certainly feel like you learned the basics of the software, although you wished that it had not been so stressful. The grades for the first

two presentations are about average for the class,
and you and the others wished that they were higher,
given all the work that you had put in.

Which of the teams in these scenarios would you describe as successful?
The first team gets high grades but team members have a pretty bad experience
working together. The second team does poorly on its graded assignments but
members like one another. The third team also does not perform as well as it
would like but its members learn skills that they each needed to learn. So which
is successful? The answer is important. It helps you decide where, exactly, you are
going when you take a trip on a project team.

Students make different choices in answering this question. I suspect that
members of the teams just described would describe their respective teams as
more or less successful, according to different criteria.

Success Is Determined by Grades

Members of the first team might think they were successful because their team
received high grades. Students often feel that the purpose of the team—the
reason it exists—is to complete a course requirement, as determined by the professor, and that doing so well is a matter of receiving high grades. Indeed, performance in the context of an academic course is measured most clearly and
simply by grades. To the extent that students believe that grades are the ultimate
measure of success, they are often willing (presumably within the boundaries of
ethical behavior) to have the ends justify the means by which the team worked
to achieve those ends. The students in the first scenario that I described might
well say that they were quite successful, indeed, the best in the class, based on
the criteria of grades.

Success Is Defined in Terms of the Health of Team Interactions

Members of the team described in the second scenario might say that their team
was successful because they enjoyed working with one another and were able to
create healthy ways of working with one another. Members treating one another
respectfully, communicating easily and openly, and focusing on what is good
for the common enterprise mark healthy team processes, generally speaking.
So, too, does the simple enjoyment that members take in working and being
together, to the point that they might become friends as well as teammates. The

students in the second scenario might well say that being a member of a "good team," free of disastrous struggles for control or wide gulfs between those who truly contributed and those who did not, was a success that they were glad to have, even if their final grades were not as high as they might have liked.

Success Is a Matter of How Much Individual Team Members Learn

Members of the team in the third scenario might define their team experience as successful because they personally learned a lot because they were on that team. Such learning can be of several types. Students can learn the course material more deeply, based on what occurs on their teams, such as study sessions or in-depth explorations of dimensions of their projects. They can also learn about aspects of project team management, presentation skills, meeting facilitation, and other dimensions related to the team process. Measuring such learning is not easy. The deeper learning of course material can be measured, at times, by how team members perform on the individually graded assignments. To the extent that students in the third scenario felt that they learned course material or team process and performance skills more deeply, they might well say that their team was an absolute success.

None of these students would be wrong. Yet none of them would be fully right either. Each of them is making an assumption that the criteria for team success are mutually exclusive—that is, that high grades, a healthy team process, and the deepened learning of individuals cannot occur together, and students must choose among them. This is a common assumption, but it oversimplifies the complexity and depth of the team experience. Students too often believe that there must be trade-offs between high performance, good team process, and individual risk-taking and learning. They might not say this, of course. But the choices that they make as they go about their teamwork suggest that they have too little faith in the possibility that the drive for excellent results, the creation of a healthy set of relationships, and individuals trying to learn new skills cannot coexist, easily or at all.

Research shows, however, that group effectiveness is defined by multiple criteria. Richard Hackman (1989), the foremost organizational psychologist studying the nature of group effectiveness, identifies three criteria in his book *Groups That Work*. One criterion, *group performance,* is defined in terms of services or products that meet or exceed performance standards, as measured by those who receive or evaluate those services or products. For student project teams, performance is mostly a function of how well their collective work satisfies those grading their assignments. A second criterion, *group process,* is defined as interactions among group members that enhance their abilities to work together as a performing unit. For student project teams, this would translate into team members increasing their capacities to work well together, to the point that they would like to continue doing so even as their projects ended. The third criterion, *personal development,* is defined in terms of members experiencing personal learning and growth as a function of their group experiences. For students on project teams, such development might be measured in terms of their own self-evaluations ("How much did I learn or develop during this course as a result of my team experience?"), as well as the individual grades and feedback from their instructors.

Given these criteria it would be wise to understand that the success of student team project experiences is not simply a matter of grades, or the social life of a team, or the extent to which individual members learn. It is the healthy balance of the three that is the key to a team that we would define, ultimately, as successful. The notion of a "balanced scorecard" for student project teams is useful here (see Box 1-1). To the extent that a team is unbalanced—that is, emphasizing one dimension and significantly downplaying other dimensions— the team does a real disservice to itself.

Some students might argue that as long as there is agreement on the team about its collective purpose—to get the highest grade in the class, for example, or to have a lot of fun and not take the grades too seriously—success should be simply a function of how well the team does on that dimension. On the surface this seems a reasonable argument. Yet there are real, if hidden, costs to that strategy that are rarely surfaced and discussed on student project teams. Consider, for example, a team (as in the first scenario described earlier) that aims for high grades. The costs of that strategy are always borne by those who feel marginalized, their ideas discounted or pushed to the side as those anointed as leaders control the flow of the work. Or a team (as in the second scenario) that creates a warm, social atmosphere in which the challenging of one another's ideas and the giving of performance-related feedback to teammates are discouraged. The costs of that strategy are to team members' self-esteem, as they receive lower grades and feel less successful than other teams whose members push to perform well. Or a team (as in the third scenario) whose members decide that they will try and improve their individual skills even though they know that they could do better by just doing what they are already good at. The costs here are not only to members' sense of collective achievement, to the extent that they do not perform well on assignments, but to their desires to contribute their expertise to their teams and to be recognized for such.

The point here is that students invariably wish for all three dimensions—to perform well, to enjoy their experiences with one another, and to learn what they do not know—and that to focus on one at the exclusion of the others always causes some sort of pain, to individuals and, sooner or later, to teams. Trade-

BOX 1-1   THE BALANCED SCORECARD OF STUDENT PROJECT TEAMS

In the 1990s, Professor Robert Kaplan of the Harvard Business School developed an innovative management tool, the Balanced Scorecard (Kaplan & Norton, 1996). Based on the notion that what you measure is what you get, Kaplan developed a measurement system that takes into account more than just the financial measures that tend to drive businesses. The scorecard presents managers with four different perspectives from which to choose measures: traditional financial indicators, performance for customers, internal processes, and innovation and improvement activities. Kaplan's insight was that senior executives do not rely on one set of measures to the exclusion of others; they understand that no single measure can provide a clear performance target or focus attention on the critical areas of the business. The balanced scorecard thus brings together the many elements of a company's strategic focus.

Two aspects of this framework are particularly important for our purposes. First, the Balanced Scorecard puts vision and strategy at the center of the measurement and evaluation process. It is effective only to the extent that people first decide what they wish to accomplish. The particular measures that people then use are designed to pull them toward the overall vision. Second, by focusing on multiple dimensions of effectiveness, the Balanced Scorecard helps people understand the interrelationships between those dimensions. Leaders are thus able to see whether improvement on one area may have been achieved at the expense of another.

What does this mean for student project teams? First, it suggests a process. Students need to first develop a vision of what they collectively want from their team experience. (Chapter 2 discusses the visioning process in more detail.) They then need to decide on a strategy by which they will achieve that vision, in terms of how they work together. Second, the balanced scorecard framework requires students to look closely at the dimensions by which success is measured—group performance, group process, and individual learning—and assign relative weightings to those dimensions. Third, the model requires students to evaluate how they are doing on those dimensions—to look at the results of their teamwork, in terms both quantifiable (such as grades) and qualitative (such as how positive or negative are their experiences with one another). Finally, the Balanced Scorecard offers a way for students to make clear choices about how they wish to continue to operate, given what they said they wished from the team experience (their vision) and the actual results of their work together. Students can look closely at the trade-offs they are making, in the light of their success on multiple dimensions, and choose to continue or alter those trade-offs.

offs must be made, of course, and you will have to figure out how and when to make those. Such is the nature of any healthy relationship. Teams, like people and the relationships that they create, develop over time. They do not simply appear, fully formed and perfectly successful. They take work. Much of that work involves making constant adjustments to the team processes, ensuring that how members are interacting with one another fits with the reasons why they are together and what is it they wish to accomplish.

Team Development

Successful teams develop. They grow over time, like any relationship, slowly developing their capacities to operate effectively. Such development occurs when teams effectively engage certain issues that invariably arise as their members go about figuring out how to work together and achieve their individual and collective goals.

The traditional language of group development is that of stages through which groups must progress, like bicyclists who complete stages of a race. There are the classic stages identified by Tuckman (1965)—*forming, norming, storming, performing,* and *adjourning*—that students feel that they should move through, often as quickly as possible. These stages pose a particular type of problem. Although they are generally correct—that is, teams do indeed need to form around agreed-on goals, develop norms to guide team processes, learn to deal with conflict productively, create systems to guide effective performance, and terminate appropriately—the idea of stages implies that such issues, like the hurdles over which runners leap, are confronted and then left behind. This is, unfortunately, not the case. How your team resolves issues of development matters a great deal, shaping its ongoing development. Your team might resolve the issues inherent in its development in ways that are partial. Those often-fragile resolutions remain with your team and continue to shape its work even as you try and forge ahead. Partially resolved issues continue to show up until they are fully resolved, or the team ends.

Each step in the life of a project team thus requires its members to complete certain tasks—pieces of work that need to be done in the service of creating an increasingly effective, high-performing unit. This work is not about content, or what your team does. It is about process, or how your team works. I think of these tasks as *tolls* that each project team must pay to continue on its trip. Unless those tolls are paid—fully paid, rather than partly, or avoided altogether—the team will have difficulty continuing along the main road that will take it to where you want to go. The team will stay stuck at the toll until it can pay what it needs to pay. Or, hoping to get away without paying the toll, the team will speed away to another road. Inevitably, it will be a road that is far bumpier, more confusing to navigate, and quite frustrating to travel. The farther that you travel down that other road, the more difficult it will be to find your way back to the right road.

The tolls are really important. The first toll, for example, involves figuring out why your team exists—its mission—and how to accomplish it. I discuss this in more depth in the next chapter. If you and your teammates do not develop a shared belief about your purpose together, the underlying disagreements, like fault lines beneath the surface of the earth, will leave your team vulnerable and easily shaken should difficult moments, such as a poor grade on an early assignment, occur. Without a shared belief in what you are trying to do together, your team might well split apart, with different members choosing different paths—some bearing down harder and others giving up. Your team either needs to regroup and decide what is collectively important—to go back and pay that first toll—or continue along a path that will make your journey far more difficult.

There are a number of such tolls along the way. Each is complicated in its own way. Paying the toll is not always easy. There are two types of obstacles: obstacles that individual members must confront and resolve for themselves and obstacles that the whole team must confront and resolve. The two types are linked. For example, for team members to join themselves to a shared purpose, the team has to figure out how to reconcile real differences in members' needs and agendas. At the same time, you and your teammates must each choose how honest to be about what each really wants from the team experience. Such honesty is difficult, given our initial desires to fit in with others and not make waves early in the life of a student team. Each member has to deal with the press for conformity and speak truthfully. The whole team also has to make sense of what each member says and create a collective mission that makes sense. How these obstacles are dealt with determines the first stages of your trip. Overcome them, pay the toll, and you move ahead. Don't overcome them, and you stay at the toll, fumbling for the payment, or you take off to find another, slower road. The tolls are the path to real progress.

Consider the first toll, clarifying the team's real purpose. A strong resolution might be for you and your teammates to openly agree on a primary purpose, such as efficient teamwork with good results or a particularly high-performing team based on lots of work and interaction. The strength of the resolution is based less on its content than on the process by which it was achieved—through you and the others talking openly with one another about your true interests and needs, exploring areas of disagreement, and developing collective strategies that would satisfy, to a reasonable extent, all of you. You've paid the toll, and can proceed on a reasonably clear road to the next place in your team's development.

You and your teammates might be tempted to jump that toll and try to avoid payment. You might publicly agree with one another about your joint purpose and privately disagree. You might stake out radically different approaches to the team and refuse to search for common ground. You might split into factions reflecting different versions of the team's purpose and refuse to bridge the gap. You might subjugate yourselves to one member's needs or ideas and then resent the direction you allowed. These processes are sure to create weak resolutions to your team's purpose. Each will create fissures in your team's foundation. Over time, left unidentified and unaddressed, those fissures are likely to widen and deepen, to the point that your team might get stuck completely, unable to overcome any further obstacles. That is too bad, and it is entirely preventable.

Teams That Learn

Teams that develop into truly high-performing units, whose members grow personally and get a lot from the team experience, are defined by a singular quality: They learn. It is the ability to learn that separates those who increase their capacities—to think, act, and perform—from those who do not. So it is with teams. Unless teams spring forth absolutely perfect from the moment of their creation—and we are still waiting for that possibility to occur—they must learn. This is as true for the New York Yankees, Manchester United, the Beatles, the President's Cabinet, and the U.S. Treasury Board of Governors as it is for a student team responsible for putting together a research analysis project and presentation. Unless each of these teams is able to learn, it will fail to perform to its potential.

There is much to learn. Teams must learn how to be teams. I focus here not on the content that members must learn—their course material, or how to analyze data or use software—but, again, on the processes by which they develop into teams. We know something about the types of processes that enable people to work well in teams. There are certain ways in which people work with, engage, and communicate with one another that enable them to create high-performing teams. Box 1-2 lists such processes. During the course of this book you will have the opportunity to learn more about each of these processes and how to instill them on your team.

The premise here is that working effectively in teams is an acquired skill. It is a skill that must be practiced. You can learn how to work well in teams, but this knowledge is useful only to the extent that you apply it in the context of your teams. Here, too, teams are like relationships. Ideally, as we each grow into adulthood, we get better and better at creating relationships with others that allow us to get our needs met—for intimacy, challenge, personal growth, and

BOX 1-2 EFFECTIVE TEAM PROCESSES

High-performing project teams are marked by certain dimensions of group process, that is, how members work with, engage, and communicate with one another. These include the following:

- Information flow among members that is accurate, open, honest, and evenly distributed.
- Members work toward common goals, rather than engage in competitive, win–lose behaviors.
- Control is shared among team members, according to the nature and demands of the particular task in which the group is engaged.
- Members each have an individual commitment to the goals of the team, even as they have differing ideas about how to achieve those goals.
- The team has norms that encourage members to display both individuality and adherence to group standards.
- Members engage differences—in ideas, perspectives, backgrounds, cultures, affiliation group, and the like—productively.
- The team encourages members to share risky ideas and feelings, and engage in innovative thinking and experimental behavior on behalf of the team's work.
- Team members perceive one another as competent in particular ways, able to contribute differently to the team and its work.
- Members are eager to adapt behaviors to meet new demands or respond to changed conditions.
- The team has a supportive, friendly, warm emotional climate.

love. We get better because we are able to learn. From each relationship we take some insight, some behavior, or some new way of being with others. We practice those lessons in the next relationship, deepening them and learning new lessons. This is a nice template for how you develop your capacities for teamwork. You try and learn as much as you can about how teams work, and how your teams can be what they should be, and you test out and add to what you know in later team experiences.

Such learning requires you to allow yourself to learn. This is not as simple as it seems. It means that you need to be truly open to the possibility that you do not fully know how teams work and should work, or how you might even contribute to flawed team processes. You need to truly engage in discussions about how your teams are working. You need to take responsibility for who you are as team members and for the choices that you make. To learn about yourself in these ways you must care more about that learning than about protecting yourself from feeling inadequate about what you do not know.

You must also join with your teammates to learn from your experiences as a team. You must review successes and failures, assess them systematically, and record the lessons in ways that are open and accessible. You need to recognize the value of productive failure, as contrasted with unproductive success. Productive failure leads to insight, understanding, and additions to the commonly held wisdom of the team about how it should proceed. Unproductive success occurs when something goes well but nobody knows how or why. The team just goes on, not quite sure why it was successful and therefore not fully knowing how it can reproduce its successes. Teams that truly learn are those that seize on experiences and events that hint of failure and try to understand as much as possible about what happened, and why, and what they can do to create more desirable processes and outcomes. The next chapter focuses in more depth on the processes by which you can join with others to create a truly learning team.

People vary in terms of their abilities and willingness to try and learn about team processes. This might be partly a matter of previous experiences. If you've been on "bad" teams before you might feel quite cynical about project teams. This greatly undermines your ability to contribute. You could create self-fulfilling prophecies: Believing that the new team experience will be negative in some fashion, you disengage from others to protect yourself from that occurring, and in so doing, help set in motion the exact negative dynamics that you feared and predicted. Or you might fear that it is just "not worth" investing much time and energy into making your teams work well, as it is "only school" and not "real life." You thus withhold feedback from others, refusing to speak honestly and openly, and decide to get by as best you can until the project or semester has ended. The problem here is that you do not actually learn how to successfully intervene in teams and render them more effective. Rather, you learn how to avoid difficult conversations. You will continue to do so when you join teams in organizations where the stakes for failure are much higher.

I wrote this book for students who are willing to try and learn about how to create successful project teams. Your motives might vary. Some of you might understand that putting the energy into creating effective teams will pay off, in terms of the quality of your team's work and its performances. Some of you might realize that the skills involved in mastering student project team dynamics are directly applicable to working in teams in the workplace. Others of you might want to have good experiences on your student project teams, unwilling to suffer through bad experiences. Still others of you simply believe in the importance of learning how to be in relation with others, and want to learn as much as possible about that process and about yourselves as well. Each of these reasons is valid, and as an impulse, should be followed and stayed with in the reading of this book and the implementing of its lessons.

Why Bother?

There is likely to be a lingering question for some of you, about how the experience of working in (and learning about) a student project team is relevant to the teams in which you are likely to spend a good portion of your careers. Student project teams are temporary. They have no assigned leaders and no real hierarchy. The consequences for failing are not as high, which means that you have less control or influence over what other team members do. The team is just a facet of a course that you're taking, among other courses and activities in your life, and is not as central as your work life is likely to be. Given these factors, why should you bother spending much time and energy figuring out how to make these teams much better, given the other areas in your life in which you could invest your efforts?

I have three responses to this question.

Work Teams Are Not All That Different

There are often more structural similarities between work teams and student project teams than you might realize. Although there are clearly hierarchical influences in organizational life that spill over into teams, there are also situations in which those influences are minimized. You are assigned, for example, to represent your department on a cross-functional task force that needs to make a recommendation to senior management about a certain strategy or product. There is a project leader, but he or she has no formal authority over you, as he works in a different division. Team members were selected on the basis of particular skills and perspectives, and represent distinct functional areas, but the team is self-managing and needs to figure out how to organize itself and integrate its members to get its work done. Like you, they were given a project and a group of others, and asked to complete it, given a certain time frame and set of expectations. Like you, they are collectively responsible for meeting the standards set by others not on the team who have authority. And like you, they have to create themselves into a reasonably cohesive team in spite of all the other demands that are pulling on them.

The Same Behaviors Are Required for Success

The fact that your student project team does not operate within the same sort of hierarchical system as do work teams does not alter the types of behaviors that you must perform if you are to contribute effectively to your team and help it succeed. In each setting you are responsible for working with others, even if you also work for them. In each setting you need to act in ways that enable your teams to work effectively. What does this mean? It means communicating effectively, listening well, and giving and receiving feedback. It means following through on your commitments, and developing trusting relationships. It means celebrating successes and learning from failures. It means recognizing and dealing with differences before they devolve into destructive conflicts. It means accommodating others and standing firm according to what the team most needs from you at any particular moment. It means acting with humility and respecting what others can offer. It means understanding when to lead, and when to follow, and acting accordingly. Such behaviors are integral to your ability to help create successful teams, regardless of their contexts. Hierarchies and bosses do not excuse you from the responsibility of the integrity of creating strong relationships, just as working with a group of peers does not relieve you of the need to work hard on behalf of others.

You Play as You Practice

Your student project team is, in many ways, the practice field, with the real events happening later, when you're on work teams with stakes that matter a great deal to you and your organization. What happens on the practice field is crucial, however. The habits that you form at practice are inevitably the ones that you perform later, when it matters more. This is what the great coaches teach: You play as you practice. Your project teams are therefore excellent places to develop and practice skills and behaviors. You will, at some point in your career, face a situation in which you truly need to exert thoughtful leadership even though you are not explicitly authorized to do so by a hierarchical structure. You will need to follow others as they do so as well. There will be other situations, many of them, when you need to help make bad teams good, and good teams better. You can practice these skills here. You can make mistakes, and learn from them, without suffering too high a penalty. That's what practice is for: to try new behaviors, fall short, and try them again, until you learn them so thoroughly that they are instinctual when you get into the higher stakes arenas.

It makes sense, then, to consider your project team experience as relevant to what you might artificially distinguish as the "real world." Your team exists in that world. Your interactions with one another are real, and have the potential to create real feelings, good and bad. The anxiety of being on a team that is stuck in ineffective patterns is real. The behaviors that you perform are real, and so are the skills that you do (or do not) develop during the project team experience. You mislead yourself if you believe otherwise. This team is not just an exercise; it is a relatively safe setting in which to learn how to create and sustain excellence on a team. If you don't learn that now, when might you?

Plan of the Book

This book is written to help you and your teams have the conversations that you need to have if you are to create teams that perform well, have healthy processes, and enable members to learn. Conversation is crucial. By conversation, I mean meaningful dialogue, based on team members speaking as openly as they can of their experiences. I have constructed this book in ways that I hope will provide a structure for these conversations. No one can force you to engage in such conversations. The extent to which you do so is entirely up to you. Horses can be led to water, as the saying goes. Whether they drink, and how deeply, is a matter of how thirsty they are. My hope is that you are thirsty for some knowledge of how your teams might be more effective, but not so parched that you are too late to use that knowledge to make much difference.

In each chapter I describe a particular task—the toll—that project teams need to pass through. I also discuss the obstacles to paying those tolls. I list these in Table 1-1. The chapters follow the general course of development of student project teams: forming teams, creating the foundation for trust, establishing team roles, exerting influence, managing conflict and differences, managing group dynamics, team maintenance, and ending the team. My purpose in naming the tolls is to help you become familiar with them, to understand them as normal rather than abnormal. To the extent that you see the issues that teams must inevitably confront as an integral part of team life, rather than as some indictment of failure, you are more likely to move toward them purposefully and engage them thoughtfully.

At the end of the book there are various exercises that support the development of your team. These exercises help your team pass through the tolls. They help you look candidly at your team and discuss the choices you have made about how to work together. We are often naturally reluctant to speak openly with one another about how we work as a team. We would rather talk about the content of our work than our team processes. Those conversations are often difficult. They involve speaking openly, giving and receiving feedback, and dealing with real differences in how people work with one another. I hope that the exercises are just in time, showing up at precisely the point at which they can be most useful for you. This will not always be the case, of course, but I am confident that whenever you are able to make the time and space to talk about your team's processes, you will have the conversations that you most need to have, when you

Table 1-1 The Project Team Journey

Dimension of Team Life	Tolls	Obstacles
Team formation	Develop common mission (what the team exists to be and do) and initial structures (how members should work together on behalf of their shared mission).	Significant differences in members' agendas, needs, commitments, and willingness to compromise. Lack of safety necessary to speak openly about personal agendas.
Roles and responsibilities	Create and assume roles that allow for all aspects of teamwork to be performed fairly and equitably.	Member's unwillingness to openly acknowledge their own roles and abilities, and provide feedback regarding those of others. Variances in participation and contribution to teamwork.
Influence and decision making	Enable team members to assume appropriate authority that allows for shared responsibility and effective decision-making processes.	Individual differences in need of power and influence. Difficulty in creating collective ways to collaborate across roles.
Process improvements	Identify initial patterns of team interaction and choose which patterns to maintain and which to alter or terminate.	Anxiety of speaking openly about patterns of interaction. Collective pulls toward conformity.
Useful conflict	Create effective ways to acknowledge, respect, integrate, and learn from differences among team members.	Anxiety and threat triggered by differences, creating individual and collective defensive patterns and routines.

Continued

Table 1-1 The Project Team Journey (Continued)

Dimension of Team Life	Tolls	Obstacles
Full engagement	Identify and alter patterns of team interaction to enable members to be fully engaged in their work together.	Members' unwillingness to openly acknowledge and change their perceptions of one another based on relevant data.
Final examinations	Finish project team experience in ways that enable individual and collective learning and allow for closure.	Members' desires to avoid difficult conversations and emotions related to endings.

most need to have them. The exercises at the end offer a reasonably safe structure in which those conversations can usefully occur.

The Essential Gesture

None of what is written in this book will make much difference in the life of your team unless you decide to move toward rather than away from the anxiety that lives beneath the surface of all teams. I note throughout the book what that anxiety is about—it shifts as teams move ahead and confront different aspects of their development—but, generally speaking, it involves the ongoing fear that you could, at any time, be marginalized by or in conflict with others. To understand this, to not hide from that fear, to examine what the team is doing to facilitate and undermine its own processes, to stay open to learning about your self as a team member—all this takes courage.

I do not mean this lightly. It is an act of courage to move toward what makes us anxious. I am constantly impressed by students who are willing to approach their team experiences as opportunities to develop insights and understandings, even when it is difficult to do so. These students understand, in a way that they might not be able to articulate, that it is only in talking about their relationships with others that those relationships have a chance to develop as they should. Such understanding is not enough, however. To say what you think and feel, even when you believe that it might be hopeless to do so, when others seem to have checked out, is an act of courage, even as it feels futile.

It is also the only healthy choice. It allows you to practice a way of being in the world. Student project teams are, contrary to what some would like to believe, "real life." How you engage in them—how you move toward opportunities to learn who you are and the choices you make in relation with others—says much about how you engage in the other dimensions of your lives as well. What you do with that understanding, and with the opportunities before you in your project teams, is up to you, individually and together.

Summary

This chapter introduced the nature of the student project team as a relatively complex social system that can work well, or badly, depending on the choices that you make about how you work with one another. The team experience is filled with many choices, ranging from how much you truly engage with one another to how you divide up work, give and listen to feedback, and care about the team's work. The choices that you make are partly determined by how you define success, in terms of grades, personal learning, and relationships with others. The chapter also introduced the idea that high-performing teams are defined by their members' abilities to learn about their teams, and thus continuously improve team processes and outcomes. Teams evolve when you confront certain obstacles and adapt how you work together to overcome them. You will need to learn how to adapt in such ways, for the success of your team—and, more compellingly, for the success of the real-world teams on which you will later be members.

Chapter 2

The Learning Team

This book is like the maintenance part of the instruction manual that comes with a new gadget—the section that describes how to keep everything working and in order, with tune-ups, inspections, and warm soapy water. Your team needs maintenance. The steps are routine, which is not to say that they are easy or quick. Without them your team might well break down, slowly grinding to some kind of halt or suddenly falling apart. It pays to read the manual and follow some sort of maintenance program. The image is, of course, partly misleading, as you will need to learn about your team before you understand completely how to maintain it. It will become clear over time, however, what sort of maintenance program is necessary. In this chapter I offer some elements that are often useful in such programs.

First, however, we need to define what we mean by team maintenance. To maintain something is to work to keep it in proper condition. It is to see to its care and upkeep. This has different meanings in different contexts. For a new gadget, warm soapy water might actually be correct; you clean to restore the thing to its original state. Maintaining your team, however, is a different matter altogether. You cannot simply restore your team to *its* original state, nor should you wish to. Your team will develop, change, and grow in its collective abilities. Maintenance is thus about enabling that evolution. When you do not maintain the team, you prevent yourselves from moving forward as you should. The gunk accumulates and clogs the gears, to the point that you get stuck, as if caked with rust.

So what's the solution? Simply put, learning. The liberal application of learning is the key to maintaining the health and welfare of your team. It is when you learn about your team, when it functions well and not so well, and how to get through difficult issues and moments, that you are able to do better work and enjoy one another. It is when you learn about yourself, as member and as leader, that you are able to engage more deeply and meaningfully.

This learning is not simply academic. You don't just learn some new words or concepts to show on a test. You have not really learned something unless your *behaviors* change. The learning that matters here is when you try to figure out what's happening on your team, or with yourself, develop ideas that might be helpful, do something differently, and see what happens. This process drives the maintenance—the care and upkeep—of your team. Keep doing the process, and the learning becomes ongoing, ending only when the team itself has completed its work and no longer has a reason to exist. Continuous learning is the analogue to regular applications of—yes, again—warm soapy water and other ingredients necessary for tune-ups.

Your team thus needs to become a team that learns. Your team will get stuck in ineffectual patterns, habits, and routines when you are unable or unwilling to learn why and how you act as you do. When you do become aware of what lies beneath the team's actions (and your own), you then have the opportunity to make conscious choices about whether you want to actually learn, that is, to try new behaviors and see what happens. Throughout the book I point out such choice points. The process of learning is filled with them, marked by them as a road is marked by opportunities to take different turns. At each point, the learning choice is clear: You can choose not to try to act differently, hoping to live with the way it is and get by, or you can try and change what each of you does and how you see one another. These choices represent different turns in the road.

Learning is a process, with particular dimensions. In his book *Experiential Learning*, Kolb (1984) suggests that learning occurs through a four-stage process in which you reflect on your experiences to develop concepts, the validity of which you test through action in further experiences. Action and reflection follow each other in a cycle that you enter at any point. The learning cycle thus provides feedback, which is the basis for new action and evaluation of the consequences of that action. You'll often go through the cycle several times, so it might best be thought of as a spiral of cycles. All this may happen in a flash, or over days, weeks, or months, depending on what you're trying to learn and how much time you devote to the process.

This model suggests several types of mechanisms that ensure ongoing learning. Simply as a matter of working on your project, you have a number of concrete experiences. You meet, make decisions, and do work. The learning cycle requires you to create mechanisms by which to reflect on those experiences—to observe your actions and try and interpret what they mean for your team's effectiveness. The cycle then requires you to step back and try and place your interpretations into a larger conceptual framework for greater understanding.

This book offers concepts and frameworks for that very purpose. Your learning commences with your attempts—guided by a conceptual understanding of what might be more effective—at behaving differently.

The experiential learning cycle is particularly useful as a way of preventing you from falling prey to two common project team pitfalls—too little reflection or too little action. In the former, you just act, making decisions without thinking them through. One of you has what seems like a good idea—or one that is good enough, which will get the team moving in some direction—and the others just accept it without evaluating its strengths and weaknesses. In the latter, you analyze your work and processes endlessly. You spin into cycles of analysis that lead nowhere, like dead ends, and are surprised when you find you have not made much progress on actual work. You are in "analysis paralysis." Each of these traps—action without reflection or reflection without action—represents a lack of moderation. Each represents the inappropriate disconnection of reflection and action, a discounting of the importance of cycling back and forth between the two. The learning cycle wisely keeps action and reflection in constant tension and relation, and so should you.

Certain conditions enable you to get into learning cycles. You learn when you are motivated, and very much want to do things better and differently. You learn when you have the capacity to absorb experiences and develop skills and abilities. You learn when you have support, in the form of others who can and will help you with expertise, coaching, feedback, and cheerleading. You learn when you have adequate resources. You learn when you have safe landings, in the context of environments in which it is okay to take risks and fail. You learn when you are reinforced for doing so, with experiences of success that refuel your motivations.

The "learning team" is aided greatly when you and your teammates share the desire to truly get good as a team. If so, you will find ways to overcome the difficulty of creating trusting, open communications that allow for ongoing feedback and learning. You will create and use structures that help you to reflect on your experiences and experiment with newer and, you hope, more effective ways of working and interacting. Finally, you will try and use rather than be held hostage by the differences in how each team member prefers to learn. You will benefit from rather than get paralyzed by the fact that some of you like to reflect more than act and others the reverse. You will try to communicate openly about the importance of each phase of the learning cycle, and let those most comfortable with each phase take the lead when that phase is necessary.

This chapter focuses on the nature and practices of "the learning team." I examine the ways in which it keeps members on the learning track amidst the pushes and pulls otherwise. Embedded within this chapter are some specific tools and practices that you can apply to give your team a real chance to learn and evolve.

The Learning Team

Your team learns when you are able to modify behaviors to reflect new knowledge and insights. New ideas are essential if learning is to occur. You'll need new ideas or insights to help you figure out what to do differently. You'll need to be able to create, acquire, and transfer knowledge. Learning then becomes possible, but you must apply that knowledge as well. Without changes in the way that work gets done, only the potential for rather than the reality of improvement exists. The learning team is thus marked by its ability to cycle through reflection and action. This involves three general types of activities.

Systematic Problem Solving

The learning team is more or less methodical about how its members solve problems. The process relies on the philosophy and methods of the scientific method, rather than guesswork, for diagnosing problems. The scientific method imposes a certain logic that, if followed, prevents you from making decisions in ways overly influenced by emotions and biases.

You begin with a problem that you need to solve. Say, for example, that when you look at a report that the team created, you can see that different members wrote different sections and that the sections don't really support one another all that well. The instructor commented on this when she looked at an earlier draft, but the problem remains. You would then generate hypotheses to explain the problem. Perhaps not all members were aware of the larger point that each of them had to help get to in the report. Maybe the team had not worked hard to figure out the transitions and bridges between the sections. Perhaps there was a basic disagreement within the team about what the report needed to say. Once you've generated such hypotheses, you can test them. You change some element and see what happens. You might, for example, appoint one member to lead a conversation about the transitions within the document, with an eye toward the larger point that those transitions help build toward. Based on the ideas that emerge, the report would change. The instructor's response would help you evaluate the success of your intervention.

Moving from problem definition to hypotheses, to tests, and to results grounds your discussions in data rather than often misleading assumptions. You might assume, for example, that the problem of disconnection among report sections is the fault of the team member assigned as the final editor. This assumption—perhaps based on your dislike or distrust of the editor—would lead you to believe that you simply need another member to take on that role. If the problem is rooted in a general lack of agreement on the report's primary focus, however, your intervention will be unsuccessful. Generating and testing various hypotheses helps you get to the right interventions. It also enables you to create a culture in which you become disciplined in your thinking.

Experimentation

Embedded in the scientific method is the systematic searching for and testing of new knowledge. This involves experimentation. You see if some new way of working together is effective. Your team has another report due soon. You have an extra meeting to make sure that each of you understands exactly the flow of the overall argument that you are making together in the report. You create an outline together, showing the points that add up to that argument and the transitions that connect those points in a logical and compelling way. You assign a member to track the argument by reading the sections and ensuring that they conform to what the team agreed on. These are experiments. You are trying new ways to work and thus creating knowledge about problems—how they get created, how to solve them, and how to make sure that they do not reappear. Such experiments create a steady flow of new ideas.

Learning From Past Experience

Learning teams review successes and failures, assess them systematically, and record the lessons in ways that are open and accessible. Their members look at outcomes they did not like and try to figure out what they might learn from them. Say, for example, that you decide that it really is the fault of your team editor that the report sections did not flow together. Your team changes editors for the next deliverable. The instructor again provides feedback about disconnection between the sections. You've now learned something important: The problem is rooted not in the editor's competence but elsewhere. You can now look at your team's structure, or its culture. Contrast this sort of productive failure with a time in which something goes well but nobody knows how or why. There's not much you can learn from these instances.

Learning from your team experiences rarely occurs spontaneously. You have to create structures that press you to do this sort of learning. There are several useful structures that you can use to create learning forums—settings in which you use reflection as a way into increasingly thoughtful action. *After-action reviews* offer the opportunity to reflect on your work together after you have completed an assignment and identify lessons to help you in the next assignment (see Box 2-1). *Process checks* occur more frequently. They are moments when you take a break from doing your work and discuss how you are going about that work. You are checking in to see how well your process is working, in terms of tasks getting done effectively and members feeling reasonably good in doing so

BOX 2-1   AFTER-ACTION REVIEWS

The after-action review (AAR) is a structured review or debriefing process that analyzes what happened, why it happened, and how it can be done better, in a forum that includes participants and those responsible for the project or exercise. AARs in the formal sense were originally developed by the U.S. Army and are now used throughout many organizations as a tool for continuous learning. The AAR offers a simple way for individuals and teams to learn immediately, from both successes and failures, at the end of a project or activity or after each identifiable event within a project or major activity. The AAR is a professional discussion that includes the participants and focuses directly on the tasks and goals. It is not a critique, in which team members judge success or failure, but rather an attempt to discover why things happened. The effectiveness of the AAR depends on team members speaking truthfully about events and the important lessons they can learn about how to improve their work toward their tasks and goals. The learning is by the team, for the team.

The AAR involves team members examining together recent events, framed in terms of four questions: What was supposed to happen? What actually happened? Why were there differences? What can we learn from that? These questions are best examined by following certain guidelines.

- Hold the AAR immediately after the completion of a deliverable, at a time when all team members are available.
- Appoint a facilitator. The facilitator helps keep team members focused on the task of learning as much as they can about how they worked together and how they can improve their performance. The facilitator draws members out, ensuring that each team member contributes his or her perspectives and ideas for improvement. The facilitator needs to remain unbiased throughout the review. He or she must maintain a focus on learning and continuous improvement, not allowing personal attacks.
- The facilitator begins by asking the team, "What was supposed to happen?" Begin by dividing the event into discrete activities, each of which had an identifiable objective and plan of action. All members participate in this—and subsequent—discussions.
- The facilitator asks the team, "What actually happened?" Team members must focus on facts—timelines, behaviors, communications, work accomplished—and not opinions. The focus here

is on identifying problems or learning points, rather than apportioning blame.

■ Team members compare their plans with the reality of what actually occurred. The real learning begins as members try and determine the sources of the gaps between what they planned and what actually happened. The guiding questions here are "Why were there differences?" and "What did we learn?" These questions enable members to identify and discuss both their successes and shortfalls.

■ Record the key elements of the AAR to clarify what happened in relation to what was supposed to happen.

■ Create action plans to sustain the successes and to improve on the shortfalls. These action plans are, in some way, experiments—in the spirit of the learning team—that members try to explore alternative courses of action that might have been more effective.

■ Try the experiments, following up on needed actions.

(see Box 2-2). These conversations show you the places where you want to try and experiment in your work together.

Each of these three types of activities—systematic problem solving, experimentation, and learning from past experience—is useful only to the extent that you are able to foster an environment on your team that is truly conducive to learning. Making time for reflection and analysis, to think about strategic plans, to dissect your individual and collective needs, and to assess your work practices and their results helps create that environment. So does your sincere desire to learn about your team. It is your *stance* that matters here. If your stance is to get in and out of this project team with only the effort required to complete the work, learning about how to work as effectively as possible will be, at best, secondary. If your stance is truly that of a learner, who wants very much to figure out how to get as much as possible out of the team experience, you might well inspire others to join with you to do so.

A final word is in order about what it means to create and work in a learning team. Learning involves humility: the understanding that no one knows everything or can do everything perfectly. Underpinning the notion of learning, of experimenting, of figuring out what's not working and how to make it better, is forgiveness. You must be willing to forgive if you are to have the capacity to learn. Absent forgiveness there is blame and remorse, either of which destroys the possibility of learning. You must forgive yourself, and you must forgive others, for not being perfect, for being human and making mistakes, for trying and

BOX 2-2 PROCESS CHECKS

Process checks are ways in which your team can quickly and relatively simply get a sense of how your team process is working. You can use process checks routinely (at the end of each meeting, say, or part-way through each assignment) or whenever a member senses that it would be useful to do so. The purpose is to insert brief periods of reflection into teamwork that more typically revolves around action and performance.

There are a number of possible formats for conducting process checks. The format presented here is quite common, and offers a tool that is reasonably uncomplicated yet quite useful. The format is known as the Stop–Start–Continue process. The following steps take you through this process. You can do this reasonably effectively in 15 or 20 minutes.

1. Select a facilitator. The facilitator's role is to structure the exercise, record information, and facilitate the team's discussions of its processes and how they might change.
2. Each team member draws three columns on a piece of paper, labeling the columns with the headings Stop, Start, and Continue. Each member then lists three items in each column, according to the behaviors, activities, or practices that the team should stop, start, or continue doing to work more effectively toward its goals.
3. Members take turn reading their columns. The facilitator creates— on a flip chart, whiteboard, or computer screen—a public record of the information in each category.
4. The team examines the pattern of responses in each category, and selects those responses that are more commonly repeated or that seem the most crucial.
5. The facilitator asks members to think of examples that will help the team understand more completely the items under discussion and explore the reasons for existing practices.
6. Team members discuss possible ways to change behaviors, activities, or practices identified under the stop or start categories.
7. The facilitator records agreements about changes that the team has decided to try and make.

This process should be reasonably brief, particularly if your team has had previous conversations about its processes. The focus remains tightly on behaviors, activities, and practices (rather than attitudes or personalities) that ground the discussions in concrete, observable changes in what members have done and should do to work effectively together.

failing, and for flinching at difficult moments and then realizing what could have been done differently. If you cannot forgive—let yourself and others off the hook—you and they cannot learn. You cannot allow yourself and others to look clearly at what you are and are not doing, and to get better at achieving your individual and collective goals.

The Problem With Grades

Grades are, for better and for worse, a necessary part of the student experience. Grades provide your team with feedback about its performance. They also provide a unifying goal: Team members are typically joined around their desires to get good grades, yet grades can complicate your ability to learn how to help your team function better. The problem is rooted in how powerfully grades affect your perspectives on whether your team is working well or not, as a result of the cultural emphasis on grades as the goal of the student experience—an emphasis rooted in both the tangibility of grades, relative to the more intangible notion of learning, and the habit, developed from early childhood, of regarding grades as the real currency of the school experience.

Grades thus threaten to overwhelm your best intentions to focus on your learning, in the same way that the amount of money that you earn as an adult threatens to overwhelm your sense of the quality and success of your life. In each case the habitual pull to compare yourself against others draws you to believe that the point is to do "better" than others. As long as you maintain that perspective—that what really matters is to compete, and win, against other people and other teams, based on some tangible marker—it is less likely that you will look more deeply at how you can get better at, and feel better about, what it is that you do. A different perspective holds grades as but one source of feedback, albeit an important one. Grades offer data about the team's functioning, but there are other data as well, related to how you and your teammates are working together and your experiences of doing so.

This other perspective requires you to separate the *results* of your team's work from its *process,* and to take each seriously. Consider the following.

Scenario 1

Your team works really well getting ready for an oral presentation to the rest of the class. The team met after receiving the assignment, figured out what angle to take, divided up the labor, assigned one individual to manage the project and another to make the presentation, and met regularly in the 3 weeks leading up to the deadline. You were one of the researchers and really liked interacting with the two others assigned to that role, e-mailing ideas back and forth and meeting to figure out how to fill in the holes in your information. The team reviewed the final argument. Two members developed the presentation. The presenter practiced in front of the group 2 days before the due date, receiving constructive feedback about how to improve the delivery. The presentation itself went well. The presenter did a smooth job with the slides, and other team members stepped in to answer questions. You and the others were pleased to get an A grade.

Scenario 2

Your team really struggled with its first assignment. In the beginning most of the members got together and talked briefly about what to do and then divided up some of the research and writing tasks. Since then, not a lot of work was done. Your team kept putting off getting together. There were some e-mails, sent by a teammate who seemed anxious to get the project done, but not a lot of replies. The team finally got together 3 days before the project was due. Some of the members brought the work that they had done and showed it to the team. Some of the work was reasonably complete, but other pieces were shoddily done or irrelevant to what you thought the team had decided to do. One member had done nothing. You like this class and want to do well. You grudgingly take the lead doing the assignment. You spend the next 2 nights working very late. With the help of another member, you take whatever the others had done and try to make a report out of it. You know something about the subject matter, and work hard at making a good argument. You're exhausted at the end of it but the project got done and handed in on time. You're frustrated with the other members. The team is thrilled when this first assignment received an A from the instructor.

Scenario 3

Your team works badly. Indeed, it is not really a team at all, just a collection of individuals who have little sense of connection with one another. You do have a friend on the team, and the two of you commiserate with one another about the others. A team assignment is due soon. It's not a huge assignment—the team has to analyze a case and write a report suggesting the best way to handle an issue—but it is the first of a number of deliverables that will get more complex as the course progresses. The team has not yet met to discuss the case and how to complete the assignment. Your friend on the team sends an e-mail to the others, suggesting times to get together. There is no time that works, given the schedules of those who bothered to respond. Your friend sends out another e-mail, with a clear message: Those who show up to either of two meetings will have their names on the assignment, and the others will not. You're impressed with your friend, who tells you that it's the only way he's found to get people together for group projects. Each of the other members shows up to one of the two meetings. The meetings are not particularly productive—there were arguments that didn't seem to lead anywhere—so you and your friend make the decisions and complete the assignment. You send it to the others, with little response, and you hand in the assignment. The team receives a grade of C+ on the assignment.

Scenario 4

Your team works really well together. Members like one another. They get together and figure out how to get the first assignment done. You each seem to take the work seriously. Members do what they say they will. Two of you create an outline. Others do research and fill in the appropriate gaps in the outline. The team gets together and reviews the research and has good discussions about the argument they want to make in the report. One of you drafts the report. The others review the draft and make a good number of comments and suggestions. You incorporate the comments into another draft, distribute it, and receive several useful comments about how to improve the report. You turn the report in to the instructor. You and the others are disappointed when the paper receives a grade of B– from the instructor.

These scenarios point directly to the double-edged nature of grades. Grades are powerful reinforcements. Good grades tend to reinforce how your team worked to get those grades, irrespective of what that process was actually like. In the first scenario, this is fine. The grade fit team members' *experiences* of working on the project. Communication was constant. Workload was shared. Roles and responsibilities were clarified, and individuals were delegated particular tasks. Members supported one another. Team members all felt that they owned the final deliverable. They had a good experience, and were left with positive rather than negative feelings about how they worked together. The high grade confirmed their experiences. It cemented their sense of how they should go about working together on the next assignment.

In the second scenario the good grade is more problematic, as it goes against what team members actually experienced in the process of getting the grade. The process was dysfunctional. Members procrastinated. Some did too little, and others did too much. Communication was haphazard. The team was little more than a collection of individuals who barely joined to do the project. Frustration was the predominant feeling. Yet that feeling—and the negative experience of the team more generally—was discounted by the high grade. Members of student project teams typically interpret high grades as a sanctioning of their processes: If the grade was good, the logic goes, the process that produced that grade must have been right, and if they want more high grades, they should follow the same processes in the future. High grades thus lock in the seeming rightness of team processes. Team members begin to reframe their actual experiences: They were inspired by deadlines, not procrastinating; they were putting the right people in the right jobs, not just scrambling to cover for disengaged members; they were delegating the finishing of the project to a leader, not just giving up and letting the person who cared the most do the most work. The ends not only justified the means, they obliterated memories of those means and substituted more flattering ones in their places.

Good grades thus tend to lead you to believe that the ways in which your team worked to get those grades, no matter how destructive, were good (or at least good enough) and therefore not worth examining more closely. In the second scenario, this is an example of what I referred to earlier as an "unproductive success." The team was successful, in terms of its grade, but it is not clear *why* that success occurred—and thus it is not clear how, exactly, to reproduce the result on the next project. Was it because the team chose the right topic or approach? Or the member who ended up doing most of the work knew a great deal about the topic or was a great writer? Or the weaker members of the team did nothing at all? What did the team really learn about how to achieve high performance in the future, other than, perhaps, to coerce a smart member to do the work? Productive successes are reproducible, in two senses: Members know how to perform well, and they want to do so. In the second scenario, the team might know what to do—get one member to do all the work—but it is not likely that the member will wish to do so given his or her frustration and resentment. The team might well convince itself that "it was worth it," but there will linger the sense of something askew between the lousy experience of going through the process and the high grade itself.

It takes a lot to resist the tendency to avoid looking closely at how the team worked to improve its processes, and good grades make this more difficult. What of poor grades? Well, it depends. If team members wish to get good grades, and do not, they are more likely to want to learn why they did not do well and how they can do better next time. This falls into the category of "productive failures." An undesirable grade leads the team toward a productive inquiry into how it can improve. The nature of the inquiry depends on how closely the poor outcome fits members' experiences of their team process. If some or many members indeed felt that their process was flawed (the third scenario) they are more likely to use the poor outcome as just the excuse they need to try and get better at working as a team. (They could, of course, choose to avoid this work by blaming one another, the instructor, or their circumstances, or by giving up and resigning themselves to poor performance.) If members sincerely felt that they worked together quite well (the fourth scenario) they are more likely to ask their instructor for more detailed feedback and revisit their choices in completing their assignment. In both cases there are still attempts to learn how to do better in the future. The question is how broken the team process is and how much work is needed to fix it.

Grades thus complicate greatly the ways in which you learn to improve the functioning of your team. The complications arise in the relation between two variables: the grade and the experience of the team process leading up to that grade. When the two are mutually reinforcing, the path is reasonably clear. A team process that feels good to all members and results in a high grade (the first scenario) needs to be reproduced. A team process that feels badly to a number of members and results in a low grade (the third scenario) is a spur to team learning and development. The means and the ends fit appropriately. The other cases are more problematic. A team process that feels badly to some or all members and receives a high grade (the second scenario) creates dissonance within members. They have to choose between "believing" the positive grade or their negative experiences of working on the project. The team that had a uniformly positive experience working together and yet received a poor grade (the fourth scenario) must make a similar choice. Internal experiences and external outcomes are in conflict.

It is difficult for learning to occur in the context of such dissonance. Because the relationship between process and outcomes raises dissonance, it is the relationship itself that must be deemphasized. In practice, this means thinking less about grades and more about team process. The tendency to overemphasize grades means that your experiences of working together—of fairness and equity, of how decisions are made, of how members' voices are heard or dismissed— tend to get overshadowed by the grade that your instructor gives. Yet the instructor cannot evaluate your process; it is only you and your teammates who can do that. If you focus only, or mostly, on the instructor's evaluation, you lose the ability to evaluate other goals, such as the health of your team's interactions and your own real learning of course material.

I am assuming here that you care about more than just the grades that you receive. For some students, this is a flawed assumption, as they care far less about what they learn or how functional their teams are than they do about their grades. For others—and I hope that it is the vast majority—there is usually some desire to make their teams better, and in the process, learn more (about creating functional teams, about themselves, about the course material) and get better results. If you are such a student (or you are willing to go along with others on your team who are), you will look at your team processes in terms of what you and the others experienced while working on an assignment rather than in terms of the grades that you've received. You will separate means and ends.

There are three ways to do this. First, you can do process checks while your team is working together. At the end of a planning meeting, for example, take 5 or 10 minutes for the team to discuss how the team is working together. A slightly longer process check format involves using the *Pit-stop form* (described in Team Development Exercise 5). Second, you can conduct after-action reviews. Third, in the process of preparing for your deliverables, you can review the insights you had about how the team has been working together. Taken together, the process checks, after-action reviews, and planning conversations help offset the often overwhelming power of grades to determine your willingness and ability to truly learn from your experiences of working together and improve your performances.

No-Fault Teamwork

Creating a learning team also depends on your ability to resist the temptation to assign blame for events (and grades) that go wrong. Learning teams get tripped up when members tell stories of blame. A team member misses a deadline, and the rest of you blame her for having to work late into the night before the assignment is due. Or two members, assigned to edit the report, change an important transition; your team receives a poor grade, for which you blame the pair of editors. In such cases you're laying blame for disliked events onto particular members. This harms your team in multiple ways: You create casualties of one another, get into patterns of attacking and defending, split into factions of allies and opponents, and communicate in ways that harm relationships and task performances. Laying blame greatly diminishes your opportunities to really learn how to get better at what you're doing.

Learning requires you to be open, to consider different possibilities, to reflect on what you and others did and did not do. Laying blame—or avoiding it—requires you to be closed to any possibilities that do not fit the story that you most wish to tell, about yourself (as innocent, heroic, well-intentioned) and about others (as guilty, incompetent, badly intentioned). The two stances are opposed. You simply cannot learn when trying to protect yourself or blame others. You are substituting the goal of self-protection for that of learning what you do not already know or think you know. You have less need to protect yourself and thus more chance to learn when you create a "no fault" zone on your team.

In their book *How the Way We Talk Can Change the Way We Work*, Kegan and Lahey (2001) suggest how you might create such a zone. They describe the difference between what they term the "language of blame" and the "language of personal responsibility." You use the language of blame when you seek to hold others responsible for gaps between what you would like to see occur and what actually occurs. The language comes relatively easily to us; we use it to tell stories that leave others at fault and ourselves looking relatively good. As you might expect, this language frequently leaves those who are blamed frustrated and alienated. It does the same for you, as it leaves you attacking and defending rather than working to understand and resolve issues. The language rarely gets you anywhere: It deflects your attention to places where you have little or no direct influence. You might momentarily feel better or more self-righteous when you blame others, but there is little lasting benefit to doing so.

The language of personal responsibility is quite different. Kegan and Lahey (2001) note that what occurs in organizational life is usually complex enough to involve many players and conditions. They suggest that in any situation of which you are a part you have contributed to the events of that situation by what you did or did not do. The language of personal responsibility becomes the way in which you acknowledge whatever your contributions are. This does not assume that you bear the greatest responsibility for difficult events, or that you are doing little or nothing to try and make situations better. It assumes only that each of us is part of a *contribution system*, that is, had some hand, small or large, in creating events as they have been created. Your work becomes identifying anything that you are doing or not doing that has led to your present circumstances.

The language of personal responsibility is diametrically opposed to the language of blame. You focus on yourself rather than others. You disarm others by identifying your contributions, enabling your teammates to drop their weapons as well and join with you in figuring out what happened. You direct your attention to places where you have influence and can actually do something productive. You tell stories that are complicated rather than simple, mirroring the real complexity of team life. You create productive conversations that move beyond attack-and-defend exchanges and into dialogues where learning and change become possible. Finally, you explore problems rather than simply solving them and making them go away. Exploring problems leads to learning and insights that you might not otherwise attain. It leads to a more sophisticated understanding of your own contributions to the situations in which you find yourself.

Consider, for example, when your teammate missed a deadline, which you felt led to the rest of the team working late into the night and rushing to complete an assignment. Assigning blame is easy enough: It was her fault for delaying her work. The team solved the immediate problem by just working hard to get the assignment done, and took care of the potential long-term problem by making sure that the teammate at fault did not have an important task on the next assignment. What if you knew, however, that events are rarely so simple, and that the other team members—including you—probably contributed to the problem in some fashion? You would think differently about the event and look more carefully at what happened. You might discover, for example, that a chain of events on the team led to your teammate's delay: Another member missed a meeting, which led to a series of missed communications and deadlines, which prevented your "at-fault" teammate from having the information necessary to complete her part of the assignment on time. She might have procrastinated, of course, or not been proactive in seeking out the information from another member, but she was not fully to blame. Each of you presumably contributed to what occurred, through what you did or did not do in the period leading up to her offense.

Consider the example of two members, assigned to edit the report, who change an important transition. Your team receives a poor grade, for which you blame the pair of editors. You resolve to make sure that these two members are not paired again, because they failed, and that they should not be in charge of the final product. That story is easy enough to formulate, but it is also a cover story: a story that you tell to distract attention from what might be going on under the surface. If you believe in the notion of shared rather than isolated responsibility in teams, then the story must become more complex and inclusive. You might look at the state of the report before your teammates did their editing. You might discover that the two members who wrote adjacent sections neither communicated nor shared their plans with one another, making it difficult to create a workable transition. You might find that the poor grade had little to do with the transition at all, but reflected the poor argument that the team was trying to make more generally. You might even discover that you were a part of the problem as well, because you suspected some of this during the process but kept silent, hoping that it would all just work out. These discoveries would require you to distribute the blame more carefully across the whole team.

Telling more complex stories about events on your team is not, however, simply about redistributing blame. You need to tell more complex stories because it enables you to act differently, more effectively, and indeed, more responsibly. If you simply blame the team member who misses a deadline, and punish her in some fashion, you leave the real problem unsolved: the more general lack of commitment to the team or its project, which gets acted out in members missing meetings, not communicating clearly, or withdrawing from one another. Talking about that problem would lead to a different set of actions, such as reconsidering whether the project idea is compelling enough to hold members' interest or whether the team's coordination and communication patterns are working well enough. If you blame the two members who edited the final report, and punish them, you also leave the real problem unaddressed: the lack of communication among members whose work should be more integrated, or the lack of effective team decision making that led to the initial project idea or argument. Again, talking about that problem would lead you to act differently, focusing more on the whole team's patterns of work and interaction.

Building more complex narratives about your team—and thus identifying the ways in which all members contribute to what happens—thus creates a more sophisticated foundation for action. It's like a physician developing the right diagnosis for an illness; the right diagnosis leads to the right course of action, which will cure the illness and make sure that it does not reappear. The problems that your teams have are rarely, if ever, located in one person. Solving those problems thus means that you need to develop a diagnosis that takes into account the whole team. Individual members will surely contribute to those problems, in terms of the styles with which they approach their work and one another. Do not get distracted by those styles, however. Look beneath them to discover the substance of the team itself, the patterns that each of you have helped put in place and maintain. It is only by looking at those patterns that you can truly learn how to get better as a team.

So what does this mean, practically speaking? The focus here is on learning as much as you can to help your team be as effective as it can. Such learning happens when you take time to pause and reflect on events and their causes. Reflection is part of the learning cycle, enabling you to move from action to insight. Process checks and after-action reviews are your vehicles for reflection. They give you moments of pause, during which you develop complex rather than simple stories of what happened and why. The stories are complex because you are developing a sense of how each member contributed to noteworthy events. You record the ensuing lessons and insights. You refer to them when planning the next stage of work. Repeated over time, this becomes a process of continuous learning. You thus build your capacity to learn how to work better and more effectively, and to get more of what you want from the journey on which you and your team have been sent.

Good Problems

Kegan and Lahey (2001) also describe in their book what they term "good problems." Good problems, they suggest, are not those that you simply solve, but those that solve you. When you move too easily to simple solutions—deciding to give unimportant tasks to teammates who have seemingly let you down, for example, or to start your projects earlier—you rob yourself of opportunities to learn much more about yourself and your teams. You do not give yourself the chance to figure out how you might keep getting in your own way. The underlying issues having to do with you and the team cannot be surfaced and looked at, learned about, and solved. It's like treating symptoms without understanding their underlying causes. The symptoms might improve, but the causes remain. Inevitably, they will generate further symptoms, which will prove irritating if not downright destructive to your team.

This chapter points to learning as the process of identifying and solving good problems. Without learning how to improve its processes, your team will get stuck, doomed to repeat patterns and mistakes. It's like the movie *Groundhog Day,* in which the main character wakes up every day stuck in time: Every day is, endlessly, the same day from which he cannot escape. It is only when he learns the lessons that he most needed to learn—about how to communicate openly and effectively, work with rather than against others, and take himself more seriously—that he makes a key change in his behavior and is released from the place in which he was stuck. Your teams are not so different; you just need to figure out what you need to learn, individually and collectively, to keep getting better at working together.

The problems and issues—in communication, division of labor, decision making, trust, and the like—that might develop on your team will not simply disappear. They might lie low for a while. They might present themselves in ways that seem minor, not worth the effort. You can try and make them go away by blaming them on particular members, but even if those members go away the issues will not. They'll stay buried within the team. They'll continue to present themselves through the actions and nonactions of you and your team-mates. Like a child whose cries of distress are ignored, they'll get more insistent, demanding attention. On teams with clear inequities in the division of labor, what might begin as bits of sarcasm grow into extended periods of hostility as the underlying inequities and frustrations are unaddressed. The underlying chasms never disappear; they simply lie in wait, like fault lines beneath the ground that cause earthquakes.

You have choices to make here. You can hope that you and the others can hang on until the end of the project, getting by without having to explore difficult issues and have difficult conversations. You're hoping that the earthquakes don't happen or that they won't be too destructive. Or you can approach issues on your team as good problems, as opportunities to learn how to get better at what you do together. This is the choice that will present itself time and again throughout the life of your project team. Indeed, it's a choice that you'll face—or not—throughout your career, and your life, as you encounter potentially good problems. This book offers you ways to make your choices with as much awareness as possible about their consequences. It also offers the tools with which you can help your team continue to learn and improve as much as you can. What you do with these offerings is, as always, up to you.

Summary

The underlying premise (and hope) of this book is that your teams can become more effective as you learn how to reflect on what occurs, develop insights about what to do differently, and act on those insights by trying new behaviors.

Repeated over time, this process drives the creation of a learning team. This chapter focused on the nature of such a team: its use of methods by which to identify and solve problems, experiment, and learn from results. It also focused on the underlying culture of the learning team: the shared belief among its members that they should, and can, learn about how to make teams better and stronger. Anchored by that belief, you can allow yourselves to move past the impulse to blame others for difficult situations or unwanted outcomes. You can allow yourself to delve into more sophisticated understandings of how all members share responsibility for creating and changing your teams. You can also make good use of the insights and tools contained in the rest of the book.

Chapter 3

Team Formation

If you have any hopes of getting to where you want to go, you have to figure out where that place is and how to get there. This sort of planning is very much the work of team formation. It is crucial to the success of your team, much as the underlying foundation of a bridge is crucial to its strength and resilience. Done well, that process begins the creation of a real team; done poorly, that process limits your abilities to become anything more than a group of individuals who happen to be cast together. In this chapter I describe the team formation process, and ways in which it can be functional or dysfunctional, using illustrations from actual student project teams.

The formation process is complicated by the fact that two processes are occurring simultaneously. You are figuring out how much you really want to be part of the team—how much time and energy you will invest, how close you want to get to other members, and how many risks you want to take to say things that might improve how the team works. Your group is also trying to figure out how to be a team—how to organize itself to get work done in ways that are effective and efficient. These two processes each shape the other. You must personally figure out how much you really want to engage in the team even as all of you, together, are making verbal commitments about how to work together.

The problem here is that of too little information. You do not really know one another well enough at the very beginning to make fully informed choices about how much to invest in your relationships. At the same time, your new team does not have enough information about how committed are its members to make fully informed choices about how to structure your time together. Any commitments that you make during formation are thus likely to be provisional in nature. They cannot help but be so, really, given how little information you have on which to base decisions. Decisions are made, however, individually and collectively, and the decisions matter. They matter for the trip that you plan, and for the trip that you actually take.

What Do We Exist to Be?

This is a provocative question. Answering it is the first toll. To pass through that toll you must think past the simple answer: "We exist because the professor told us that we have to do a project together." This is an answer to a different question: Why or how were we formed? I am posing a more challenging question here. I am asking you to think carefully about all that your teams might become, if you so choose. I am asking why you are going on the trip at all.

In posing this question I am making certain assumptions. First, I assume your teams can exist for different purposes. I reviewed these purposes in the introductory chapter. Teams can exist for you to perform well and get high grades. They can exist as settings in which you learn how to work together well and enjoyably. They can exist as vehicles for your personal growth and learning. Second, I assume that you can make choices about the extent to which your teams exist to serve these purposes. These purposes are not, or should not be, mutually exclusive, and you need to figure out the varying emphases that you wish to place on each. Third, I assume that the choices that you make matter, for what you do in your teams and for your experiences during the life of the team. Our experiences—on our teams, in our relationships, in our lives—are always a matter of the choices we make about what we exist to be, alone and in relation with others.

The more traditional language here is that of "mission." Your new team's first task is to develop a common mission—what the team exists to be and to do—and the initial structures by which you will work together on behalf of that mission. A mission statement is a *destination*. It allows everyone to know where they, as a team, are headed. It answers the question, "What is this team meant to be and do?" Team missions provide a common ground. They offer common goals and directions that anchor members. They shape the choices that you make in relation to what your team does together. And they are touchstones, to which you can return, reaffirming them, even changing them as you work through difficult decisions and choices. In healthy teams members struggle well together. They return, time and again, to the specific missions that hold them together, serving as a collective source of meaning and purpose. It matters less the particular answers to the question, "What do we exist to be?" than it does that teams have answers to the question, and that the answers make sense and matter to members.

This is what missions do: They gather people's energies, point them in some direction that matters to them, and send them on their way. Military missions focus soldiers in just this way. They instruct, guide, and lead people toward or away from certain acts. Indeed, compelling missions help people sharpen and make choices. The world of the student project team is filled with choices: how to invest time and energy, divide up and integrate work, spend time together, and make trade-offs between work and play. Clear and succinct statements of the team's mission clarify those choices. Mission statements, used well, divide what is pursued from what is not.

Missions that compel people are simply put. They are immediately graspable. They contain a few rather than many ideas and purposes. They represent consensus rather than compromise, the result of team members struggling to articulate the essential nature of what keeps them together. Mission statements that represent compromise are large and unwieldy. In an effort to make sure that all members and all purposes are represented, these statements are too loose: There is no particular, special mission that people can sign on to that will engage them fully, that will both orient and limit their work in useful ways. This is what we are after: deceptively simple statements that hold people together, represent what they most wish to do through the instrument of the team, and create divisions between what they will do and what they will not.

It might seem like a waste of time to develop a mission statement for a team that exists just for an academic course. The project will come and go, after all, and missions seem like they are meant for "real" organizational teams. What too many students have discovered, however, is that they have wasted far too much time by not developing clear and agreed-on statements about what they will do as a team. Working at cross-purposes, they end up wasting time working against or around one another. Students have also discovered that course project teams are very much like organizational teams, and that the more that they practice developing missions for their project teams, the better they are at it when they join organizations and the stakes are much higher. The real learning from your project teams is not simply a deeper investigation of course content but the chance to develop skills of how to be on teams.

So what does this mean for the first conversations on your new project team? It means first allowing yourself to speak truthfully about what you really want from the team experience. You need to speak honestly about your priorities. You might care deeply about grades, your social experience on the team, doing as little as possible so you can focus energies elsewhere, or really learning course material in depth. Crafting a mission is a process of identifying what it is that each of you cares about, and how much. Second, you need to examine the costs and benefits of these values. You must explore together the trade-offs that each of you is willing to make, and what those trade-offs will mean to you personally and to the team more generally. Third, you then need to work together to craft statements that reflect true consensus, to the extent that is possible in the first moments of a team's existence.

The resulting project team mission statements look deceptively simple. Some examples might be the following:

- The purpose of our team is to enhance the learning of our members, to the point that each of us feels comfortable with course material and performs well in the course.
- Our team exists to create a first-class project on which we work together and equitably.
- We agree that the primary purpose of our team is to complete the course project in ways that leave us enjoying our work together.
- The mission of our team is to get a high grade on the team project without sacrificing our relationships with one another.

These are missions. They are foundations on which to build. They contain values and beliefs. They suggest trade-offs between various purposes, which are implicitly arrayed in terms of importance and priority. The statements reflect choices that you and your teammates are making about who you are and wish to be as a team, what you wish to do, and the nature of the conversations and relationships in which you wish to engage.

What you actually do with these mission statements will determine the extent to which they are, in practice, vibrant and compelling. Some mission statements are fully lived. They orient team members consistently, compel them to move toward certain behaviors and away from others. Others live only symbolically. They are written down but have little to do with what people actually do. Mission statements are thus meaningful only to the extent that you routinely invoke them, and use them to help anchor important conversations and guide difficult choices.

Initial Structures

Once you have created a mission for your team, you need a vision of how members should work together on behalf of that mission. This involves creating the initial structures that will help the team begin to function effectively. Their usefulness will depend on how clear your mission is. When team missions are clear—that is, when all members of your team understand what you will and will not pursue, and where you wish to end up as a team—it becomes possible to create paths that take you to those spots exactly. When those missions are diffuse, and people wish to go many places simultaneously, you will likely struggle to remain together on any path. Such struggles are often difficult. You may work at cross-purposes and maneuver against one another in the absence of mission statements that ground you in a specific set of values, purposes, and rules for making choices.

The initial structures that you need to create are of three general types—ways to divide and integrate work, to coordinate and communicate, and to make decisions. I work through each of these structures in turn, and the types of choices that need to be made. In many ways, these choices all point toward a primary decision that you need to make: Are we to be a working group or are we to be a team? The differences are not simply semantic. Box 3-1 offers a way to conceptualize the differences. The choices that you make will inevitably answer this larger question and shape your relationships with one another.

Dividing and Integrating Work

A significant set of decisions involves figuring out how the team's work gets done. Your team must develop structures that fit the nature of the work that you need to do. A research project, for example, requires you to identify the different areas that need to be researched, assign different team members distinct areas, and bring them together to integrate your efforts into a coherent report. Creating something new—a product, a design, a plan, a process—requires you to spend much more time together, brainstorming and playing off each other as you develop one rather than many ideas. Each of these tasks requires your team to develop particular ways of getting the work done. To figure out those ways, your team must answer some specific questions.

What Roles Do We Need to Get Our Work Done?

Different roles are necessary for effective, efficient work. These roles will change according to the nature of the task. Research projects require researchers—people who will go out and gather information, in libraries and through the Internet and in interviews. They also require integrators—people who will pull together the information gathered and shape it in ways that offer effective arguments. They also require finishers—people who will create reports or presentations that effectively represent the work that has been done. Creative projects require different sorts of roles. They require brainstormers who will lead others in thinking as creatively as possible, researchers who will find out what similar ideas or products already exist, and implementers who will perform analyses related to the feasibility of the ideas that are generated. Analytical projects, which focus on analyzing a problem or issue and making recommendations for action, require

BOX 3-1   THE NATURE OF TEAMS

Working groups and teams are not the same thing. Katzenbach and Smith (1993), in their book *The Discipline of Teams*, describe the differences in terms of performance. A working group's performance is a function of what its members do as individuals. A team's performance includes both what individuals do themselves and what they do together on collective work products that reflect real, joint contributions. They define a team as a small number of people with complementary skills who are committed to a common purpose, set of performance goals, and approach for which they hold themselves mutually accountable.

Katzenbach and Smith summarize the differences more generally in the following ways:

Working Group	Team
Strong, focused leader	Shared leadership roles
Individual accountability	Individual and mutual accountability
Individual work products	Collective work products
Runs efficient meetings	Encourages open-ended discussion and active problem-solving meetings
Discusses, decides, delegates	Discusses, decides, and does real work together

The working group is thus most suited to individual performance tasks, which can benefit from coordination and communication. Departments and functional areas use these groups to coordinate work that needs to get done that does not depend on collaboration in the service of joint products. The team, on the other hand, is most suited to collective performance tasks, which can only get done when people work together—develop ideas and solutions, solve problems, and create products and presentations.

Katzenbach and Smith point to the commitment that team members hold—to a collective purpose, and to one another in the service of that purpose—as the crucial distinction between working group and team. Student project teams are most successful, as teams, when they are able to generate and sustain such commitments.

members to be different sorts of analysts—social, financial, organizational, environmental, business, and the like, depending on the nature of the project.

It matters less that you choose precisely the right label for certain roles than that you have the conversations necessary to understand the sorts of roles that should be played and who should, at least initially, perform them. Without those conversations, your team will have too many members doing some things and not enough doing other things.

How Should We Be Led?

One particular role that you need to decide on concerns leadership. This is a tricky area, particularly in the beginning of a team's existence, but it becomes less tricky the more openly it is discussed. Your team needs leaders. I focus on issues of leadership in much more depth in Chapter 5, but it becomes important even at this early stage that you discuss how you should be led. Neglecting that conversation damages your team's ability to do its work. Too many project teams in organizations have discovered that without a project leader, people drift or work at cross-purposes. The question that needs to be addressed at this initial stage concerns the model of leadership. What does the team require for its mission to be accomplished?

Ideally, your answer to this question allows for leadership to be defined in multiple ways. Your team will require different types of leadership at various times. Different members are likely to provide those different types. The two most effective types of leaders are the *facilitator,* who, like a traffic cop, helps monitor the flow of conversation, ensuring that team members participate appropriately and move through agenda items; and the *project manager,* who coordinates and schedules the project-related activities of team members, ensuring that their work is integrated.

How Do We Divide Up the Work?

Teams exist because, in theory, it is more efficient and more effective to have multiple people working on the same project than to have one person trying to do so alone. Such efficiency and effectiveness is a matter, however, of making sure that your team is dividing up the work in ways that make sense and seamlessly integrating its efforts. Complex projects have multiple aspects. There might be different areas to research, paths to explore, designs to create, and the like. It often makes sense for teams to adopt divide-and-conquer strategies, assigning different pieces to particular individuals or subgroups. To have the whole team working together on all aspects of a project can be frustratingly inefficient and ineffective. Your team needs to be mindful of the choices that members are making in regard to such strategies.

There are several dimensions to consider. One dimension has to do with the relation between expertise and learning. Your team might ask particular members who are already quite skilled—at research, say, or finance—to perform those functions. There are trade-offs here. Those individuals will likely do a relatively better job at those tasks than other less knowledgeable members, but opportunities for other members to apply and deepen their learning about those areas will be lost, as are opportunities for the selected members to try other, less familiar tasks. A second dimension has to with the nature of subgroups. Your team may split into smaller clusters, with members joining together in subgroups to work on particular pieces of the project. These subgroups are often useful, enabling individuals to work more closely with several others on complicated tasks. At the same time, they pose a potential threat. If you spend a great deal of time in a subgroup, you might begin to identify more closely with a few others than with the team more generally. This gets problematic when subgroups compete with or withdraw from one another. You need to be careful to divide up work in ways that allow for both discrete pieces of work to get done by subgroups and for those units to join together and integrate their work.

Coordinating Efforts and Communicating Information

Another set of decisions involves figuring out how to coordinate your efforts and communicate with one another. There is, in any relationship, the potential for slippage—that is, for people to act on the basis of misguided assumptions about what others are thinking or doing, misinterpret others' communications, and drift along in less-than-ideal ways of working or relating. Teams are no different. Slippage in project teams is almost always a matter of members not figuring out how to coordinate how they should be working together or staying closely enough in touch with one another to make sure that their efforts are useful. This is particularly tricky when teams are working virtually, using technology (Web spaces, teleconferences, e-mail) a great deal and only infrequently getting together face-to-face.

In figuring out how they should connect with one another, project teams must answer the following sorts of questions.

How Often Do We Meet as a Full Team? What Should Happen at Our Meetings?

These questions are, of course, interrelated, and tied to the larger issue of why your team is meeting. Teams meet for different reasons, according to the nature and flow of their projects. In the beginning, they meet to develop shared understandings of what you need to do, visions of what your final products will look like, standards of quality and efficiency, timelines, and the processes by which you work. There should be a fair number of these meetings. These issues are not simple. They require you to develop a well-articulated grasp of what, exactly, the project requires, and how you want to satisfy those requirements. As you begin to work in subgroups on specific tasks, you will probably meet less often as a whole team, or for less time. At those meetings members will check in with one another about their progress, and give and receive assistance as necessary. You need to make sure that you are continuing along the same path, in terms of the vision of what you are doing and how you are working together. You need to make sure as well that everyone knows how their pieces of work are connecting to one another. Later, as the team completes its work, you will meet to stitch together the final products. This too might take a fair amount of time, as you work together on conceptualizing the transitions and bridges between different parts of the project.

We do know something about what makes meetings effective. First, you need to know why you are meeting. Each meeting should have a clear purpose. If each member knows exactly why the team is meeting—for problem solving, decision making, planning, reporting, or feedback—the time is likely to be productive. Second, a clear agenda distributed in advance of the meeting enables you to remain focused on the purpose and enables the team to work efficiently. Third, adequate preparation by each member of your team means that you can actually do real work together. Fourth, you need to ensure adequate participation in discussions by all those present at a meeting. Fifth, start and end meetings on time by sticking to the agenda. Finally, summarize action items, such that each of you knows exactly what you and the others will do prior to the next meeting.

What Should Happen Between Meetings? How Should We Use Available Technology?

Project teams exist even (or mostly) when members are not meeting together in their full teams. It is important to figure out what you should be doing between meetings. Clearly, you should be working on whatever aspects of the project for which you are responsible, alone or in subgroups. Yet you also need to figure out how to coordinate your efforts between meetings. This is particularly important if your team is geographically dispersed and cannot meet regularly. There are several areas to consider here. First, you can assign particular members to serve as *coordinators,* people to whom information flows from other members (about what they are working on, having difficulty with, and learning about) and who summarize and disperse that information to the team more generally. Second, you can create ways for all members to virtually "meet" for updating and planning. This involves figuring out how to use technology—conference calls, dedicated Web sites, e-mail lists—to enable members to regularly engage with one another in useful ways.

Teams that are largely virtual in nature, whose members do much of their work physically apart from one another, need to be aware of what that process means. Virtual work has a certain allure. Members might feel that they are not wasting their time by getting to and attending meetings. They might feel that they can get real work done more effectively and efficiently apart from one another. It does indeed seem more productive to just work—do the research, figure out what it means, put together an analysis, and send it off to other members—than spend time in meetings that often seem circular, boring, and inefficient. However, there are real costs here of which these team members need to be aware. Face-to-face meetings offer the opportunity for you to create together, to play off one another's ideas and build something that might not otherwise occur. Meetings enable you to give and receive real feedback that cannot be expressed any other way, given the importance of reading one another's verbal and nonverbal cues and expressions. Meetings also enable people to eat together, laugh together, and create relationships with one another that lead to trust. Without some face-to-face meetings to build and sustain such relationships, virtual teams inevitably fracture in one form or another.

Decision Making

Your team also needs to develop ways to make decisions. Unlike in work organizations, where there are established hierarchical roles, your project team has no clear procedures for making decisions. And there are plenty of decisions to make: how projects get defined, their final forms envisioned, and the approaches taken to achieve those visions; who does what on the team; how members coordinate and integrate their work; and what, ultimately, defines the final products. How these decisions get made—that is, the implicit rules by which you decide among competing alternatives—matters a great deal, in terms of the quality of those decisions. In Chapter 5 I focus in more depth on some of the complicated issues involved in how project teams make decisions. At this point, however, your team does need to address an important issue. How important is consensus—the real kind, not the false kind—and how willing are members to pursue it in practice?

It would be wonderful if everyone agreed on important decisions. Full consensus is nice. It is also difficult to achieve. In its ideal form it requires you to have full and open conversations, filled with different perspectives and ideas, and to move, through a consideration of the costs and benefits of different alternatives, toward the path that makes the most sense to all members. This takes a lot of time. It requires you to engage thoughtfully with rather than simply give in to one another. A variation is partial consensus. This occurs when many of the team members agree on a certain course of action, and those who do not agree, after a consideration of the arguments and a voicing of their reservations, are willing to go along with the others and support the chosen alternative. Partial consensus does not involve voting. It means that you are willing to agree to pursue paths on the basis of your faith in the perspectives and beliefs of others.

There is, of course, always voting. Voting is a reasonably efficient way to make decisions. Team members make their arguments and put them to a vote. The majority rules. There are costs to this approach, however. First, you might lobby one another outside meetings, trying to marshal votes for your proposals. This creates a politicized environment that undermines effective teamwork. Second, you might attack, passively or aggressively, others' proposals during discussions that would otherwise be spent focusing on analyzing the costs and benefits of all alternatives. Third, if the same people are routinely in the majority or the minority, the team might split into two—those with power, and those without—and be unable to work as one unit. These are useful cautions for an overreliance on voting.

Another solution mirrors that of work organizations: Individual members are authorized to make the final decisions, based on a hearing of different alternatives. Team members are assigned to be arbitrators—to make decisions on the basis of their expertise or experience in certain relevant areas, or as part of their role as project manager. This decision process allows for efficiency—one person is making a decision, rather than going through lengthier processes of forging consensus. The costs are, of course, related to the concentration of decision-making power in the hands of one person. The decision might be perceived as driven by one person's agenda. There might not be a full airing of the possibilities. Others might feel excluded from the process, and thus not engage in carrying out the decision.

The Formation Process

Several weeks into the semester a professor forms teams of five students. The teams are to work together through the remainder of the semester on a project. The project has several large components—a research report due midway through the course, and a presentation and paper due at the end. Project grades are worth half of the course grade, which is also determined by tests and class participation. The professor gives the students a packet of materials that describe the assignments. She asks the students to turn in a brief description of the project topic that they have chosen. She ends class 10 minutes early, giving students time to exchange contact information and figure out when they are going to meet. The description is due the week following the introduction of the project.

One of the teams in the class gathers together the next day. Members introduce themselves. One of the members, Sarah, tells the others that she had been on a great team the previous semester, and had spent some time thinking about why it had been so great. The other members were curious. Sarah says that one of the main reasons was that they spent some time talking at the beginning not just about what they were going to work on but how they would work together. She also says that it turned out that most of the members had similar ideas about what they wanted from the team. She wishes that they had talked about that earlier, she told her new team, as there were some uncomfortable moments during the course of the project, but they had finally gotten to some clear agreements about the team's purposes. Sarah asks the others on her new team if they had good experiences before. Several have, and they speak about why they thought those teams were good. Dana says that on her team it was clear what people were supposed to be doing. Joel says that people liked one another and got along, but were honest with one another, too. Raj says that people did their assignments when they said they would. Stephen says that they had fun together.

Sarah expresses her hope that they can create a team with similar characteristics. She tells the others what she hopes to get out of the team, and what some of her strengths and weaknesses might be in relation to the types of projects they will be working on. The others follow her lead, talking about what they too hope the team experience would be like, what they might be able to contribute, and what they would need to learn more about to help the team on its project assignments. Dana talks about how important it is to be on a team where members think about learning and not just about grades. Raj tells her that he hopes that they can maintain that, once tests and project grades come into play during the semester.

Joel suggests that they formalize their conversation a bit more. He facilitates a discussion of the team's mission statement—what they could all agree was the purpose of the team. After discussing the importance of grades for some, and of a more relaxed social atmosphere for others, the team develops a statement that all members say they can live with: We agree that the primary purpose of our team is to complete the course project in ways that let us learn the material more fully and enjoy our work together. Everyone writes the statement down, pleased that they could, at least initially, figure out how to deal with the place and meaning of grades, learning, and social dimensions in the team project. Dana stresses the importance of the statement, telling the others that they will probably need to refer back to it and see how well they are living out that mission. Raj jokes that they should come up with a team name, based on their mission. Stephen, grinning, says he had the same idea, and suggests a name—"The Escaped"—based on their relief about no longer being on previous, horror-filled teams. The others laugh, and use the name from then on.

Joel tells the others on the team that it might also make sense to talk in more detail about how they might work together, as he, like several others on the team, occasionally travels during the semester. The team talks about meetings. They agree on a regular meeting place, near the campus, and work through their schedules until they agree on a regular meeting time for getting together. The team agrees to meet every other week for planning and coordination purposes, and then, as assignments are due, every week, with the option to add more sessions as necessary. Raj pushes the team to think about leadership and the various roles that members should play. The team agrees that there should be a project manager for part of the project, defining the role in terms of scheduling, coordinating information flow between members, and reminding members of deadlines and commitments. Raj volunteers to be the first project manager. Dana suggests that Sarah might facilitate the first few meetings, in terms of developing agendas, keeping the team on track, and reminding the team to think about its process during and after its meetings. Stephen says that he'd be happy to interface with the professor, making sure that the team is on track in terms of understanding assignments and collecting the right types of information. Dana talks about enjoying research. Joel says that he is a detail person who is pretty good at tying up loose ends and making sure that final papers and presentations are really complete. The team agrees to revisit these role assignments after the first stage of the project is complete.

Finally, after an hour of discussing how they can begin working together, the team focuses on the first assignment. They brainstorm ideas about what perspective they should take on the project. They come up with several options. The team divides into two pairs, each of which will do preliminary research on an option and report back to the others at the next meeting. Raj, the project manager, who is not in a pair, says that he will put together a timetable for the project, develop some criteria by which to decide in what direction to go, and investigate setting up a Web space for the team to share information and have discussions. The team adjourns, its next meeting established. Members are pleased with how much they accomplished in what seemed like a quick 90 minutes.

When Formation Goes Well

This is an example of a formation process that, in its first steps, is going well. Members are beginning to move from a group of individuals to a team. They do this not as a function of their being fortunate enough to have been thrown in with others who think alike, are nice people, or skilled in teamwork. Such factors help, of course, but we tend to overemphasize their importance—and in so doing, overlook the ways in which teams create the foundations for effective teamwork by focusing on three key dimensions: *missions, roles,* and *boundaries.* In our example, the team did a fine job of attending to those dimensions and positioning itself for more good work together.

Mission

The team began the process of figuring out why it existed. The members knew, of course, that they had a project to complete, as part of the course requirement. As discussed earlier, however, there are many ways for a team to do that. Our team, at Sarah's initiative, discussed what they really wanted from the team experience. They were able to develop a simple yet meaningful statement that will guide their work with one another. Such statements are the foundation for good team formation. The process of creating them forces members to think about their agendas and needs. It forces them to think about how to accommodate differences. Later, these statements will serve as guides for making decisions— about how much effort to put in, how members work together, and how to solve disputes. Articulating a primary mission brings a group together and makes it a team, giving members a shared goal large enough to overcome disparate agendas and needs that might otherwise pull them apart.

Roles

The team also began to think about what roles individuals might play on behalf of the team and its project. Roles are instrumental for work getting done. They ensure that the efforts of individual members will be in sync with one another. Our team named some basic, but crucial roles—meeting facilitator, project manager, researcher, resource, and finisher. Such roles ensure that important tasks will get done, and done efficiently, without duplication of efforts. Complex tasks, such as team projects, require an appropriate division of labor. Assigning roles early in the team formation process allows for such divisions. It also enables individual members to have a clear sense of what they are uniquely contributing to the team, which goes a long way toward offsetting the ambivalence with which they initially regard the team. Roles provide both a sense of belonging and of individuality.

Boundaries

The team also began to create boundaries around its members. Boundaries separate people from their environments. Team members began to connect with one another, as they talked about their purposes, needs, and how to work together. In so doing, they separated, if temporarily, from other groupings—their classmates, friends, and other project teams. Members began to construct a shared identity. They did so partly by articulating their common purpose, but they also shared moments—humor, truths about previous team experiences, devising a team name—that joined them with one another and set them apart from people who were not part of those moments. There is something important about the collection of such moments: Over time, they create a shared history on which members can draw that keeps them connected to one another even when they might later, when real differences emerge, wish to draw apart. These moments begin with the first meeting, as members sketch an identity—"we are not them"—that they will later develop into "this is who we are." Without boundaries that allow separation from environments that exert their own pulls, people cannot form such shared identities and join together to do good work.

Figure 3.1 graphically depicts what team formation looks like when it goes well. Initial boundaries form. A mission is identified. Initial roles are assigned. The process goes well enough that members begin to believe that others might prove themselves to be good partners. Throughout the formation process, each of us inevitably looks at others, consciously or not, to seek answers to the following sorts of questions: How committed are they to the team? What hidden agendas do they have that will affect me? How competent are they going to be in doing the work? How much can I trust they'll do what they say they will? Will they treat me respectfully? Will they help make this a safe place to take risks? How fragile or strong are they? How honest can I be with them? The team acted in ways that enabled its members to answer these questions positively. Members picked up clues indicating that they would not be taken advantage of, nor ostracized, and moved to join with one another to form a real team.

When Formation Goes Badly

Consider a much different team formation experience. In the same class as our earlier example, another team also has five members. It takes them several days to get together. When they do meet, it is for a short time. Neil looks at the others and says that he has a really good idea about the first assignment, from a friend who took the course the year before. The others let him speak. They decide to go with his approach, and divide up the work. Two of the members—Jill and Sharon—are close friends, and they tell the others that they will do the research for the assignment, as long as someone else on the team pulls it together for the first report. James agrees to do this. Neil says that he will get more information from his friend. The fifth member, Sheena, says little other than giving a vague indication that she will help James pull together the assignment. The team

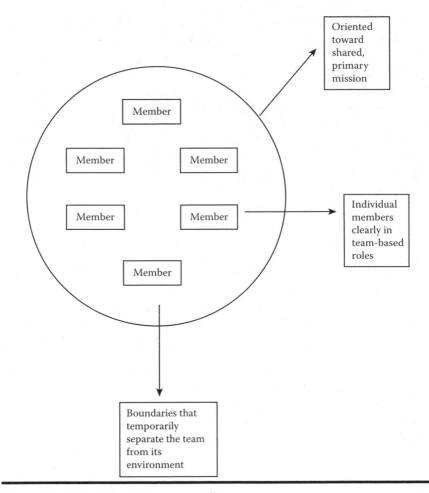

Figure 3.1   When formation goes well.

agrees to meet 2 weeks later and review its progress. The members exchange contact information before dispersing.

This is a relatively weak formation process. The team moves right into tactics and strategy for doing the first assignment without a larger discussion of the team's mission and purpose. Without that larger conversation, the group will remain a series of relatively disconnected individuals, each operating on the basis of his or her own understandings of why the team exists and what its mission should be. These different understandings, as long as they remain unarticulated, lay the groundwork for future disagreements and resentments. The team also does a minimal job of naming the roles by which the team will operate. Members choose roles to get the first assignment completed, but they

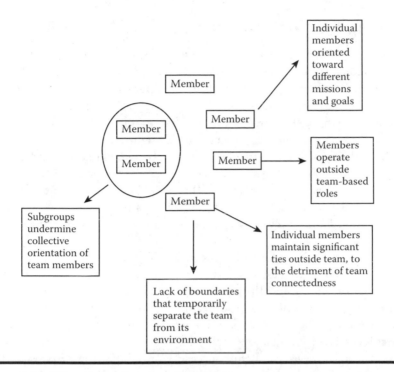

Figure 3.2 When formation goes badly.

do not focus on process-related roles, such as meeting facilitator and project manager, which aid the ways in which individual efforts are joined together. Finally, the boundaries around the team as a whole remain weak, too porous to contain and focus members on a shared identity. The team is fragmented: Two members (the friends) stay connected to one another more than with the team; one member stays connected to his friend outside the team; and the other two remain isolated. Figure 3.2 depicts this formation.

This sort of process goes badly because members do not try and discover, in their initial interactions, any compelling reasons to be together. They were thrown together by chance and make little effort to be anything more than fellow travelers forced to share a vehicle for a certain period of time. There is little in their first meeting to assuage members' anxieties about others' commitment to and competence at creating a team that will do good work, create trusting relationships, and enable real learning to occur. Individuals are thus likely to hold back, in terms of their engagements, until and unless the team forms differently as the journey continues. With no compelling mission to guide their work, and no vision for how that work should get done, it will be difficult for this team to engage its members and its project.

Entering the Conversation

It is more than likely that students in the second team, which did not form very well, had some reactions during that meeting. Some were probably uneasy with the way that the conversation went. They might not have liked the way in which Neil pressed the team to take material from his friend. They might not have felt comfortable with the two friends, Jill and Sharon, splitting apart from the team and working on the research together. They might have been concerned that Sheena said very little and seemed indifferent. They might have been frustrated that they never really talked about what they wanted from the team, or tried to get to know one another, even a little. These reactions would be pretty natural. They would be accompanied, most likely, by ideas that would have helped the situation, and indeed, would have made that initial meeting more like that of the first team.

The key to changing formation processes that seem to go badly into those that go well is for team members to share their ideas, right then and there, about how to form a better team. The key, in other words, is to enter the conversation: the conversation that will carry your team from its first moments of sitting in a room together all the way to the last moments of relief and celebration after the project is complete. The qualities of that conversation will determine the success of your team, however you define success. Conversations must be rich. They must have room for many voices. There must be truth. There must be honesty. There must be disagreements. They must be loud at times and quiet at others. They must be funny and serious. They must be brief when they should be brief, and go on for much longer when they must do that as well. They must, above all, be real rather than pretend.

These conversations are not easy to have. They are particularly difficult in the beginning, when you do not know one another very well, but it is then that they are most important. The beginning of the conversation—the warmth of the tones, the richness of the dialogue, the truth of what is spoken, the depth of the people who are revealed—shapes its middle, and then its end. You must do that which is most difficult: Enter the conversation as though it is the middle, and you are already comfortable with one another, enough to speak openly and truthfully. Doing so enables your team to form cleanly and clearly. Not doing so means developing ways to converse that will lead to a great deal of misunderstandings, frustrations, and false starts that will need to be revisited, over and again, until the conversation is right.

The formation process thus requires you to feel safe enough to say potentially risky things that might lead to your own rejection and alienation. Safety is defined by the sense that it is permissible to say what you really think and feel. In the early stages of group life, safety does not really exist, as members do not really know how others will react to what they say. Smith and Berg (1987), in their book *Paradoxes of Group Life,* describe "the paradox of safety." Safety, they suggest, does not exist until group members act as if it does, and in doing so create it. In other words, you cannot be sure that a situation is safe until you act as if it already is, and take a risk. If you act as if it is safe enough to say something risky—for example, telling Neil in the second team that you do not feel comfortable using materials from last year's class and would rather spend time brainstorming what this team might do instead—then you create the possibility of safety. A difficult thing is said, the team survives well enough, and further risks can then be taken.

So what might this look like? You might notice, for example, that in the very first meeting of your team several members talk a lot and others speak very little. You do not know the other students, but you have been on other teams with that pattern and it caused problems. You decide to say something at the end of the meeting: "I know that we've just begun, but it seems that there was unequal participation in this meeting. I wanted to make sure that we were aware of it, and I'll do my best to monitor my own participation. What do the rest of you think?" This feels risky. You do not know how others will react. You do know that if you say nothing the pattern will probably get stronger and become more difficult to break later in the semester, so you speak. Others respond. Several of the quiet ones comment that they could not find ways to break into conversations. A more talkative member says that he found the silence unnerving and wanted to make sure that the group was doing something. You all talk about feeling nervous about the project and how much time it would take. Members agree to monitor their own behaviors and not just react—by talking too much or too little—when they get anxious about the project. They feel good about talking about what happened in the meeting and how to improve. By raising the issue, you have made it safer for others to raise other process-related issues in the future. By acting as if it were safe to say what you did, you helped create a sense of safety in and for the team.

This is not easy to do. It means deciding to throw your lot in with others and risk making yourself vulnerable. It means not getting stuck in your natural desires to fit in with others and thus not say something risky. Initially we often tend to emphasize the areas of commonality with one another, showing our similarities, to find a sense of connection to others in the early parts of a relationship. This enables us to fit, or seem to fit, with others. Yet, at the same time, we also wish to establish our own identities, separate from others. We wish to keep parts of ourselves in reserve, as a form of protection and as a way to shield parts of ourselves of which we are not absolutely confident. Both sides of this ambivalence—our desires to fit in and our desires to remain apart—work against our saying things during the team formation process that feel risky and unsafe. We need to make some real choices about what we do in such situations.

I work with this idea more fully throughout the rest of the book. At this point, it is enough to know that when you move toward saying what you think during the process of formation, you are much more likely to help that process become more effective. You are more likely to create the foundation for a healthy project team. You are more likely to pass through rather than be stuck at the first toll on the journey. You are ready to set forth, reasonably clear about where you and your teammates are going and how you would like to get there.

Summary

Team formation is the process of creating a whole out of disparate parts. The process involves individuals with varying needs and agendas developing common understandings of what they might accomplish together, in the service of the tasks they are asked to do. These understandings are created when you figure out together your real purposes, the missions that you want to accomplish, and what it is, truly, that you mean to do together. Missions provide specific rationales for your team. They enable you to make purposeful decisions. Immediate decisions include how you divide and integrate work, coordinate efforts, communicate information, and choose courses of action. Such decisions are part of the team formation process, which can go well or badly. This chapter described and illustrated the differences between the two. Successful formation enables you to move from a group of individuals to a team: You have figured out what you want to do together, identified some initial roles, and created a boundary separating you from others. Unsuccessful formation lacks these elements. The first Team Development Exercise, "Contracting," enables you to begin down the path of successful team formation.

Chapter 4

Team Roles and Responsibilities

You are on a team because you cannot do all the work of the project yourself—at least, not as well or as efficiently as a high-functioning team could. This has several important implications. You have to figure out how to divide up the work of the project. You have to figure out how to make changes in who is doing what, and how well, on behalf of the team. You have to figure out how to hold one another accountable, such that all team members are working and none are taking advantage of the others. Done well, these initial steps create an initial foundation of trust among you and your teammates—the sense that you just might be able to take this trip together and arrive at the place you wish to go without too much difficulty or aggravation.

The division of labor is a large part of what your team experience will be about. Projects are usually complicated enough to require you to divide the labor in some fashion. This is partly a matter of making sure that all the necessary parts of a project are covered. It is also a matter of spreading the work amongst you and your teammates, such that none of you are overloaded. As an old phrase suggests, "Many hands make light the work." Dividing the labor gets you more hands. It not only makes good sense in terms of workload, it also gives you the sense that you are working with others. Working with others rather than alone is more fun and more meaningful. At the same time we each need the sense that we are contributing uniquely to our teams. When we divide up tasks, we can each see what we are contributing. We can see ourselves in the work and products of our team, and are more committed to it.

Teams that are unable to divide the labor in appropriate, useful ways inevitably end up themselves divided. Some members do too much, others too little. Important tasks are left undone. Too many people tackle other tasks, causing redundancy. These teams fall short—and often fall apart—because their members are unable to solve the problem of *equity*. Equity is less a matter of the exact distribution of workload—the amount of hours per se that you and the others put into the project relative to one another—and more a matter of whether you feel that everyone is pulling his or her weight and is invested equally in the team and its outcomes. Equity is a foundational issue in project teams. When you get it right, you create a solid foundation that allows you to learn how to get better and better at creating an extraordinary team. When you do not get it right, you create fissures among yourselves that, like fault lines beneath the surface, will likely split and divide under stress.

In this chapter I examine the issues related to dividing up the labor of your project. The equity issue runs throughout the chapter. There are various ways to solve this issue, and we consider useful structures and processes that can help. None will solve the equity issue, of course, if you are not willing to engage it directly—to name it, to speak honestly with one another about your perceptions and experiences, and to agree to try new ways of working together. Without such direct dialogue, your team will likely be plagued with "free riders"—those who hitch a ride on the backs of others who do much of the project work—and you will be caught within the cycles of frustration and ineffectiveness that inevitably result. There is a toll that your team must pay here to avoid these cycles. You must deal clearly and directly with who does what, and how well they do it. Pay this toll now and move on; avoid it, and you will pay far more dearly throughout the rest of your work together.

Roles

You can avert the potential messiness involved in dividing labor by identifying specific *roles* that you and others perform on behalf of the team. Roles are sets of expectations about who will do what. When you assume a particular role—say, the team member who is supposed to create and maintain a Web site for the team's use during the project—there are certain expectations about what you will do and what the results of your work will be. The role is clearly distinguished from what others on the team are doing. Such clearly defined roles provide the framework for dividing up labor. The definitions—clearly specified and agreed on collectively—create a shared language by which you can later discuss issues of workload, equity, and performance.

There are various types of roles. There are roles related to what happens at your meetings and how your project work gets done. Each of these types of roles serves important functions.

Meeting Organization

Students often complain about project team meetings, and often with good reason. Meetings can waste too much time. They can be boring. It can take too long to get anything done. We need to understand this partly in terms of skills and knowledge. You need to know something about how to hold team meetings. First, you need to know how *agendas* can help create efficient, productive teamwork. Useful agendas have several dimensions. They support the team's goals and objectives. They are developed in the light of what your team wishes to accomplish, the project timeline, and progress thus far. They use realistic time frames, according to the depth of discussion that specific items require. They are created through the input of all members.

Second, your team needs to create and use a series of basic *ground rules* to guide meetings. These include respect for time boundaries, in which meetings begin and end on time, and all members take responsibility for moving conversations forward according to meeting agendas. Members are prepared for meetings. One person talks at a time, without interruption, such that all members feel listened to and heard. All members participate in the meetings, even though the levels and depth of their participation might vary from meeting to meeting. These ground rules are basic and essential. To the extent that you and the others follow them, the team will remain focused and productive, and members will begin to create a necessary sense of basic trust in one another.

Third, your team needs a set of *discussion rules* that will allow members to explore ideas in as much depth as possible. These include making time and space for generating lots of ideas, which gives the team options from which to choose in narrowing down topics and directions to pursue. This prevents you from settling too quickly and easily on any one direction just to get done with the task. You also need to make sure that various members are playing the role of "devil's advocate." This means raising issues and concerns about the ideas that team members are pursuing. This helps you to carefully consider the costs as well as the benefits of those ideas. A third discussion rule is to seek common ground among opposing points of view, by developing syntheses of different ideas and perspectives. This engages your team in a process of learning from different views, while helping to minimize potentially negative emotions.

Finally, your team needs to create clearly defined roles for all members. Certain roles enable you to hold meetings that are both productive and efficient. These roles include the following.

Meeting Facilitator

This member leads the team through the meeting agenda, managing discussion topic sequences and timing, summarizing accomplishments and decisions, and clarifying next steps, member responsibilities, and deadlines. The facilitator is responsible for managing the time of the meetings, clarifying the issues that need to be discussed and worked out for the team to progress. It is his or her job to make sure that all members contribute to the agenda, such that no issues or topics are left unaddressed. It is a leadership role, not in the sense of having the authority to make decisions on behalf of the team, but in the posing of questions and choices that help team members to figure out how to continue moving ahead.

Scribe

This member records issues discussed or tabled, decisions made, and next steps, and disseminates information to other team members. The scribe is responsible for ensuring that all team members have the same information about what the team has discussed and decided, and what issues members still need to resolve. The scribe maintains the "official" record of the team and its work. This might also include regular updates via e-mail or maintaining a Web site that enables team members to remain on top of their work and its progress.

Process Facilitator

This member notices group processes and facilitates discussion at the end of meetings about how to continuously improve those processes. Although all members must, ultimately, take responsibility for raising issues that they feel are disrupting the team's progress, the process facilitator assumes the role of making sure that necessary conversations—about levels of participation and engagement, avoidance or engagement of conflict, decision making, and the extent to which the basic ground rules that govern team interactions—are raised during meetings.

The process facilitator is, in some ways, the group's conscience when it comes to effective group processes. There are certain commonly understood characteristics of such processes. Information flow among members is accurate, open, honest, and evenly distributed. Members work toward common goals, rather than engage in competitive, win–lose behaviors. Control is shared among team members, according to the nature and demands of the particular task in which the group is engaged. Members engage differences—in ideas, perspectives, backgrounds, cultures, affiliation group, and the like—productively. The team encourages members to share risky ideas and feelings, and engage in innovative thinking and experimental behavior on behalf of the team's work. The team has a supportive, friendly, warm emotional climate. The process facilitator helps the team reflect on the extent to which it exhibits such characteristics during its meetings.

Project Work

The work of the project differs from that of team meetings. Team meetings are the places where you come together to discuss your progress. It is during meetings that you figure out what you have done collectively, what still needs to be done, and how that might happen. It is during meetings that you discuss the obstacles that you need to surmount to do the project well and create strategies for doing so. It is also in meetings that you raise objections, have the right arguments in the right ways, and join together as a team trying to accomplish the same objective together.

It is between meetings, however, that much of your project work actually gets done. You will most likely spend much more time actually doing the project—collecting information, writing and editing papers, creating and revising presentations—than you will in meetings about the project. It is difficult to actually produce work together—to write sentences or prepare presentation slides with others—without frustrating or isolating others. That work mostly happens when you are away from the team. For you to be able to work productively, however, you have to be very clear about what it is, exactly, that you are doing, relative to one another.

You can get that clarity by taking on roles directly related to dividing up and doing the actual tasks necessary to get the project done. These roles include the following.

Project Manager

This member organizes and coordinates everyone's efforts, turning strategies into manageable tasks. These tasks are scheduled and charted in ways that are easily understood and communicated. There are spreadsheets with deadlines and timelines. Members are clear about who is doing what and when their pieces are due. The project manager ensures that members are communicating and coordinating with one another appropriately. He or she makes it clear where, in the flowchart that shows how the various activities of each member intersect, there are jams and how specific team members need to resolve them. The project manager keeps everyone on task, based on agreed-on timetables and deliverables.

The project manager should not also function as team facilitator. Even though the meetings are about the project itself, there is some danger of having those meetings run by the project manager. The reason? The project manager tends to focus on deliverables, timelines, and commitments made and honored. This focus is crucial. Yet it is also crucial for your team to have the license to range a bit widely in the meetings, at least occasionally. Tangents need to be followed for a bit to see where they lead. Brainstorming needs to occur. Differences must be allowed to exist among members, and resolutions pursued in ways that allow for creative problem solving. It is a great deal to ask of a project manager to attend to both the press of deadlines and the need for a team to be nonlinear during portions of its meetings. It is easier to split those tasks. It is thus the meeting facilitator's role to locate the balance between focusing on getting deadlines met and allowing members to pursue seemingly tangential issues and ideas.

Resource

Regardless of how smart you and your teammates are, or how much experience you have with your topic, your team is unlikely to have all the ideas and information necessary for your project to be a success. It is important for at least one member of the team to become a resource that brings insights and perspectives into the team's orbit. This person scans the environment and seeks out others outside the team who can provide useful perspectives. The resource person brings new contacts, ideas, and developments to the team. The other team members work to figure out whether and how to use that input, and how to integrate it with what they have already learned and considered. Your team needs someone to make sure that you are not ignoring important, sometimes obvious dimensions of the project environment.

Researcher

The researchers are the real workers on the team. Each member should take this role at various points in the life of the team, as each person will have a different way of accessing information. The researcher searches for data. He or she looks into various topics, following leads and clues like a detective, getting more and more deeply immersed into trying to solve problems and piece together puzzles. The researcher looks into topics, background, histories, and other dimensions of project assignments. Researchers are also responsible for checking the validity of what they discover, cross-checking sources until it is clear that the facts are substantiated—an increasingly important task in the age of the Internet. The researcher ensures, finally, that the team has appropriate information to analyze, until the other team members agree that there is enough, that all the important questions have been answered.

Quality Inspector

Your team might move along quite nicely, meeting agreed-on deadlines for deliverables. Members are pleased that they are getting the work done without a lot of difficulty or disagreement. However, the quality of the work itself might not be that high. Members are handing in incomplete or irrelevant research. Those charged with integrating different sections do a lousy job with the transitions between sections. Members are accepting analyses of data from one another that are relatively simplistic or represent sloppy thinking. The role of the quality inspector can help a great deal here. The person in this role is authorized to initiate team discussions of the extent to which deliverables meet standards of quality. To the extent that your team is open to those discussions, the quality inspector is crucial to the success of your project.

This is a tricky role. The quality inspector can all too easily be cast as the "bad guy," the one whose standards of quality are so impossibly high that the rest of the team dismisses whatever he or she says about the deliverables. The inspector is thus isolated from the others. Several outcomes are possible here. The inspector might remain isolated, a source of tension on the team. The inspector might capitulate, going along with the rest of the team in believing that its work is good enough even when it is not. Or the team might explicitly revisit its contract, its definition of success, and in doing so, reach an agreement about what its standards should be and whether or not those standards are, in fact, being met. This latter option enables the quality inspector to represent the team's wishes rather than be at odds with its members.

Writer/Presenter

Finally, the results of the project must be readied for dissemination. Your team needs members who will do the work of synthesizing information and analysis into appropriate forms, through writing reports or preparing presentations. This role requires a certain amount of skill, including the technical skills of using various software programs for integrating documents and creating presentation slides and the literary skills by which members are able to weave together the different pieces of writing—some with quite different styles—into some coherent whole. Members who possess such skills are invaluable. They help the team become greater than the sum of its parts, locating as they do the nature of the key ideas and arguments that move throughout the results of the project.

This role, too, is tricky. The writer or presenter of a project inevitably makes decisions about what gets emphasized and what does not, about the ordering of ideas and arguments, and about the framing and phrasing of conclusions and recommendations. Some members of your team will agree with certain decisions, whereas others will resent them. The other option—all of you on the team sitting down together to write sentences or develop slides—is, however, often a painful process, filled with large and small arguments about the prominence of ideas, the choice of words, and the ordering of information. Your team needs to authorize its writer or presenter to make choices. At the same time, members in those roles need to do the work early enough, and be open enough, to seek and use feedback and advice. Do this well, and the dissemination process, although never completely free of anxiety, proceeds. Do this poorly, and the process might well undermine all that has gone before and that which is to follow.

Clarifications

Each of these roles is crucial for project teams. They are useful, however, only to the extent that you clearly and explicitly define the behaviors for each one. If you appoint a member as project manager, for example, and do not define precisely what that person needs to do—and how others need to work with and respond to him or her—you are setting in motion a series of disappointments. The project manager might well play the role on the belief that the team works best when all communication goes through her. This might frustrate you and several other team members. You might believe that her job is to help schedule meetings and keep track of outcomes, and members should communicate directly with one another to coordinate their work on pieces of the project. Your team is thus operating on the basis of different beliefs and assumptions about how to work together. Because you had not agreed on the exact definition of the project manager role, you and your teammates are left disappointed with and frustrated with one another. Unless you are somehow able to directly engage the issue of role expectations, you are likely to fall into a self-reinforcing cycle of disappointment and blame. It is precisely such cycles that leave project teams stuck and ineffective.

This sort of process holds true for each of the roles already noted. Each role must be spelled out in some depth and detail. People have different ways of facilitating meetings or scribing notes. They also have different images of what it means to do research or be a process facilitator. These images are neither right nor wrong. They are simply different. Some members will find these differences acceptable. Others will find the differences disturbing. Your team needs to minimize such disturbances by developing role definitions that are acceptable to all members. Each team must take on this work, such that each member is quite clear about what it means to take on a certain role. Each of you must have a good sense of what each of you are expected to do and not do once you are cast into a certain role.

Your agreements are, of course, inevitably speculative. Your team might agree to a certain definition of a role and then struggle with how much you actually like that role once a member puts it into practice. You might have agreed, for example, that the meeting facilitator should "drive the meeting." When the

first team member in that role "drives" in a certain way that disturbs others—
he overly directs the conversation, interrupts others, or moves too quickly to
resolution—it means that you need to be more precise about what certain terms
actually mean in practice. Such on-the-job recalibrations are crucial for all of the
roles. You must frame these conversations as part of continuing to define roles,
not as disappointment with particular members. Team members are simply taking up new roles in the ways that match their taken-for-granted assumptions
about how those roles should be played. Those assumptions should be challenged, in the spirit of what the project team needs, in the course of making role
definitions as precise and useful as possible. This process trains both current and
future holders of team roles.

The process of clarifying what the roles require leads right into figuring out
which members should take on specific roles. First, of course, you must decide
which roles need to be filled. This will vary according to the precise nature of
your project. Projects that demand a great deal of research will require several
researchers. Projects that culminate in important presentations will require several presenters. The roster of roles thus needs to fit project requirements. The
resulting framework of roles enables you to make sure that you have the right
amount of people in the right roles. Too many members occupying a limited
number of roles results in a lack of balance among necessary roles. Too few
members occupying the necessary roles means that the relevant tasks will not
get done.

You then need to match the right people with the right roles. There are several choices involved. You must decide whether team members should play roles
for which they are already naturally suited—the ones that they are already good
at—or roles for which they are not as prepared and from which they can learn.
You can make an argument for either choice. It is certainly more efficient, and
usually more effective, to assume roles for which you have aptitude. On the other
hand, school offers relatively safe opportunities for learning, and you should
have the chance to learn what you do not already know. A similar trade-off
involves the extent to which members remain in particular roles for lengthy periods—indeed, throughout the project—or switch with one another at various
points. Staying with the same roles allows you to learn those roles deeply, with
payoffs for the team as a whole. Switching roles enables different members to try
new behaviors. Each project team will need to make its own choices here. Some
might create hybrid forms, such as pairing members who are already skilled
with those who are not, or switching some roles and not others. In many ways,
it matters less exactly what resolutions you settle on, as any of them can work
quite well, according to who is on the team and what the project is. It matters far
more that your team has the conversations, makes explicit choices, and settles on
solutions that all members understand quite clearly.

Identifying necessary roles, clarifying expectations for role performances, and assigning individuals to perform those roles are all necessary in dividing the labor of the project team. Such structural solutions are not, however, always sufficient to solve the equity problems that bedevil some project teams. On some teams, individuals almost inevitably enact roles poorly, leaving others to pick up the slack. If that is your team, you face some choices. You can simply accept what seems inevitable, that some members will do more and others will do less, and go forward. You can split into different, perhaps warring factions, and let the team fracture or dissolve. Or you can try and adjust the roles, and go through a period of calibration, marked by your team members having the opportunity to learn how to work better and more effectively.

This latter process—of learning, of improving performance—makes the most sense, if we want our teams to be successful, however we define and measure success. It might also be the most difficult. It only occurs when we are able to give and to receive feedback. It is through providing feedback to one another that we are best able to eliminate ineffective patterns of behavior and create new, more effective patterns. This takes work. It takes practice and a clear understanding of what feedback is and how you can use it in the context of your project team.

The Nature and Practice of Feedback

Feedback is the relaying of information to others about how they and their work are perceived, what influence they and their efforts have on others, and other information that will help them learn about themselves in the team. Feedback allows you to grow and learn. We each have blind spots, places where we cannot see and thus act very effectively. Without others to help us see what we need to see—like passengers in a car who alert us to oncoming traffic—we run into trouble. You and your teammates are in the vehicle together, and able, should you choose, to help one another see past blind spots. Without feedback, you remain insulated, self-sealing systems, aware only of what you think you already know. Without feedback—some input from somewhere outside your own head—you cannot know what it is that you do not know. This can get you stuck, doing the same things over and over even though they are not that effective. It also hurts your team. It is difficult to imagine a team being effective, learning, and changing without its members learning how they affect and are perceived by others. Your team can get stuck if you and others are not provided honest feedback.

It might feel like it is too soon to give feedback to one another. You might wish that you had more evidence on which to base your feedback. You might wish that others had more evidence on which to base their feedback to you. It is often the case, though, that beginning with the first moments of your time together, you have already noticed behaviors that you knew would be problematic. The longer that you wait to discuss those behaviors—the ways in which people work with or against one another, take on or avoid work and responsibility, or act as if they care about or dismiss the project itself as important—the more difficult it becomes. It is always useful to raise issues earlier, when patterns of behavior have been established, than later, when it might be too late for people to change. Sooner rather than later is always better. Your other strategies are to act as a prosecutor (waiting until you have enough evidence to confront and convict a teammate) or an ostrich (pretending or hoping that the behaviors just go away). Both are far less effective in terms of actually helping your teammates change, grow, and become better contributors to your team.

Feedback Assumptions

Effective feedback is built on a certain set of assumptions. These assumptions include the following.

Providing Effective Feedback Is Difficult to Do

It takes a lot of conscious effort, at least for most of us, to figure out exactly what we need to say and how to do so in ways that others can and will hear. You must therefore be very aware of the impact of what you say and how you say it. You cannot develop that awareness in a vacuum. It means thinking carefully about what you most wish another person to understand, in terms of the effects—positive as well as negative—about his or her behavior. With that in mind, you need to consider how to frame that message such that the other person will hear it, and get interested in changing behavior. Notice that this process—of thinking carefully about what you want the other person to truly hear and how you need to speak—is different than simply lashing out at or dumping information on others. The task here is to help others change and become more effective, not to hurt them, make them feel badly, or drive them away.

Feedback Is an Investment in Others

It takes a lot of time. It is a relationship, not simply the delivery of a set of observations and judgments. When you allow yourself to give thoughtful, well-considered feedback to others, you are investing something of yourself in them, in their learning and development. When you back away from such a relationship, you divest from others; you pull away from them, preferring to live with rather than seek to change what they do and how they impact you and the project team. This is neither good nor bad; it simply is. Given the limits on your resources—your time and your energy—it is probably not reasonable to expect that you will invest in each of your team members precisely the same. You are likely to invest in those who you believe will take feedback well, and do something positive with it, and back away from those who you believe will defend against your observations. And you are likely to invest in those who matter to you most.

Feedback Provides Opportunities to Learn

Thoughtful feedback, delivered respectfully, gives people the chance to learn something, often about their selves. Whether or not they actually do learn, or make some sort of change, is up to them. Your task is to keep providing such opportunities, aware that it might not make a difference now but might do so later. You may tire of this at some point, as we all do. It could feel as if you are hitting your head against a wall, and only by stopping will you feel better. There are clearly some people who do not wish to learn about themselves. They defend against the possibility that they are imperfect. They do not wish to do or do not feel themselves capable of doing the work required to change. They push you away, blaming you, making you feel badly for your efforts. Your desire to back away from these teammates is understandable. But if you continue to give others opportunities to learn, they just might do so. Your job as a teammate is to give them the chance, and then another, and perhaps another.

To Withhold Feedback From Others Is Disrespectful

It assumes that they cannot learn, that they are not strong or capable enough to change. We often tell ourselves cover stories for why we withhold feedback from others: We decide to believe they're too fragile; they're just like that and can't change; or they've been told this before and haven't changed. You harm others when you allow yourself to believe these cover stories without a significant amount of evidence. It is one thing to discover, over time, that a team member cannot listen or act on your feedback, particularly when you have diligently varied the conditions—time, setting, tone, language, context—in which you engaged in those conversations. It is something else entirely when you act on flimsier evidence that lets you off the hook from truly testing out others' abilities to learn from your feedback. Like incomplete evidence in a courtroom, your suspicions that others will be too defensive, guarded, or fragile to learn might well convict them, and do an injustice to the truth of what they are capable of.

Withholding Feedback From Others Often Protects Us

The cover stories that you tell about others might mask your own reluctance to see where the feedback might lead. Others might well come back at you in ways that you do not want and might not like. You might, for example, want to tell a teammate that she participates too little and does not contribute as much as others, but a part of you fears that she might well tell you that you and other "team leaders" shut her down and leave no room for her to participate. To the extent that you are unconsciously anxious about receiving such feedback from others, you avoid opening the conversation. Rather than acknowledge that, however, you might act as if it is she who does not wish to receive feedback. You therefore think of her in certain ways—as too defensive, too fragile, too stuck in her ways—so as not to think of yourself in those ways. The technical term for this is *projection*. We unconsciously project onto others the parts of ourselves that we do not much like, and act as if those traits—defensiveness, fragility—belong to them, not to us. We do this, at times, to protect ourselves from learning something about ourselves.

Feedback Doesn't Often Feel Good to Give

Confronting others directly—holding up a mirror so that they can see the impacts of their behaviors on others—might not feel good. You might wish to protect them from feeling badly about what they see, or you might not want to risk disrupting your relationships with them. It is often the case, however, that you strengthen your relationships with others by believing that they are both capable and willing to learn about themselves. Others might not like you very much if you tell them things that they do not want to hear, but they will respect you. More important, although having difficult conversations might not feel very good, it often feels worse to pretend that everything is fine when it might not be. It also feels worse to work around someone and feel powerless to try and change their behavior.

Effective Feedback Can Start a Cycle of Learning

Feedback is not simply a one-way, hit-and-run process. It occurs in the context of relationships. When you provide feedback to your peers, you are implicitly inviting dialogue. Those who receive begin to give as well. Effective teams are characterized by such cycles of feedback, which tend to release a great deal of energy into the team. These cycles take time and require much patience. They require you to remain open to the possibilities of learning something yourself when you decide to give feedback to your teammates. They require you to want to engage in two-way conversations, as others are most likely to accept your observations and insights when they sense that you are open to receiving theirs as well. Continuous learning marks successful teams. Such learning occurs, ultimately, among teammates who are open to challenging and supporting one another, and do so by moving toward rather than away from giving and receiving feedback.

Feedback Techniques

These assumptions ground the process of providing effective feedback. Acting on these assumptions requires you to offer some combination of positive and negative reflections to your teammates. There are some specific techniques that you can use here. Make sure that you describe specific, concrete behaviors that led to the feedback. Provide feedback as soon as appropriate after the behavior, rather than waiting until it is either too distant a memory or so many examples have built up that when you finally do offer feedback, your pent-up frustration or anger gets in the way of how you deliver the feedback, and therefore, how others receive it. Speak directly to others rather than using a third party. In this vein, it is important to note that e-mail is not an appropriate mechanism by which to provide feedback. You can and should use e-mail for offering information. You should not use it as a means by which to conduct dialogues likely to generate emotions. It is simply too easy with e-mail to misinterpret tones, and without an ability to read others' faces and other nonverbal gestures, too much miscommunication occurs.

In providing feedback you can also include your own real feelings about others' behaviors insofar as they are relevant to the feedback (e.g., "I get frustrated when you show up late for meetings, which makes it more difficult for me to pay attention to what you say"). You also need to check for clarity to ensure that the receiver fully understands what you are saying. This is a tricky process. It is condescending to say to someone, "Now, repeat back to me what I said so I can be sure that you understood it." One way to check for understanding is to ask others what they now plan to do, in light of the feedback. Their answers will reveal the extent to which they truly understood and absorbed the messages that they were given.

Effective feedback is, at its core, a process of discovery. In giving feedback, you cannot simply assume that you know exactly what was driving others to act as they did. This is an arrogant belief. Instead, you must seek to discover the other person's perceptions and experiences. Ask relevant questions that seek information. Look for the gaps between what others believe and what you believe about behaviors and consequences. Those gaps are problematic; that is, they become problems for you to solve, through dialogue. Your feedback is offered in the spirit of helping to identify and solve those problems, but you also need to make sure to get others' attention by specifying the consequences of their behavior—particularly consequences that matter to them. This is not about threatening others; it is simply making clear how their behaviors are leading them away from what they want, whether it is good grades, their peers' respect, or not wasting time.

Finally, you provide effective feedback when you refer to behaviors about which your teammate can actually do something. It accomplishes little to tell another team member that you do not like the sound of his voice, the way that she clears her throat in the midst of presentations, or how he leaves team meetings without standing around and engaging in small talk about the class and professor. Focus on those items that people can actually change—and give them the benefit of the doubt that they can do so. Effective feedback thus means raising difficult issues, such that the receiver is not left wondering about what is left unsaid during the conversation. When you dance around the issue, hinting at but never directly engaging it, hoping that the receiver will simply figure out what you are (not) saying, you create rather than solve problems. Instead, use direct, clear language that communicates caring and respect.

Receiving Feedback

These techniques for providing effective feedback go a long way toward creating a productive process, but they are only part of the story. The other part involves how you receive feedback. People who receive feedback well manage to do so in spite of their own tendencies to defend against the notion that they are not doing something well. They value the opportunity to grow and become more effective at working with others more than that of proving to themselves and others that they are without flaws. Receiving feedback well takes some courage. You must risk learning something about yourself that you do not know in a public, potentially embarrassing, forum.

There are several techniques involved in successfully receiving feedback from others. Listen to others without interrupting. It helps to record what others say. Taking notes concentrates your attention on capturing others' thoughts and stops you from defending yourself. Seek to understand what others have to say, on the assumption that it contains some truth. It is relatively easy to simply dismiss feedback from others, on the notion that their perceptions are in some fashion faulty, biased, or incomplete. If you can hold that notion aside, and look for how others are right rather than wrong about their perceptions, it becomes possible to learn from their feedback. You will always have plenty of time later to dismiss what they say, to tell yourself all the ways in which others are wrong, biased, or misinformed. But while they are talking with you, look for ways in which they are right. They might well be, and you might learn something important about yourself.

You do not have to be completely silent when others give feedback. Feedback is indeed a dialogue. Ask for specific examples, but be careful about your intentions in doing so. Examples can help you become clearer about the larger point in what others are saying. But when you dispute those examples—offering excuses or rationales about why you were completely justified doing or saying what you did in those particular circumstances—you do not allow yourself to learn from the feedback. It is, perhaps, more useful to ask others for the specific behaviors that you did or did not perform that led them to their perceptions. This lets you look more carefully at your behaviors and their consequences. Ideally, you would invite others to help you understand how to act more effectively in problem situations. Once you are able to identify which behaviors you would like to change, ask others to provide future feedback after performance of new behaviors. You also need to acknowledge to others the risks they took in providing candid feedback, and thank them for their help. This helps make the experience a positive one, which makes it more likely to be repeated.

The effective giving and receiving of useful feedback is the mechanism by which project teams move from being stuck in repetitive patterns of behavior to those that enable you and your teammates to develop truly successful units. Feedback is an intervention. It interrupts negative cycles, and creates positive ones. It is not necessarily a smooth process. There will be hurt feelings. There will be people who do not say what they mean. There will be those who cannot hear what is meant. People will tiptoe around important items. Others will defend against hearing anything negative. All of this will occur, in different forms and at different times. The key issue is whether you can stick with the process, understanding that it takes time for people to assimilate the truth of what others tell them. This occurs only when you feel that others are not out to wound you or make themselves feel superior at your expense. When you approach the feedback process with good intentions—with the desire to improve yourself and others—you are more likely to create the conditions under which that process will be constructive rather than destructive.

Persistent Inequities

There are times, of course, when you or your teammates are unable to provide or receive feedback, or to make appropriate changes in how you work together. This sets in motion certain patterns. You do not hold one another accountable. You avoid certain conversations. Your team gets stuck in persistent inequities, with some people contributing a lot and others not much. You give up on one another. This sort of pattern—with lots of variations—remains in spite of your good intentions otherwise.

Take, for example, the case of participation in team meetings. Participation is a tricky subject. Ideally, members participate when what they have to say can move the conversation and the team's work ahead in some fashion. This might not mean that each of you speaks for exactly the same amount of time. Indeed, that probably should not be the case, at least during the course of any single meeting. You should participate when you can contribute in useful ways to the discussion. Some members will clearly have more expertise with some topics, but every team member should be able to contribute, as each member brings to the table a different set of ideas and experiences. If that is not the case, and a team member feels that, over time, he or she does not have appropriate influence on the team, his or her sense of inequity will inevitably undermine the team's health and effectiveness.

Patterns of participation vary, of course, but there are two that are quite prominent. In one pattern, there are several members who participate quite a lot. They drive the group's agendas, offer their opinions without hesitation, organize the team's efforts, and generally move the team in certain directions that they prefer. Other members participate little. Some offer very little, withdrawing into relative obscurity; others contribute a bit here and there, taking up the role of followers. A variation of this pattern is when one individual dominates a team, and others fall completely into the role of followers. In the second pattern, there is more equitable participation. Members participate about the same, with some leading some conversations, and others leading different conversations, according to expertise and familiarity. A more diffuse leadership structure characterizes these teams.

The first pattern presents more difficulty, in terms of members' sense of how much effort different people are putting into the group. The question, of course, is how such inequity is understood and dealt with. There are various ways to frame such clear differences in participation. You could point to those who participate a lot as too dominating. You would thus tell a certain story about those team members: they take up too much space; they are controlling; they are extraverts; they have large personalities; they are natural leaders; or they just cannot help taking over. You could point to those who participate little as too subordinate. You would thus tell a certain story about those members: they take up too little space; they are shy or frightened or weak; they are introverts; they do not care; they are freeloaders; or they cannot help but be just followers.

Each of these stories focuses on the particular natures of those who lead or those who follow. Your explanations for why those members act as they do focus on their individual characteristics—their personalities, traits, and tendencies. The problem with such explanations is that they do not lead to useful interventions. As long as you believe that people act as they do simply because that's the way that they are, you will believe that there is little that you can do, and you let yourself off the hook of even trying. It is true: You cannot change other people's personalities. Like all of us, you have enough difficulty changing parts of yourself that you would like to change. What hope do you have of changing how shy, dominating, or controlling your teammates are?

You can, however, tell yourself a different sort of story that offers the possibility of changing inequitable patterns. It offers hope. Such stories begin with a certain premise: Each and every member of the team has gone along with the creation of the current patterns of participation. This premise is important. It suggests that each member of your team bears some responsibility. It suggests, indeed, that each of you has implicitly gone along with—has allowed and agreed with—the ways in which others are participating. Those of you who are relatively quiet are allowing those who participate a great deal to do so. Those of you who are relatively dominant are allowing those who participate little to do so as well. The premise here is that each of you is making a certain choice about how to participate. Each of you can also make a different choice.

This premise opens up another way to approach the problem of inequitable participation. Rather than assume that you are helpless to change others' personalities ("they just can't help it, that's just how they are"), you can take steps to change their behaviors—by taking the radical step of changing your own behaviors. Say, for example, that you are frustrated by how little your teammates participate in team meetings. You could make some specific changes yourself. Rather than ignore the issue or speak of it outside the meetings, you can point out the inequitable patterns to the whole team. Rather than blaming the "quiet ones," you can take responsibility for your own behaviors. You could talk about the pressure that you feel—from yourself, from others—to participate a lot. You can then make sustained, careful efforts to participate less, and to make room for others to participate more. The same sense of responsibility, and action, can occur in the opposite situation, if you are one of the quiet ones. You, too, can point out the patterns that the whole team has created. You can take responsibility for the choices that you are making to let others participate more. You can also make real efforts to participate more, even though it might feel risky and unfamiliar to do so.

Another sort of persistent inequity might have to do with how much work different members of your team are doing. You might simply tell a story that blames individuals for being too lazy (not working hard enough) or too obsessive (and working too hard). This story creates real divisions on your team that are difficult to bridge. This story can also be reframed. You can understand this issue not in terms of individual personalities, but in terms of the whole team struggling to figure out what "good enough" means. This is not a simple process but is still one in which you must engage together. When has enough research been done to answer questions adequately? When are case analyses complete? When are presentations fair and balanced? When is project management useful without being overly demanding? When are the scribe's notes complete? Answering such questions is precisely the process by which you figure out your shared standards and expectations. These conversations might take longer than you wish, but getting them right is crucial. Box 4-1 offers a more in-depth look at such conversations. You must have them, as a whole team, if you are to move past the seemingly endless struggles between individuals with seemingly irreconcilable styles.

Such conversations require you to move beyond the typical stories and explanations with which you often feel most comfortable—the stories that blame others, absolve you of responsibility, and let you avoid potentially difficult moments of honesty with yourself and your teammates. When you tell those typical stories, you allow your project teams to get stuck. You split into subgroups, with those who participate too much arrayed against those who participate too little. Each side grows increasingly frustrated and upset with the other, and acts out that frustration in ways that maintain the splits. You might isolate yourself from some of your teammates and you might well create scapegoats within your teams. Scapegoats are team members who you blame (and then reject) for your team's failures to figure out the issues of equity. These members are driven away, not physically, but in all the other ways that are important on a team. The scapegoat becomes a casualty of stories that leave you and others blameless.

Persistent inequities do not need to remain so, however. Feedback is one way in which you could intervene—or others could intervene with you—and try to change how team members work together. Another way is to talk together about shared standards so that individual members are not stuck fighting about how much work should be done. The problem, of course, is when individual members don't seem to care about the inequities. How can you get their attention and increase the chances that they might work effectively with others? The answer is related to the issue of accountability.

Accountability

Ideally, everyone on your team is working together well, and equitably. Your team takes some time at the end of meetings for members to discuss how their work is progressing. Each of you asks for feedback and it is given, freely and constructively. You use that information to change how you work. The process is repeated. This is the cycle of continuous quality improvement. It drives the creation of effective team performance, and solves problems of equity and contribution.

BOX 4-1 WHEN ENOUGH IS ENOUGH

There is often a great deal of variation in opinion among members of student project teams about how much is enough when it comes to working on course deliverables. Some students have high—some might say impossibly high—standards. They are uncomfortable with work that is not clearly excellent. At the extreme, these people are perfectionists, with all that the term implies: committed to high quality, driven, impatient with what they perceive as incomplete or inconsistent work, and somewhat unforgiving of themselves and others. Other students are more comfortable with putting in enough time and effort to create good results, but not so much that the costs of investing more energy outweigh the benefits of doing so. These students are willing to stop short of excellence—or, to their minds, unattainable perfection—to move on to other arenas commanding their attention. At the extreme, these people are minimalists, willing to settle relatively easily for work that is "good enough" and focusing their efforts elsewhere.

Each perspective represented by this split—the desire for excellence, the desire for efficiency, and reasonable cost–benefit ratios of effort to outcome—is perfectly understandable. Each side comes at the same question from different starting points: When is enough, enough? It is a question worth asking. Indeed, it is one of the most crucial questions that team members can ask themselves, as the ways in which it gets answered will shape how members work together and how much they like doing so.

The discussions about when enough is enough—that is, about how much effort to put into various pieces of work—should take shape in the following ways.

- Team members need to begin by acknowledging their shared desires to maximize both quality and efficiency. This shared acknowledgment goes a long way toward easing some of the tensions among members who have different views. The tendency is to identify specific team members as perfectionists or as minimalists (or worse). The team then acts as if the issue is personal ("it's that person's problem") or interpersonal ("those two just fight about it all the time and hate each other"). Although specific individuals will stake out different positions, the larger truth is that the whole team is struggling with the trade-off. It is a disservice to individual members who speak up and defend a position on the issue to believe otherwise.

■ Members also need to acknowledge that there are trade-offs between quality and efficiency. The crucial conversations therefore need to occur as members are working on each deliverable. At some point in the work, the team needs to talk candidly about the point of diminishing returns to locate that point. They need to ask: What is likely to occur if we were to spend more time working, both in terms of outcomes and in terms of our relationships? The answers need to be grounded in both a good sense of the project and its goals, and in members' openness about their experiences working together.

■ Members can also consider the possibility of introducing certain structural elements that might help them find the point at which enough becomes enough. One structural mechanism is the clock. The team can decide on a certain amount of time that members will spend working on a deliverable. This becomes the boundary, and whatever work gets done in that period of time will automatically be defined as good enough. A second mechanism is to appoint a member as the quality inspector. This member is authorized by the team to periodically pose the question of diminishing returns, and to gather a census from the team about whether they have yet reached that point. Each of these structural mechanisms is meant to push team members to find the balance between quality and efficiency when it is difficult to do so.

Team discussions about the issue of defining "enough" are healthy and constructive to the extent that the whole team is on board with ultimate decisions. This will not be easy. Individuals might have quite real, and strong, disagreements. They will have to find ways to compromise, however. The perfectionists among us will have to be okay with stopping short of what we perceive as excellence; the minimalists among us will have to be okay with putting more time and effort into the work. We do this because if we do not, we maintain unnecessary and unhealthy splits in our teams that are likely to do significant damage, ultimately, to both the quality of the work and the efficiency with which we complete it.

If only if it were so easy. What seems like a perfectly clear, logical process is more often avoided than used. The problem is that a number of the assumptions behind continuous quality improvement do not necessarily hold in the case of student project teams. Students vary in terms of how much they care about outcomes. Some are committed to performing well, to learning course material, and to learning about and improving their own skills and abilities. Others simply want to get the project done with minimal effort and inconvenience. Many are somewhere in the middle, willing to go along with those who seem to sway the team the most in one direction or another. You will vary as well in your ability and willingness to change how you perform your roles and in how well you are able to help one another, by giving and receiving useful feedback.

We thus have to consider the issue of how you hold one another accountable for not performing well. This is a relatively straightforward process in work organizations, at least in theory: The boss gathers information from various sources and provides feedback to subordinates (directly, through dialogue, and indirectly, through performance evaluations and financial rewards) about the extent to which they have met performance expectations and standards. Your teams do not have a similar option. You have no formal authority over one another, you cannot impose organizational sanctions, and you have few points of leverage over one another, particularly over teammates who care little about course project grades.

Consider these situations. On one team, two members take over a project as a deadline approaches, largely ignoring the valuable contributions of others. On another team, several members are late with their assignments, leaving the project manager to integrate and rewrite a paper the night before it is due. A member of a third team attends only a few meetings, and contributes little to the midsemester presentation. How do you hold one another accountable in these situations? What leverage do you have? How can you get one another's attention, to get one another serious about the team and its work?

Course instructors can help here. Because they assign grades to project team deliverables, they can also create a system for team members to evaluate one another's contributions, as a way of distinguishing those who contributed a great deal from those who contributed little. An example of this system is shown in Box 4-2. The system allows, in effect, for variations in the grades that team members receive. Although all members receive the same grade for a team project deliverable, systems that enable group members to evaluate one another's contributions enable instructors to modify individual grades as appropriate.

Instructors can also create systems that enable you to remove underperforming peers from your team. This is, of course, a serious matter. It might occur only in the most extreme cases, such as students never attending team meetings or refusing to do any work on projects. Yet the fact that the system exists usually acts as a deterrent. It also helps you not feel so powerless in the face of peers who

BOX 4-2   SAMPLE TEAM CONTRIBUTION SCORING SYSTEM

Students are asked to evaluate the contributions of their team members. Students should focus on all aspects of their teamwork together: coaching, researching and analyzing case materials, developing and presenting project assignments, and general overall cooperation.

The evaluation process is as follows:

1. Multiply (the number of people on your team *minus one*) times 10. The result is the number of points that you will allocate among the members of your team, not including yourself. If there are 6 members on your team, for example, multiply 5 (i.e., 6 − 1) by 10 to get 50 points.
2. Distribute the points according to your assessment of each member's contribution to the team's work. The distributed number of points cannot exceed the total points available for distribution.
3. **The points may NOT be distributed *completely* evenly.** That is, every team member must not receive 10 points. **If everyone on your team receives a 10 from you, your own score will be penalized. Also, you may only use whole numbers when allocating points.**
4. Please offer rationales for scores that indicate extraordinarily high or low contributions to the team. These comments will be used by faculty for grading purposes only, and not shared with students.

Your Name: _____

Team Member Name	**Points**	**Comments**
_____	____	_____
_____	____	_____
_____	____	_____
_____	____	_____
_____	____	_____
Total Points	____	

flagrantly violate the basic contract by which your team operates. It gives you some leverage in a context where you otherwise have none. Box 4-3 presents an example of a team warning and termination process.

You also have another source of leverage: appealing to people's desires for positive relationships. We usually want to be liked and respected by others—by peers and by our teachers. We typically wish to feel that we are inside rather than outside of our groups. These natural desires to belong are, for many of us, a powerful source of motivation. We will do what is necessary to not let others down, and face their approbation and rejection. If members of your team feel that they are in danger of such rejection by others who they would *like* to have like or respect them, they are more likely to step up and do their parts. This is the power of peer pressure: People fall in line when they fear being left out in ways both subtle and direct. None of us thrive in isolation, at least over any significant period of time. Your leverage here involves helping underperforming peers realize that they are risking your friendship and respect. This is rarely spoken of directly and clearly. It is not necessarily an easy conversation, but it can have a powerful effect.

Seeds of Trust

In the previous chapter I wrote about how important it is for you and your teammates to speak honestly to one another, even when it does not feel safe to do so. I introduced the paradox of safety: A sense of safety does not exist among you until you act as if it is already safe enough to be reasonably honest with one another. Once you act as if it is okay to be honest, and others respond accordingly, you actually *create* safe-enough places to continue to be honest. Developing this ability to be honest becomes crucial as you have the conversations discussed in this chapter. Deciding what roles you and others should perform, giving one another feedback about your role performances, and discussing issues of inequities in effort and participation all require you to speak clearly, openly, and directly to one another about what you notice and experience. The choices you make about how openly you communicate mean a great deal for how safe it is for your team to discuss important issues.

Those choices also mean a great deal to the *trust* that gets created among your team members. Trust is a big deal on project teams. If you look closely enough at teams that are hugely successful at doing great work, building strong relationships, and enabling their members to learn, you will discover a great deal of trust among members. Members on those teams believe in one another's good intentions. They know that others will work hard and back each other up. They are confident in one another. They know that they can rely on one another for whatever it is that they, and the project, need at any particular point in time. If

BOX 4-3   TEAM WARNING AND TERMINATION PROCESS

Sandra Deacon of Boston University's School of Management, with colleagues, developed a process by which to hold team members accountable for their performances as team members. To reduce the "free rider effect," in which individuals coast by on the work of others, teams are provided with the leverage to warn and, if necessary, terminate members who do not contribute to the team's work.

FIRST WARNING

This is the first stage in responding to a team member who is not meeting the team's expectations for performance. This written notice developed by the team is given to the team member. This warning must

- Describe the poor performance, defining the unacceptable behavior (i.e., rather than stating that the team member "has an attitude," state "the team member has missed many deadlines").
- Describe the behavior that the team needs or expects from the individual.
- Include a specific time limit during which the team member can correct his or her behavior.
- Be signed by all other team members.
- Be copied and given to the course instructor.

SECOND WARNING

The second stage of the process involves providing a second warning to the team member, delivered both in writing and verbally. The warning must again contain the following components:

- Include a specific time limit during which the team member can correct his or her behavior.
- Describe the poor performance, defining the unacceptable behavior.
- Include a specific time limit during which the team member can correct his or her behavior.
- Be signed by all other team members.

The written warning must be presented to the team member in the context of a meeting, which the course instructor attends.

TERMINATION NOTICE

The team may choose to dismiss a team member if his or her behavior continues, following the warning stages, to violate the expectations set forth in the performance plan. A 48-hour written notice of intent to dismiss must be signed by all other team members and delivered to the team member.

- This notice must define the member's inadequate performance.
- This notice should include a statement of remediation and redemption (i.e., a plan for the team member to make up missed work within a short time period to avoid official termination).
- A copy must be given to the course instructor.

Termination of a team member is serious and should be done in consultation with the course instructor. However, the instructor **will not override** the decision of the team. An individual who is dismissed from his or her team will be required to (a) join another team willing to have him or her as a member, or (b) complete team assignments on his or her own to get credit for those assignments.

you look closely enough at teams that clearly fail to meet members' goals, conversely, you will see a great deal of mistrust. Members doubt one another's intentions. They are suspicious of one another's commitments. They do not believe in one another's competence. They do not believe that others will follow through on stated intentions. They do not find one another trustworthy.

Trust is difficult to create. Deeply held trust builds slowly over time, in contrast to infatuation, which is quick to form and quicker to dissipate. It builds through interactions among team members that signal their intentions, commitments, competence, and consistency—indeed, their trustworthiness. As you talk with one another about your project, about dividing up the work, and about how you will work together, you are looking for such signs, even as you emit your own. This mostly occurs outside conscious awareness. Most of us are not explicitly thinking about how much we can trust others when we first begin to work with them (and we are certainly not aware of how we are signaling our own trustworthiness). Tacitly, however, you are paying close attention to your teammates, scanning them for signs that they care about their new team, might be good at the work, seem to be interested in the project and in you as a person, and will do what they say they will do. If you sense that the answers to these questions are positive, you are more likely to begin to give them the benefit of the doubt and start to trust them a little. You open yourself up a bit; you give others leeway to do work that you might otherwise do yourself. Like testing the strength of a frozen lake, you will put some weight on a foot and see if it holds, and if it does, you will inch out farther, ready to retreat should you sense the ice might give way. You look for signs to guide how much you should let yourself depend on your new teammates.

In various chapters in this book I return to trust as a key component of project teams. There is more to say about how trust develops, in terms of our propensities to trust or not, and what it means for others to prove themselves trustworthy, and I discuss those issues later on. The point here is how important trust is to the lifeblood of the team. When you trust your teammates, the journey that you go on together is much richer and far more sustaining. You don't waste energy trying to figure one another out. You don't keep track of each member's efforts and outputs for fear that some are not pulling their weight. You don't worry about team members' inability to put the time into the project on a particular week, because they have proven in the past and will certainly prove in the future that they are willing and able contributors. You are free to focus on the mission of your team, secure in the knowledge that you are in it together. You have faith in one another.

The seeds of trust are sown in the first few conversations among your team, those related to what you will do together and how you will go about working together. Within those conversations there are signals sent and received about intentions and capabilities. You are all suddenly thrust into this new relationship, the project team. There you stand, you and your new mates, filled with questions about one another: Who are you, in this relationship? What are your intentions? Are you in, or out, or straddling the fence in between? Do you, will you, care? Are you, can you be, loyal? These questions get answered early, in the conversations that you have about what your team will do, and how it will divide up the labor. They get answered again between the lines of feedback given and received. They get answered all the time, until they no longer need to be asked, until you and the others have made up your minds once and for all. Until then, your job is to do the best that you can to be worthy of other people's trust— following through on your commitments, seeking and providing useful support and feedback, and learning as much as you can about the project and how to do it well. That's not a lot, and it is everything.

Summary

Developing clear expectations and agreements about who does what on your team becomes the foundation on which you construct appropriate divisions of labor that lead to equity and fairness. This chapter described the various roles that your team needs. Two types of roles are important: those related to how meetings are organized and function, and those related to how projects are managed and completed. Your team must clarify these roles, in terms of what specific members need to do on behalf of your team; otherwise, your team is likely to experience confusion, uncertainty, and frustration. Your team also needs to help members get better at performing their given roles. This is a matter of feedback. This chapter described the nature and practice of feedback on student teams—when to provide it, how to do so effectively, and how to receive it from others in ways that allow learning and changed behaviors to occur. Indeed, it is only through feedback, thoughtfully given and received, paired with systems of accountability, that real inequities in what members of your team do can be altered in healthy, constructive ways. The second Team Development Exercise can help you implement the suggestions from this chapter. The exercise— "Clarifying and Improving Roles"—offers a process by which to create necessary roles, and later, improve how they are performed.

Chapter 5

Influence and Decision Making

You simply cannot get around it: Your team will have to figure out how members influence one another. This can be a struggle. You might be reluctant to cede control over what the team does and how it does its work to others you do not know well or trust very much. Yet you might not wish to take control of your team either, for that brings with it a great deal of responsibility and, perhaps, resistance from others. So you have to wrestle with how to take up the appropriate amount of authority on your team while enabling others to do so as well. This matters a great deal for your experiences on the team. You are looking for ways to have your voices heard, have your views taken into account, and shape your own destiny on the team. At the same time, you do not want to be completely responsible for the team. The difficult work here is to find the right balance between having too little and too much authority and responsibility, a balance that works for you and for the team. This is the toll that your team must go through: how to enable members to assume appropriate authority and influence that enables good direction, shared responsibility, and effective decision making.

This toll is avoided only at great cost. Your team must figure out how to get the right members to have the appropriate influence at the right time. Your team needs drivers, members who will steer the wheel and help the team get to where it needs to go. People want to be led well. If you feel that your input does not matter, you will withdraw or be disruptive. If your team cannot put the right people in the driver's seat—that is, those with the correct expertise and ability to facilitate others—the team will drift along. The driver's seat might be empty, with everyone on your team wanting to be a passenger. You don't want the responsibility, perhaps, or don't want to appear to want to control the team, so you hang back. Perhaps too many on your team are fighting to get into the driver's seat. You don't trust others to drive, perhaps, or you don't feel good when you are not in control. Members spend more time trying to drive then they do on the project itself. Each of these represents a failure of your team to configure appropriate ways for members to wield exactly the influence that they should. Each also represents a failure of you and your teammates to be willing and able to step forward, or backward, based on what the team most needs. Each has the potential to end in a great crash.

You will work through (and often struggle with) these issues in ways that teams in work organizations do not. Workplace teams are usually led by project managers, task force leaders, quality control officers, and the like, who everyone agrees are supposed to assume more responsibility than others for leading teams. These leaders draw their legitimate authority from the hierarchical organizations in which they operate. They are authorized—that is, given the legitimate right to do work—through accepted hierarchical channels. This makes questions about authority and influence simpler to answer: The default position is that those who rank higher on the team or are officially responsible for its work wield more power in the affairs of their teams. This is not always an effective proposition, of course. Project leaders might take the lead on all aspects of a project, heavily shaping what occurs on the team throughout all phases of its work, when in fact other, less formally authorized members could have more skills and experiences. In such cases, the process by which influence is wielded is clear and efficient, albeit misguided. The rules of influence do not need to be negotiated—they are quite clear—even as the team's work suffers.

On your teams, however, the processes of authorization are far less clear. There is no organizationally sanctioned default position. You are not hierarchically related to one another. This complicates matters. You must figure out your own patterns of influence. You have to *authorize* one another, that is, empower and allow specific members to influence conversations, take on tasks, make decisions, and make judgments on behalf of the team more generally. This can (and should) be a transparent process. You assign influential roles, such as project leader or facilitator. More often, it is not so transparent. You covertly authorize some members by attending to them greatly, giving their words weight, following their leads in team conversations, and supporting their actions as they attempt to influence you. When you do this, you are also not authorizing others, at least to the same degree. You pay less attention to them, do not take their ideas as far, and resist their attempts at influence. Authorizations and deauthorizations are paired, as you turn toward some members and away from others.

Understanding Influence

Influence on your teams, then, is a matter of an authorizing process that occurs through ongoing interactions and relations. The first part of that process involves each of you making choices about whether and how to influence your team. This is partly a matter of your own internal sense of how much influence you can and should wield over the team, depending on what it is doing at any point in time. The question is, how comfortable, and able, are you to use your voice to try and influence others? Each team member varies in terms of abilities and willingness to nominate himself or herself to assume such leadership, based on individual traits and experiences.

These self-nominations are, of course, a tricky process. Some of you might have a good awareness of what influence you can and should have and be comfortable wielding that influence. Yet some might not have such a good awareness. You might think that you should have much more of an influence on the team, like a passenger who thinks he or she should be doing more of the driving. Or you might think that you should have less influence, even though it's clear that you are a pretty good driver and know the road quite well. In both cases, there is a gap between what you believe about yourself and what might be true. It is here that feedback is crucial. Feedback from others is the mechanism by which we can align our perceptions of ourselves with the reality of what we can and should do.

The second part of the authorizing process involves your team reacting to members' self-nominations. Your team needs to authorize members if work is to be done. Tasks are only completed if your team allows members to do things on its *behalf.* What does that mean? It means that your team has to let members have their expertise, and lead the team when it makes sense that they do so. Some of you will have to step back, making room for others to climb into the driver's seat and direct the team along the next stretch of road. This might mean, for example, letting a member take the lead on a piece of research, and trusting that she will do it well. If you cannot do this, your team will never allow itself to make decisions or divide its tasks—both symptoms of members unwilling to cede control to one another. Your team must thus figure out how to enable those most able to lead at particular moments to influence others. The corollary, of course, is preventing those who are not as equipped to lead from doing so.

These two processes—individuals nominating themselves as influential, and others reacting to those nominations—usually occur beneath the surface. They are mostly undiscussable. From the first moments on your team, you are developing patterns of influence. Some of you step forward, and others fall back. This might shift around, according to what your team is doing and how it develops. Or early patterns might become locked in place, resulting in the types of persisting inequities discussed in the previous chapter. The whole process can be quite complicated—indeed, a free-for-all—as you and your teammates jockey for influence in the absence of an external legitimizing system and structure. The process can also be exactly right, if your team can get to the place where members step forward and are accepted based on their expertise and usefulness to the team as it does its work.

Beneath the Surface

When the right people step forward or step back at the right times, and others cede influence according to what the team needs done and who it needs to follow, your team is well on its way to effective performance. It does not always work that way, unfortunately. There are less rational factors at play when it comes to how you think about, feel about, and go about creating patterns of influence on your team. Much moves beneath the surface when it comes to explaining how and why your team creates its particular patterns of leadership and followership.

Consider the following.

Scenario 1

A student project team is making its way through a semester-long project. Members are working together reasonably well. One member, however, differs from the others. He gets his work done reasonably well, usually meeting the deadlines that the team sets for certain deliverables. The work itself is pretty good as well, or at least good enough. Where he differs from the others is in expressing his views about what the team is or should be doing. It's as though he doesn't care enough to think about the assignment. He just waits to be told what to do by the others on the team. Other team members have tried to draw him out, to find out what he thinks and see if he has any ideas about what they should do. He doesn't engage much in those conversations. He takes notes, waits until someone assigns him a task to complete, and he goes off to work on it.

Scenario 2

The project team is a struggle for its members. People like one another and get along quite well. They like the project itself, as it involves applying concepts to an interesting real-world setting. The problem is that no one is really willing to step up and take on the project leadership role. The meetings drag on and on. Decisions are not really made, although there is some occasional voting that helps the group figure out what they should be doing. Even after the votes, however, no members step forward and try and organize the team, in terms of who will do what, with whom, and by when. There are two members of the team who are roommates, and almost by default, they tend to get stuck with pulling together the deliverables. But they are not happy about it, and truthfully, they are not always the most qualified, in terms of their abilities to see the larger picture. No one wants to lead the team. The team drifts toward the end of the semester.

Scenario 3

A member of a project team is causing problems for the other students. She cannot seem to agree with anything that the team decides. At first the other members of the team appreciate her ability to raise questions that they had not considered, which certainly helped improve their work earlier in the project. But even after they had changed their approach, she raised more and more questions, resisting the direction that she herself had helped set in motion. She was constantly going against others, seeming to argue for the sake of the argument rather than for the sake of what made the most sense for the team and its finishing the project in a reasonable fashion. She just refuses to agree. Her teammates are getting tired of trying to appease her.

You can understand each of these scenarios in terms of the personalities of the individuals involved. In the first scenario you can think of the team member who simply wanted to be told by the others what to do as shy, lazy, insecure, and other traits that might explain why he was a follower. In the second scenario you could believe that the team was composed of individuals who were laid back, overly courteous, collaborative, and conflict avoidant, all traits that led them to avoid taking on leadership roles. In the third scenario you can explain the resistant student as rebellious, cantankerous, and untrusting of others. Such explanations probably contain some truth. Our personalities certainly shape how we act within teams. However, we need to look more carefully at what occurs in project teams, in terms of how personality really shapes how people deal with authority more generally.

Psychologists have shown that people respond to authority itself—having it or not having it—in certain ways, according to their own formative experiences with parents, caregivers, and other authority figures. Each of us has certain instinctive, often unconscious reactions to authority, which get played out in a variety of settings, such as project teams. The basic idea here originated with Sigmund Freud (1989). He discovered that people tend to re-create the unresolved dynamics of past relationships (with parents, siblings, and other important figures) and act as if those dynamics are part of present relationships (with spouses, team members, and bosses). The technical term here is *transference:* We take the models that we have in our heads about authority figures and transfer (or project) them onto other people in situations that evoke them. We walk into a new project team, not really knowing others or having worked with them before. Unconsciously, we project onto the blank screens of others the old movies that run in our heads about authority. We then act as if those old movies are current reality.

Consider, for example, the person whose early experiences were with authority figures who completely dominated what he was supposed to think and do. He learned, in effect, that his opinion did not much matter. He learned that if his voice was not heard, he might as well remain silent. He adopted, much like the student in the first scenario, a style of quiet obedience, waiting for others to make decisions and tell him what to do. Or consider the person whose early experiences taught her that those in authority were loud, angry, and confrontational, and needed to be either placated or fought with. Like the student in the second scenario, she learned to placate and soothe, withdrawing from confrontation and, more generally, from others on the team. Finally, consider the person who, early in her life, had quite negative experiences with people who were always letting her down. She grew up believing that those in authority cannot be trusted. Like the student in the third scenario, she resists others' authority, refusing to give in to their influence.

The colloquial expression for such explanations is that of the personal "baggage" that people carry with them into their adult lives and unload on others. Some people do have baggage. They have their own personal "issues" with authority. There is not much that you can do about this. You do not have the type of relationship—as therapist, as parent, as teacher—that licenses you to help them with these issues. Changing such deeply rooted personality characteristics is a big deal. It requires people to look closely at their own behaviors and trace their roots, beginning with their early family experiences. It requires them to want, almost desperately, to change. It also requires others, like therapists and mentors, who are skilled in creating particular relationships in which personal explorations are possible. That is not your job on your project team. It is difficult enough to try and change yourself, to become more aware of and to alter your own behaviors. Trying to change your teammates is bound to be a frustrating experience.

Yet there is something that you can do. You can understand what lies behind your teammates' actions, and armed with some insight, treat them in ways that minimize the extent to which their personal issues with authority get in the way of the team's work. Take, for example, the teammate who always pushes for influence. She has an opinion about everything. She insists on her way. She argues with others about issues large and small. It seems like she never stops talking, never listens to others. Your impulse might be to try and shut her up. You ignore her. You interrupt her, and try to direct attention to others. You look bored when she speaks, hoping that she'll see and get the message. You avoid looking at her, so as not to encourage her to speak. You do not address her, knowing that she'll take it as an invitation to jump in once again. Although these strategies might have some limited success, they are precisely wrong. Often, people who are always pushing for influence are, deep down, afraid that they will not be heard. Somewhere in their early lives, they had the experience of being ignored in some fundamental, painful way. When you push them away, interrupt them, or avoid them, it simply increases their fears of being ignored. They react by insisting that their voices are heard, even if they do so in ways that leave them with little real impact on the team. You can be more effective with your teammate if you make her feel heard—attending carefully to her, showing her that you understand her point, clarifying how you are building on her ideas, and in other ways demonstrating that she has value. This will work, but slowly, as she learns to trust that others will attend to rather than ignore her.

You can use similar reasoning to come to a deeper understanding of a teammate who has quite the opposite problem: He never seeks to exert any influence at all. He backs away from argument. You never really know what he is thinking. He waits for others to figure things out and tell him what to do. He hides behind clichés, repeats the sentiments of others, and waits to see which way the wind is blowing before nodding his agreement. Your impulse here might be to just let him hide. You get used to him not adding much. You hold no expectations that he will participate in shaping the team's direction. You stop trying to engage him. Or perhaps you do just the opposite. You push him to add to the team. You make a big deal out of getting others to be quiet, and turn the spotlight on him. You challenge him to add value. These strategies, too, are precisely wrong. People who hide in plain sight often enough expect to not be heard. They had early, powerful experiences of being ignored, inculcating in them the deeply seated beliefs that their voices did not matter. They thus stopped using them altogether. When you ignore them in the team, you simply reinforce their beliefs. When you turn the spotlight on them, they run from it, not wanting to risk opening themselves up to rejection and even more reinforcement that they do not matter. The effective approach here, as earlier, is to create safe-enough places for your teammate to speak openly. Here, too, this means making him feel heard—creating space for him to speak, acknowledging the value in his contributions, and building upon his ideas. This will work, slowly. If you remain consistent, and make a real effort, he will learn to trust, to some extent, that others will attend to rather than ignore him.

Even these simple insights and actions can make a difference in how you and your teammates deal with one another's issues and baggage about authority and influence. I am not suggesting that you become one another's psychologists. You need not probe into your teammates' childhood experiences, what happened with their mothers, or some traumatic event that left them unable to trust others. That is not your job. Your job is to be a good teammate and help others be good teammates as well. In both of the cases that I described, different as they are, being a good teammate requires you to do exactly the same thing: to attend closely to others, to help them feel heard, and to show them that they are valued for what they say and do. That is as much as you can do, and over time, with patience, it can prove to be a lot. It is the best chance you have to help your teammates put down the authority "baggage" that they carry and leave it outside the rooms in which your team meets.

Leadership and Followership

There is no official leader of your team. The instructor did not make one of you solely responsible for the team's output. You are free to create whatever type of authority systems that you want, in terms of how members lead one another in different ways. This includes, of course, the roles that I discussed earlier—facilitators, project managers, researchers, and the others. Yet even with these roles, something interesting sometimes happens on student project teams. Members re-create the types of hierarchies that they have seen in regular work organizations. They endorse one of their members to be "the leader," and others to be "followers." This is not discussed, of course, and team members might even deny it if you point it out, but it happens anyway, in subtle ways. A member takes it upon herself to take the lead. Others fall into place around her, waiting to see what they should do. A covert hierarchy is created, with captains and lieutenants and privates. The hierarchy operates regardless of what formal roles members have taken on their teams.

This dynamic is understandable. Student project teams are odd structures. They do not resemble the teams that we see at work, where there are bosses and subordinates, or sports teams, where there are coaches and players. It is a free-for-all, like a pickup game on the neighborhood court, where, often enough, the bigger and stronger kids dictate the play and what the other kids get to do. It is not much different, on some project teams, than those pickup games. In odd situations, where there is no clear way to proceed, we often try to make the unfamiliar familiar. We impose some sort of structure. To avoid the free-for-all, students slide into familiar patterns of leadership and followership, modeled on work organizations, sports teams, and other hierarchical systems they understand. This provides a sense of order and familiarity. It takes away the anxiety of not knowing how members should relate to one another.

The problem, of course, is that the hierarchical structure is mostly wrong for a project team. You might get lucky. You might have a member of your team step forward—someone you like to think of as a "natural leader"—and carry the team. If that person is superlatively gifted—has great ideas, can inspire members to add to them and carry them out, can bring the deliverables together—the hierarchical model just might work, but that is rare. More likely, a team has someone take over who can do some things well and not others. She becomes the project manager and the meeting facilitator, in practice if not in name. As long as the team depends on this person to lead, the team itself will thus do some things well and not others. The team pays the price of following its one leader.

There is another way. The real opportunity presented by the fact that your project team is self-managing is that you can create flexible authority structures. You can create space for each member to lead at certain points in the project, according to what his or her strengths are. Members who are great at thinking outside the box or coming up with lots of creative and zany ideas can take the lead at brainstorming ideas and solutions to problems. Members who are great at sifting through data and coming up with clear explanations can take the lead at structuring team deliverables. Members who are great at dealing with contradiction and ambiguity can take the lead at reconciling different perspectives. With enough understanding of each member's strengths, and enough flexibility, your team can have the best of its members coming forth exactly when it is most needed.

Certain conditions make this sort of power-sharing arrangement possible. First, you need to get to know your teammates well enough to understand what each is good at. Second, you need to make sure that the roles that you each occupy (using the categories from the previous chapter) fit well with your respective strengths—and that everyone is clear about what roles they have. Third, you need to provide one another with feedback, in appropriate ways and at appropriate times, to enable each of you to get better at those roles. Fourth, you need to make it safe enough for each of you to step forward and take the lead at the right time. This safety is a matter of feeling valued and appreciated by one another, rather than disrespected in some fashion. Fifth, you need to make sure that each member is indeed stepping forward or stepping back when he or she should.

These conditions are necessary but not entirely sufficient for the sharing of influence. There is one another condition that your team must meet as well. You must each have an understanding of leadership and followership that *allows* for influence to move around. We typically think of leadership and followership in terms of individual characteristics. She *is* a natural leader, we say, or he *is* a follower; that's pretty much who they are. If you think in these terms, you cannot help but lock yourself and your teammates into narrowly defined roles with little hope of escape. What then happens is predictable. Leaders lead, and followers follow. As team members sink into those roles, the gap between them widens. That's when many of the problems discussed in the previous chapter related to persistent inequities of who does what on the team occur. As long as you think of leaders and followers in terms of real differences in people, you set your team up for real differences in how much responsibility team members assume.

You can avoid this by thinking of leadership and followership as behaviors that any of you can perform at different times. This perspective helps you get away from the mostly erroneous belief that people are either leaders or followers. Each of you has the capacity to lead and to follow, and each of you should take turns exercising those capacities. Doing this well requires you to have a certain *model* of leadership and followership that enables you to take turns in those roles and support one another's efforts at leading and following. The traditional hierarchical model mostly splits leading and following. Leaders assume lots of responsibility, and followers assume little. We need a model that shows how leaders and followers stay in relation with one another, so no one is abdicating their personal responsibility to others even though they are wielding different amounts of influence at various times.

David Berg (1998), a noted author and organizational psychologist, offers such a model. In his article, he notes that leadership is relational, a dynamic among people rather than as power located in one particular person. This means that we have to start thinking about followership as a part of leadership; the two must be considered together, as one cannot exist usefully without the other. The problem, Berg suggests, is that we typically think of followers in negative, even demeaning terms: as sheep, passive, obedient, or lemmings. Why? There are several reasons. Followers are often looked on as less than (and leaders as more than) in society and its institutions. We often accept these images as true. Our culture celebrates "leadership qualities." We idolize those who are out in front, the heroes, strong and brave, leading the charge. Our organizations look to promote leaders, and implicitly devalue followers. We buy into that. Yet, paradoxically, we spend much of our lives in follower roles. The less we value those roles, the less likely we are to strive to be effective in them.

Berg suggests that we need to think much more about the nature of followership and how it relates to leadership. Exemplary followers exist in relation with their respective leaders; their leaders exist in relation to them. It is in the context of their relationships that great things happen. Followers are loyal and supportive. They help create relations marked by mutual affection, which are better able to survive conflict, disagreement, and tension. The follower has a distinctive voice, which can be heard alongside that of the leader and contributes to the overall conversation. Followers are somewhat invisible to the outside world. They labor in the shadow of the leader, who is the main character of the story, the place where the spotlight shines. Yet leaders and followers create relationships that are collaborative and complementary. Followers are not simply clones but complement leaders in some particular way, through their skills, abilities, views, commitments, and perspectives. Leaders cannot succeed without that complementarity. The relationship, not the individual, is the unit able to accomplish what neither leader nor follower could do by himself or herself. Each needs the differences that the other brings to create the necessary collaboration across the roles of leader and follower.

Berg (1998) concludes his analysis by pointing out what leaders and followers need to do to set up their collaborations. Leaders need to accept their own limits and weaknesses. When they do so, they enable followers to contribute their skills, perspectives, and capabilities. Leaders must thus resist their own and others' expectations of perfection, which cause them to hide weaknesses and not learn. Leaders must allow themselves to accept help. They need to provide the direction necessary to enable followers to make their own contributions to the work, without conveying the sense that they, the leaders, know and can do everything themselves. They need to respect and rely on followers for information, perspective, and insight. They must take into account others' disagreements, which are necessary for the relationship to work. For their part, followers must find their own voices and the willingness to use them. The voice is the instrument by which we express ideas, solutions, critical views, opinions, and feelings. Followers need to find ways to communicate with leaders in ways that are uncensored and direct. They must be committed to leaders, have the desire to see the leaders'—and thus the team's—goals achieved. They must locate the courage to speak honestly, in the face of fear or difficulty, in situations that do not necessarily feel safe to do so.

So how might this work on your team? Say, for example, you are the project manager. This is a role of some influence on the team, and you have some choices about how you play that role. You could hoard that influence, making decisions yourself that leave narrowly defined ways for others to participate. Or you could share that influence, doing the parts of the role that you are good at and asking others for help in the parts that they are good at. You thus become a leader who creates ways for others who follow to join with you, to complement you. Or, to take another example, you are the presenter of the team project. The project manager is charged with structuring the presentation, which you are then supposed to translate into a compelling presentation. You again have some choices to make about how you play your role. You could act as if it is the project manager's responsibility to create the presentation and your responsibility to make it attractive and deliver it well. Or you could step up and join with the project manager earlier, offering candid feedback and advice that helps shape the material in ways that will later translate into a good presentation. In this last scenario, you become an exemplary follower, using your voice to add what otherwise could not be added and shaping what is ostensibly the manager's work.

This model of leadership and followership creates a way for each member of your team to influence the team's work. The model is necessary—along with the other conditions that I named earlier—if your team is to find ways for all members to contribute meaningfully. At the beginning of this chapter I noted that you and your teammates must go through this toll: how to enable members to assume appropriate authority and influence that enables good direction, shared responsibility, and effective decision making. Getting to know one another's capabilities, assigning roles and providing feedback that helps you get better at those roles, making it safe enough for each member to step in or step away according to what the team needs at different points, and understanding how often leaders and followers can switch around and how much they need one another help you pay this toll.

If you and your teammates cannot find ways to create these conditions, your journey is likely to be more complicated, as you miss the toll and are forced off the road. This can appear in different ways. Your team might let the wrong people have too much influence, and the right ones back far away, unwilling to be exemplary followers. You've then created an unofficial hierarchy that does not serve your team well. Your team might have too many members trying to lead, to be the most influential, competing for the loyalties of others. Or your team might not have anyone who steps or is invited forward. This, too, might be competitive, but in reverse: No one wishes to be seen as wanting influence and authority, but neither do they want anyone else to become the leader. Each of these represents a problem. Without leadership, and without followership, good work cannot get done on a team.

Unless you are able to perform some sort of intervention, these problems are likely to grow, even as you might wish for them to simply go away. There are various interventions that can work, each of which begins with naming how members are and are not influencing one another, and discussing the costs and benefits for your team. The specific interventions derive from your sense of what is getting in the way of flexible patterns of influence that give the floor to the right people at the right time. It might be that your team really does not have or does not follow ground rules that allow for mutual respect. Your team might not have a clear, compelling mission or vision to which all members subscribe, leaving members to pull toward different goals. Some members might not have received feedback that would help them be more, or less, dominant on your team. Members might not really trust one another, and cannot therefore let others take the lead. Each diagnosis leads to a different sort of intervention. In the next chapter I focus more closely on how your project team can make course corrections before it is too late to do so.

Making Decisions

On no other dimension are your team's patterns of influence and authority clearer than that of decision making. You can clearly see how influence moves around on your team by looking at how you make decisions together, and there are lots of decisions that you'll have to make. You have to figure out how you will tackle your assignments. There are usually multiple directions that you can take, in terms of areas, topics, issues, or contexts. Strategies need to change as you discover new areas or run into roadblocks, and you will likely have to decide whether and how to change course. Your team will make other decisions as well, related to divisions of labor, the nature of meetings, how you engage with instructors and other teams, the content and form of the work you do, and even what you will have on your pizzas. Team life is a series of unending decisions.

Researchers know a great deal about team decision making. The first and most important item is deceptively simple: The quality of your decisions is a function of the quality of the process by which you make them. This is worth thinking about. If you assume that good team decisions occur because the right information was shared and processed thoughtfully, then the ways in which that actually occurs, or does not occur, matters a great deal. If you cannot get members to share information and think together about what it means, you are unlikely to make the right decisions. If, however, the process by which you share and use information and ideas is good—that is, inclusive, participative, and thoughtful—then your decisions are far more likely to be right. The technical language here is that of *process losses* and *process gains*. Process gains occur when you and others work together in ways that make the team better than the sum of its parts. How you interact creates intangible but crucial relational outcomes— trust, respect, excitement, hope, and the like—that bind your team together and create real units. Process losses, conversely, occur when you go about working together in ways that make the team less than the sum of its parts. The classic case of groupthink is a compelling example of a process loss (Box 5-1).

Process gains and losses occur routinely in the course of team decision making. Indeed, one way to understand your team's productivity is the extent to which its process gains outweigh its process losses. As long as your team is going about working and making decisions together that enable members, generally speaking, to capitalize on one another's strengths, capabilities, and ideas more often than not, your team will be productive. Ideally, of course, there would always be process gains. You and your teammates would only work together in ways that brought out the best in each of you. You would always follow the principles by which the best decisions are arrived at on the basis of complete information analyzed completely.

Again, researchers know a bit about what that ideal process looks like. Project teams approach decision-making situations in clear, rational ways. They begin by setting their objectives. With those objectives firmly in mind, they talk about their basic assumptions and strategies before making specific decisions. Consider, for example, the team assigned the task of creating a strategic plan for a new business. Members begin with a clear sense of their agreed-on objectives: to create a business plan that draws as much on their previous experiences as possible, is realistic, and can be easily researched. Using those objectives, they discuss their assumptions about what "realistic" means, finally agreeing on a working definition that emphasizes reasonably low barriers to entry into a new market. Members spend time talking of their experiences with different industries, and discover significant overlap in a particular business. These initial conversations serve as the foundation for those that follow. With the larger objectives and landscape firmly in mind, the team can approach the tactical decisions involved in figuring out more precisely the actual work that they will do.

Tactical decision making is very much a process of identifying and solving problems. Once a team understands what it needs to accomplish, the work becomes figuring out the obstacles to doing so and overcoming them. This is a process familiar to engineers and scientists: You break problems into manageable parts. You understand and research them thoroughly. You devise strategies. You consider alternative strategies. You discuss adverse consequences. You choose a strategy and try it out, as you test a hypothesis. You insist on data as the

BOX 5-1 GROUPTHINK

Groupthink describes a decision-making process in which group members go along with what seems to be a consensus position, even though that position is not the wisest course. Groupthink causes groups to make irrational decisions that do not fit available data. Members ignore their own personal doubts, conforming to prevailing opinions, because they do not wish to derail the decision toward which the group is heading. Groupthink represents a diminishment of a group's resources: Group members' ideas, perspectives, and critical thinking are partially withheld rather than fully shared.

Janis (1971), in his classic book *Victims of Groupthink*, articulated three primary causes of groupthink.

1. *Cohesion.* Groups that are highly cohesive—that is, members tightly connected to one another psychologically and emotionally, and thus less likely to critically question one another.
2. *Isolation.* Groups that keep themselves apart from external data, expertise, and alternative perspectives—all of which might raise concerns and scrutiny about particular paths and decisions.
3. *Strong leadership.* Groups led by strong leaders—charismatic, dominant—who promote their own solutions and make it difficult for others to raise issues and concerns with those solutions.

Janis also described eight symptoms of groupthink.

1. The feeling of invulnerability—leading to excessive optimism and risk-taking.
2. Ignoring or devaluing warnings that, if taken seriously, would challenge the group's basic assumptions about its chosen path.
3. Unquestioned belief in the group's morality, which allowed members to justify the means to their ends.
4. Stereotyped views of others—particularly leaders of others cast as enemies—that rationalize courses of action.
5. Pressure applied to group members who might disagree to conform to the group.
6. Ignoring or devaluing ideas contrary to the apparent group consensus.
7. The illusion of unanimity.
8. Self-appointed group members ("mindguards") who protect the group from dissenting opinions.

Janis also suggested ways to prevent groupthink. He believed that leaders must assign tasks to groups but not intrude with their own opinions. They also need to make sure that each member is a critical evaluator, airing doubts and exploring all possible alternatives; the role of "devil's advocate" should be formally assigned and rotated. Members should check the group's ideas with trusted outsiders as well; indeed, outside experts should be invited into group meetings, in which all are free to explore the costs and benefits of various alternatives. In such ways groupthink can be avoided.

foundation for examining the results of your initial work and making decisions about ongoing strategies and efforts. You allow yourself to learn from others. Insights come not only from reflection and self-analysis, but also from looking outside one's immediate environment for new perspectives. Scientists and engineers enthusiastically borrow from and build on others' work (with attribution), knowing that inventions and discoveries are often little more than taking what is known and adding pieces here or applying it differently there. Successful project teams know this, too.

In creating the new business plan, for example, you would identify the first wave of problems, related to mission (what will the business do?), capitalization (how will we fund it?), and cash flow (how will we make money and what will be our expenses?). As you solve these problems, the plan itself might change as you encounter certain obstacles. Other waves of problems will emerge, related to managing (what skills do we need to succeed?) and growing (how do we expand the market?) the business. You devise scenarios, using what you learned from others' efforts, and test them with data from simulations that you create and run. On the basis of those data, you make adjustments. You approach each turn of the wheel dispassionately, sifting through information, solving problems, and making decisions on the basis of what you discover to be true rather than on what you wish were true.

Process gains are thus anchored by rationality. Yet, in truth, interpersonal behaviors drive decision making and determine the extent to which a team becomes more than the sum of its parts. The rational method of understanding and solving problems and making the best decisions depends on your ability to do what seems simple but can be quite difficult. You and your teammates must listen to one another. Listening is not simply a matter of hearing, of registering the words that others speak. It is a matter of understanding others' intents, the deeper meanings of what they wish to communicate—their thoughts, feelings, and experiences.

Process gains are also anchored in your support of one another during the process of making decisions. Support is a multilayered process. It is not simply a matter of agreeing with others. It is a matter of helping one another articulate what needs to be articulated, pushing and challenging one another to deepen ideas. It is a matter of pulling for others to participate, and valuing what they have to offer. It is, finally, a matter of respecting one another's potential to contribute, which makes it safe for members to put themselves forward. Process gains occur when each of you feels valued, respected, and drawn on in the service of making good decisions.

Process losses, conversely, occur when rational decision-making processes are undermined by destructive interpersonal behaviors. I noted some of these earlier. Your teams might turn to certain members to make decisions not on the basis of their knowledge and experience, but on the basis of other, less relevant factors, such as charisma and age. Some of you might insist on getting your own points made and your own needs for power met. Your team could split into subgroups, with members aligned with and against one another. You might try to influence one another in ways—such as the use of guilt, sarcasm, or belittling humor—that undermine support, trust, and respect. Or you might handle conflict poorly, arguing a lot, getting defensive, or shutting off rather than exploring differing views. Such behaviors, with repetition, can lead you and your teammates to draw away from one another. You become unavailable to and for one another. You cannot be drawn out and drawn on in the service of sharing and analyzing information in the ways that good decisions require.

One way in which to understand team process gains and losses is to consider what you do in terms of *competition* and *collaboration*. You will always have elements of both collaboration and competition in your relationships, and in social systems more generally—in groups and teams, communities, families, and organizations. The question is where your team locates those elements. In project teams with healthy decision-making processes, members locate competition outside the boundaries of their teams. Other teams in the class, other cohorts, even teams from other schools, are the competition. Collaboration becomes located within the team itself, among members. In project teams with less healthy processes, competition gets located within the team. Members compete against one another. They try to outdo one another—for influence and power, for grades, or for popularity, or they create subgroups that work against, or at least not with, one another. Subgroup members collaborate with one another, drawing the boundaries tightly around smaller units and leaving the larger unit—the project team itself—at a loss. What is otherwise healthy competition that might enable the team to draw together gets twisted in on itself, and the team collapses under the weight of its internal competition.

Decision Rules

Where your team locates competition and collaboration can be clearly seen in how it makes decisions, and more specifically, in the rules that tend to govern its decision-making processes. Every team decision follows certain rules. The rules may be quite obvious and clearly understood by all members. The rules can also be covert, operating beneath the surface, where they remain undisturbed and undiscussed. The decision rules that mark your team evolve over time. You and the others initially make decisions. If you like the results, you will naturally repeat the processes by which those first decisions were made. Soon enough, with enough good results, the decision-making processes become integrated into your team. Unless your team flounders in some significant way, you are unlikely to revisit the processes by which you make decisions.

Decision rules dictate who makes the decisions for a project team, and how those decisions get made. The most important dimension to the rules involves the nature of authority. Who has the power on the team to make the decision? Who has the authority, ultimately, to chart the course for the team? Ideally, you would discuss and decide on certain structures that locate decision-making authority in particular regions of the team, using criteria that matter to you (e.g., minimizing time commitments, ensuring widespread participation). There are four such structures that you might use. Each has its benefits and costs, and each fits certain situations. Some are quite familiar.

You might authorize a *single team member*—a project leader, for example, or the report writer or team presenter—to make decisions on behalf of the team. A version of this involves you asking a member to be an *expert* for a certain area of the team's work. This member gathers certain information and, on the basis of particular knowledge, skills, and experiences, makes decisions on behalf of the team. Authorizing single members has the advantage of minimizing the time necessary to make decisions, particularly in the case of a member's unquestioned expertise. With little team interaction, however, this sort of structure makes it less likely that other team members will be able to help implement given decisions.

Second, you could delegate decisions to *subgroups*. A minority of the team makes the decision. Two members, for example, are asked to prepare a presentation and are granted the authority to decide what that presentation will look like. Or two members are asked to research different possibilities and make a presentation to the rest of team, which defers to the subgroup's judgment. This sort of structure, in which authority is located in committees, is familiar in work organizations. It is quite useful when there are large numbers of decisions to be made and limited time in which to do so. The dilemma, of course, is that not all of your team may be committed to a subgroup's decision, particularly if you feel manipulated (e.g., presented with only one alternative with downsides not presented). It is also the case that, to the extent that decisions are located in multiple subgroups, they might be at odds with one another, leading to contradictory or competing courses of action.

Third, you could depend on *majority rule*. You and the others discuss particular issues, come up with alternatives, and then vote. The option with the most votes wins. This process is often the accepted fallback position, the taken-for-granted way to move reasonably quickly through decisions in which all members at least nominally participate. Voting does not, however, enable complete agreement. The process creates winners and losers. Minority opinions are swept away rather than investigated for what they might contribute to the creation of new, better options. The quality of your decisions suffers, as useful disagreement is avoided rather than explored. Implementation suffers as well. If you "lose," in terms of what you wanted as an outcome, you could feel less ownership over the team's decisions and thus feel less responsible for making those decisions work out. Competition thus replaces collaboration. Under real time constraints, voting works, after a fashion. Your team avoids getting mired in potentially difficult areas, and something does get decided. The costs might be quite high, however, in terms of the potential to fracture your team, leaving an important minority pulling not quite as hard in the majority's direction.

Finally, you could choose *consensus*. This involves collective decisions made through effective, fair communication processes. Consensus does not require unanimity. It requires, rather, that a majority approve a given course of action with which the minority truly agrees to go along. If the minority truly opposes the decision, the course of action must be modified until all members agree, even if to varying extents of enthusiasm. Consensus decisions thus include input from and acceptance by each team member. They demand a high level of team involvement, more than any other decision-making structure. They also lead to relatively strong, well-supported decisions. Done well, the process by which you reach consensus enables you to each feel heard and understood. You are each able to point to the results of the team's decision and see your own input and impact. When you feel truly included in the process by which decisions are made, you are more likely to engage in the process by which those decisions are implemented. You want the team to succeed, for you feel part of the team rather than split off or left behind by others.

A consensus decision is a reasonable decision that all members on your team can accept, even though it is often not optimal for each of you. Getting to that decision takes time. It requires you to be reasonably good communicators. You must listen well and carefully to one another. You must build on one another's ideas. You must resist the pull to create winners and losers in the decision process. You must rationally discuss the trade-offs between various ideas and options, looking at both costs and benefits. There are several familiar techniques that help here, for generating and evaluating options (see Box 5-2). Consensus gets easier with such techniques, and with practice.

Such techniques can only lead to true consensus when you are committed to basic principles and values: mutual respect, trust in others' intents, the valuing of others' potentials to contribute, and belief that our work is best done with others. Following these principles, you avoid arguing for your own positions. You can learn from others' reactions. You seek out and value differing opinions. You do not change your mind to avoid conflict or reach agreement, and are suspicious when others do so, knowing that false consensus is dangerous. You explore reasons and look for acceptable alternatives. You change your mind when you can agree with most of the proposed decision that most of the team supports. You care about the quality of both your relationships and the team's decisions, understanding that consensus-building processes should strengthen each.

Consensus requires you to commit to spending the time necessary to work your way through consensus-building conversations—and not incidentally, to learn how to disagree well without being disagreeable. This issue of time is tricky. You will never feel as if you have enough time to do all that you need or wish to do. Given the choice, you would probably wish to spend less rather than more time in meetings, as would we all. Yet there is a certain reality to face. Although you might wish to believe that you really do not have time to invest in making sure that each of you is on board with certain strategic and tactical decisions, it ultimately, and inevitably, takes far more time to not do so. Think of all the time that it takes to get disengaged or upset members to participate in meetings, follow through on their obligations, or provide constructive feedback. It takes a lot of time to sit through unproductive meetings that are followed by countless e-mails and conversations among subgroups strategizing about how to cope with frustrating team situations. It takes a lot of time to do work that others agreed but failed to do because they did not feel truly included in the team.

The issue of time aside, consensus is not easy to do, nor is it always the right way to make decisions, particularly when the decisions are not all that important or buy-in from all members is not all that crucial. There are situations in which you should authorize project leaders, content experts, or subgroups to make decisions, but be warned: Each of you should be fully aware about what decision-making structure is being used when. Otherwise, you are likely to have misunderstandings—and thus frustrations and disagreements—about who is making certain decisions. You can only achieve such clarity by openly discussing and agreeing where authority should be located. These agreements need to be based on rational assessments of how your team should allot its resources—how

BOX 5-2   TECHNIQUES FOR TEAM DECISION MAKING

Certain techniques are useful for generating or evaluating ideas, both of which are crucial for productive decision-making processes in project teams. The most familiar process for generating ideas is brainstorming; for evaluating ideas, some version of the nominal technique is often used.

BRAINSTORMING

Brainstorming is a process by which teams generate many ideas relatively quickly and easily. A team leader and a recorder—they might be one and the same person—are identified for the brainstorming session. The leader defines the issue, problem, or idea to be brainstormed, making sure that all members share a common understanding of what they are trying to figure out. The leader controls the session, as one would direct traffic, ensuring that all members contribute in a somewhat orderly fashion. The recorder writes down all responses as they are generated; others do not interrupt, but rather, are stimulated by and build on others' ideas. Brainstorming emphasizes quantity, on the premise that the more ideas that are generated, the greater the likelihood that something valuable will emerge. Members must not criticize others' ideas; suspending evaluation enables members to feel safe enough to risk sharing ideas that they might otherwise not, for fear of embarrassment. The critical dimension occurs later in the context of evaluating ideas. In the brainstorming process, the leader presses members to share unusual ideas, which are more likely to generate new possibilities and solutions. Members are also free to improve on and combine ideas, working together toward a list of possible solutions.

NOMINAL GROUP TECHNIQUE

The nominal technique offers a process for sifting through, evaluating, and making decisions about a group's ideas. This relatively simple process involves the team working from a list of ideas that members have generated. Each idea is discussed in turn for the purpose of clarification and understanding. After each item has been discussed, the team uses voting as a way to aggregate members' judgments and determine where each idea stands in relation to the others. Team members each choose and rank the top five ideas, assigning points according to their rankings (e.g., 5 points for the best idea). Point totals are then calculated for each item, offering a quick collective ranking of all ideas and identifying the team's most favored group actions. The team can then begin to explore the different dimensions of those favored actions, solving problems related to implementation.

VIRTUAL DECISION MAKING

Decision-making techniques such as brainstorming and the nominal group process were designed for face-to-face interaction, which enables team members to build on one another's ideas in real time. Virtual decision making, in which team members generate some form of agreement electronically, might seem more efficient—members do not spend as much time in meetings—but, in the long run, yields decisions that usually do not represent the team's best collective thinking. Monologue replaces dialogue, and there is no simple way to test the depth of any consensus that seems to emerge. Virtual communication could, however, be useful as a step in decision-making processes. Members can distribute necessary information for positioning decisions and offer ideas that, although not quite brainstorming sessions, help create collective lists of possible options. It is when teams try to prioritize and then select courses of action that face-to-face interaction is vital, and virtual decision making gets more complicated.

it wishes to spend its available time, how to best use the varying knowledge and skills of its members—in light of its tasks and objectives.

Decision making gets messy without such open discussions, rational assessments, and collective agreements. The messiness is produced by *covert decision rules* that remain undiscussed, and therefore unchanged, even as they prove dysfunctional in terms of enabling teams to achieve their objectives. These rules emerge not from explicit conversations about how decisions should get made but from how your team actually makes decisions. You might, for example, agree to forge consensus, but in actuality, the consensus might be more false than true. The actual decisions might come from particular individuals or subgroups that wield outsized influence, with the others letting them have their way by being unwilling to invest the time or energy in controlling the others. The decision rule in play here is that of an overpowering minority. Your team might use coalitions based on outside friendships to wield influence, or your team might split into opposing camps on any major decision, leaving members who are somewhere in the middle to fashion relatively weak compromises to which few are committed. Such covert decision rules are in play during actual decision-making processes.

Making the Implicit Explicit

Influence happens. You will have more or less power and authority, depending on your team and how members work with one another. This can be transparent. You are assigned certain leadership roles, having to do with project or meeting management. It is also, inevitably, less transparent, as you and your teammates give and withhold power to one another in ways that are not publicly acknowledged. You will do this subtly—looking at or away, listening attentively or superficially, building on or ignoring contributions, or smiling warmly or not at all. You will probably not be conscious of doing these things. Nevertheless, you will send and receive signals that create patterns of authority and influence over one another. These patterns might or might not be productive. Your team might create precisely the right authority structure, in which the right members influence the team at the right times, not too much and not too little. Your team could also create patterns that are precisely wrong, giving some members too much and other members too little influence, in terms of their respective capabilities and what your team needs.

There are reasons why teams create and maintain ineffective patterns of influence. Some of you will simply insist on your authority. You will take up a great deal of space in the team. Perhaps you like power, or you believe your ideas are simply better. Some of you will take up too little space. You withdraw, not wishing to impose. Perhaps you feel better having others tell you what to do, or you do not want the responsibility for the team. In both cases, these choices probably have something to do with the natures of you and your teammates. There are issues of ego, insecurity, trust, and the desire to be seen in certain ways. Such psychological matters are quite real, but they do not have to be insurmountable. Your team can try and improve how members work together. The difficult work here is making the implicit—how members actually go about making decisions and wielding influence on the team—explicit. It is only when you are able to openly discuss how you make decisions, without attacking or defending, that it becomes possible to create different, more effective processes. In the next chapter, we look more carefully at how such course corrections occur.

Summary

Your team must develop appropriate ways in which you influence one another. You need to be well led: The right person needs to exert influence at the right time, and others need to step back and let that influence occur. This chapter examined the process by which teams authorize certain members to lead, and how that process goes well or badly. When it goes well, leaders and followers shift over time, and create ways of interacting with one another that allow for partnership, flexibility, and mutual support. The patterns of influence that your team creates are most visible when you are making decisions together. Certain processes, described in this chapter, result in effective decisions, and others do not. These processes are implicitly codified in various *rules*—some overt, others covert—that your team follows in making its decisions. The third Team Development Exercise—"Decision Rules"—enables you to reflect on how you have thus far gone about making decisions, and offers you the opportunity to make choices together about how to do so in the future.

Chapter 6

Process Improvements

You have now been on your team for some time. You know what you're trying to get done. You've figured out some ways to work together, and how to make decisions. Your team has settled into various roles, and into ways of leading and following. Whether you are aware of it or not, you have developed certain patterns on the team. These are the result of the initial decisions that you've made, which helped you solve the problems that you encountered along the way so far. These patterns might be fine. They might have set in motion exactly the types of interactions that you need to get the best work done and the clearest communications flowing. Yet these patterns might also not be so useful. They might be limiting the possibilities of what your team can do. They might be getting in the way of having a good experience on the team. They might even be leading you down the wrong path.

It is important to try and interrupt patterns that get in your way, and sooner rather than later. Dysfunctional patterns, like newly poured concrete, can set and harden if left undisturbed. Patterns are important. They help make the team experience familiar and help you know what to expect as you work with one another. They form in predictable ways. You start to develop certain routines: Your team meets in certain places. Your meetings begin to assume a certain familiarity, with particular members taking the lead and others participating in increasingly predictable ways. Over time, and with repetition, these routines ease into patterns—familiar, taken-for-granted ways in which you work with one another. Embedded within these routines and patterns are unspoken rules that organize your interactions. Such rules make the strange and unfamiliar—

relations among peers with differing motives, needs, and skills—understood and familiar. These rules are rarely discussed, or for that matter, acknowledged.

We can understand this using the language of organizational culture. Edgar Schein (1999), a prominent organizational psychologist, developed a particularly useful theory of organizational culture. His theory suggests that members of a newly formed unit have certain problems to solve, such as how to go about getting resources, make decisions, divide up labor, and use authority. The unit pursues certain courses of action to solve those problems. To the extent that those actions are successful (i.e., they effectively solve the problems and members achieve their goals), they become the acceptable means by which the unit operates. Over time, and with increased success, those actions—and the assumptions that drive them, about how members should work together to solve problems of external adaptation to the environment and internal coordination—become taken for granted. Beliefs about how to solve these problems have become taken for granted because they have worked repeatedly and reliably.

Consider, for example, a new project team that needs to pull together a research report. They spend some time meeting to talk about the report and what it should look like. There is some disagreement, which they do not fully resolve, but they decide to let the most vocal member, who is most passionate about the project, make the decision about which direction to take. They also divide up the work, with different pairs taking different aspects of the research, synthesizing, and writing. The team works reasonably hard, gets the work done just in time, and receives a high grade for the report. The members are pleased with the result. The following month, the teacher hands out the next research report assignment. The team follows the same routine as it had before: letting a more vocal member decide the nature of the report, splitting the work among pairs, working to the last minute, and receiving a reasonably high grade. They have now created a set of rules to guide their work together.

Over time, and with repeated success, there comes a point in the history of a project team whose members have successfully solved particular classes of problems over and over when the same class of problem arises and members do not even pause to wonder if they should solve this one as they solved all the others. They just do. They just assume that they will use the same processes of working together and making decisions that have led to their previous successes. These processes become so woven into the fabric of the team's culture that behavior based on any other premise becomes inconceivable, as well as nondebatable. As long as those processes—and the rules that guide them—are effective, in terms of members' experiences and learning as well as outcomes and grades, team cultures enable members to instinctively move in positive directions together. If those processes are less effective, team cultures might ultimately slow members' collective progress toward the creation of a healthy, successful group.

These patterns and their underlying rules form over time. They are not pre-existing. They emerge through the interactions among team members. Indeed, they emerge tentatively, at first, mere hypotheses that team members check out and see how they work. Over time, unless interrupted and replaced with different patterns, they begin to take hold; later, they calcify, and become unquestioned basic assumptions that guide members' behaviors. At that point, the team has a strong culture set in place and more or less immovable.

What does this mean for you and your team? It means that there is a toll that your team must now pass through, a crucial one that successful teams slow down and pay, and unsuccessful ones do not. The toll is this: You must look at and identify the patterns that define your team, and together, choose which ones to maintain, which to modify, and which to discard. This process will enable your team to have certain patterns, rather than certain patterns having, and thus paralyzing, your team.

Many teams avoid paying this toll. They just keep on keeping on. They figure that the project will end soon enough, and that the course will, too. This is, of course, true. You do not have to work with your teammates forever, or even for a very long time, as you might in a real job. Yet there is a real opportunity here to practice and develop skills that you will surely need in your jobs, indeed, throughout your careers and your lives. I refer here to the skills of trying to make things better, in how you and others are working together. You could certainly avoid learning and practicing these skills, but you do not need to. There are not many places in our lives when we do have the chance to practice interrupting dysfunctional patterns, and trying to get them to be more functional. The student project team setting is a relatively safe place to do this, given that the costs of failure are, relative to other places in our lives, low. Why not try? The typical protests to this—it's just not worth it; the team just isn't that important; it's too much hassle; it's not worth creating more problems, or different problems than what we have now—are too easy. They let you off the hook of doing the difficult work of trying to make things better through difficult conversations. They rob you of the chance to practice a lifelong skill.

You and your teammates thus have some real choices to make: Will you look at whether your team is going the right way? Will you speak honestly about your experiences, to try and learn about and improve how your team works? Will you let yourself listen to and learn from one another, such that you—not just the others around you—take responsibility for trying to change certain ways of working and communicating? These are choices that each of you makes. To the extent that you choose not to try and change patterns, you create self-fulfilling prophecies: Expecting not to improve team processes, you shy away from doing so, and therefore create exactly what you expected—unimproved processes. To the extent that you choose to try and change patterns, you open up the possibility of real success in doing so. It's your choice.

Professor Jerry Harvey (1989) wrote a wonderful story, "The Abilene Paradox," about the difficulties involved in managing agreement in groups and teams. The article derives its title from a story that Harvey tells of his family and himself deciding to drive to lunch in Abilene, 2 hours away, one hot, dusty day in an old car that lacked air conditioning. After their return, they discovered that, indeed, none of them had really wanted to make the trip but, thinking that the others did, went along with the idea. Harvey realized that the story encapsulated a larger truth, a paradox, about groups and organizations. He stated the paradox as the following: Groups and organizations frequently take actions in contradiction to what they really want to do and therefore defeat the very purposes that they are trying to achieve, partly because of people's inability to manage agreement.

The Abilene Paradox offers a useful way to understand some of the difficulties related to project team members speaking openly about how they are going about working together. Harvey describes six symptoms that are worth noting.

1. Team members agree privately, as individuals, as to the nature of the situation or problem.
2. Team members agree privately, as individuals, as to the steps that would be required to cope with the situation or problem.
3. Team members fail to accurately communicate their desires or beliefs to one another. In fact, they do just the opposite and thereby lead one another into misperceiving the collective reality.
4. With such invalid and inaccurate information, team members make collective decisions that lead them to take actions contrary to what they want to do.
5. As a result of taking actions that are counterproductive, team members experience frustration, anger, irritation, and dissatisfaction with the team.
6. If team members do not deal with the generic issue—the inability to manage agreement—the cycle repeats itself with greater intensity.

Harvey identifies four factors that propel individuals toward the Abilene Paradox: the *anxiety* that gets created when they think about acting in accordance with what they believe needs to be done; the *negative fantasies* that they have about what will happen if they act in such ways; the *real risks* associated with those actions; and the *fear of separation,* that is, the anxiety related to separation, alienation, and loneliness should they be rejected by and isolated from their teammates. These factors shape and constrain the abilities and willingness of project team members to speak openly about what they see, think, and feel about their team processes, even as those processes lead them down paths—like the hot, dusty road to Abilene—that take them to undesirable destinations. To the extent that you are aware of these factors, you have some choices about how much influence those factors will have on what you say and do, as you look at and try to make changes in the patterns that you have thus far created on your teams.

Choice Points

There are particular moments when the choices that you must make come into sharp focus. These moments demand that you act: that you acquiesce to following the patterns that you and the others have created, or try to interrupt and change them by addressing them directly. If you do not address them—call them to others' attention, and lead a conversation about why they exist and whether they are in the service of what you are trying to do together—you are implicitly sanctioning them. You are agreeing with them, simply because you have decided to not disagree with them. You want them to exist, even if you protest to yourself that you do not much like them. Your silence is, in fact, your consent.

Consider the following situations.

Scenario 1

Your team is working on a presentation. The team has divided up the work, making sure that all the various pieces of the presentation are well researched before they are put together into the final product. One member, James, did less of the research work, and seemed to promise that he would take the lead on preparing the presentation itself. When it came time to work on the presentation and translate the research findings into slides, James told the team that he did not have time to do much. You had suspected this might happen, because James had, from the very first meeting, begged off from doing much for the team. He gave very little, and seemed to just want to coast along. You decide that you do not want to be taken advantage of by another member in such ways. You say something to him, away from the others. You tell him that everyone on the team has other things to do, and for the sake of fairness and equity, every member has to do a reasonable amount of work. James gets defensive. He lashes out at you, saying that he does not see you contributing all that much, and that his ideas are just as good as, if not better than, those of other members. You do not respond, saying that you just wanted him to know how you felt about his contributions. At the next meeting, he is withdrawn, offering very little.

Scenario 2

Your team has met a number of times, working on a report. There are six members, placed together in a team by the instructor. None of you have much experience with the topic of the report. You have noticed that the team is dominated by two of its members, who tend to do a lot of the talking. You try and participate, even though you feel that you have to interrupt the two to do so. The other three members are pretty quiet. You are not sure if they are naturally quiet or shy, or whether they just don't feel like fighting for airtime. One of them, Susan, missed the last meeting, without letting the others know or checking in afterward to see what she missed. You are getting a bit worried, because you have seen this happen in other teams, and it usually does not work out very well. Indeed, the last team that you were on felt like it was really two groups, one whose members were dominating and talkative, the other silent and withdrawn. That group got through the semester, but each group was upset at the other and barely made it to the end of the class without full-scale conflict. You do not want to see that happen again. You are not sure what to do, except for trying as hard as you can to try and bridge the gap in the meetings themselves. You make it a point to interrupt or slow down the two dominating members, as politely as you can, and turn to the quiet ones for their input. This is getting tiring, and also leaves you little room for sharing your own ideas on the project.

Scenario 3

The team project due date is only a few weeks away. It seems that all the professors are piling on the work now, and you feel pretty overwhelmed with all that you have to do. The team is behind on getting this project going—it seems that most of the other teams are much further ahead—and you are getting nervous. One of the members of your team, Ignacio, had agreed to do the initial piece of research, which the team needed to figure out the direction of the project, and then to schedule meetings and coordinate the project. This was a week ago. The team has not heard from him since then. You are beginning to get a bit worried, but frankly, you have so much other work to get done that you put it out of your mind for a few days. Finally, after not hearing from Ignacio and not having him reply to an e-mail that you sent, you find out his phone number and call him. He seems surprised at the urgency and tells you to relax, that there is plenty of time. You tell him that the project might take more time and require more effort than he thinks, and it might make sense for the team to at least meet and try to figure out together what needs to be done, by whom, and when. He agrees, and the next day sends out an e-mail to schedule a meeting. At the meeting, Ignacio does not have the research that he had promised. Other members of the team seem worried about this as well, and several suggest that Ignacio might need some help finishing the first piece, given the time pressure. Ignacio takes offense at this, telling the other members to relax, and promises to send them the work in the next few days or so.

Scenario 4

You are glad to be on a project team with one of your closest friends in the program. The course is a bit boring, and you do not know the other team members particularly well, but at least you have your friend to hang out with during team meetings. The project is pretty complicated—it is a semester-long project, with several deliverables along the way. You are happy to go along with the rest of the team when one member suggests that the team simply divide into smaller groups, each of which will assume responsibility for a separate part of the work for each deliverable. You and your friend quickly volunteer for a certain piece of the first project; the others form into pairs as well. You and your friend have at least some fun working on your assignment, to the extent that is possible given the subject matter. Several days before a deliverable is due, you realize that the team had not established a meeting, or any other mechanism, by which to put the various pieces of the first deliverable together. You quickly send an e-mail to the others, and arrange for all of you to meet the night before the due date. It is a crazy, long night, and you are exhausted the next day, and not too thrilled with the final product, which you think does not add up to a coherent whole. You worry that the rest of the semester will be like this, in terms of being on a team that is little more than a set of barely connected subgroups.

These four scenarios, each of which has occurred on real project teams, deal with different issues in team project life: equity of workload among team members, splits between those who participate too much and too little, the failure of members to do what they say they will do, and the overreliance on subgroups. Each of these issues, if left untended long enough to grow to full strength, has the potential to undermine the abilities of project teams to develop into high-performing, healthy units. The question of whether that potential will be realized—that is, whether such issues will destroy the fabric of the healthy team—is answered only by what you would actually do in the exact moments when faced with these situations. These are choice points. How they are engaged or avoided determines the fates of the teams.

Consider, for example, how you could react in these scenarios. There are ways to deal with the situations that can set in motion or go along with patterns that can *weaken* the abilities of you and your team to work together.

- In the first scenario, you could simply ignore James, as he increasingly withdraws from the group. You could retract your feedback to him, telling him that you were wrong in your perceptions and feelings. You could pretend that the event never occurred. You could even act as if the whole matter is about the fact that the two of you do not like one another, and that you should simply keep that outside the context of the project team.

- In the second scenario, you can keep trying to be the bridge between the dominating and the withdrawing members. You could take the quieter members aside and tell them to speak up more, or take the aggressive members aside and tell them to speak less. You could simply give up trying to make any change and do the best you can in the group to get your ideas across and make the project the best that you can, given the limitations of the team.

- In the third scenario, you can privately urge Ignacio to work faster and get the results to the group more quickly, increasingly stepping up the intensity of your communication to the point that you show your anger and frustration. You could mount a covert insurrection, and take on the work yourself, with or without his participation. You could simply hope that all will work out and that you do not have to do anything.

- In the fourth scenario, you could simply make sure that you and your friend continue to work together on the next deliverables, so at least that part of the work is enjoyable. You and your friend could try and switch to another team. You could make sure that you leave enough time in your schedule before the due date such that you are not so overwhelmed at the end.

Each of these actions does little to strengthen the capacity of the team to be ultimately successful, regardless of your intentions. Why? Your actions prevent you and your teammates from identifying and altering patterns of interaction that need to be interrupted. To understand this, you need to look at how the issues at play in the four scenarios are not simply about specific individuals, although it might seem that way. If all you focus on is trying to fix or work around the individuals, your team misses the opportunity to change the patterns that everyone helped create.

The lack of equity (first scenario), for example, is not simply about the individual who does too little. It is also about how the whole team deals with what has been called "the free rider" syndrome, in which some team members do little and others do much of the work. This syndrome has as much to do with those who allow it to occur as it does with those who instigate it. The split between those who participate too much and those who participate too little (second scenario) is not simply about individuals who want too much airtime and to exert outsized control, or those who are too shy or introverted to speak up. It is also about how the whole team figures out how to make space for one another's ideas and inputs, value one another's different contributions, and create common ground in their work together. The failure of members to do what they say they will do (third scenario) is not simply about individuals who promise more than they can deliver. It is also about the whole team developing collective standards for the quality and timing of their work, and holding one another accountable to those standards. Finally, the danger of subgroups (fourth scenario) is not simply a matter of members who pull away to do separate pieces of work and do not communicate enough. It is also about how the whole team figures out how to divide work, such that it gets done, and integrate their work, such that it represents the collective.

The choices that team members faced in the scenarios, then, are of the same piece: the decision about whether to move forward and engage the larger issue, related to the whole group. In each scenario, there were patterns in motion. The actions that I described earlier would all keep those patterns going. Ineffective patterns cannot really change until they are identified, named for what they are and how they play out, and all members understand how they helped create and sustain them in their teams. When members identify the patterns, there is the possibility that they can actually work to change them, together.

This last word—*together*—is crucial. You might like to believe that the problems on your team are the fault of one or two members. You blame those who try and get away with not doing much work, do not live up to their commitments, dominate others, or are simply rude and obnoxious. The reality is more complicated. Yes, individuals bear responsibility for their actions, but your team as a whole is solely responsible for the patterns of behavior that it deems acceptable or not. If the whole group looked at James (first scenario), the two dominant members (second scenario), Ignacio (third scenario), or itself (fourth scenario), and said, quite clearly and constructively, that certain behaviors are not acceptable, strong signals would have been sent that would have, ultimately, strengthened the capacity of the project teams. Ineffective patterns of behavior only exist because your whole team allows them to, when you and others choose not to send such clear signals.

You have dealt with this from the first moments your team got together. You noticed then, almost without noticing, the signals that your teammates sent during those initial moments and meetings. Each of you signaled your willingness and ability to listen or ignore, contribute or withhold, join with or withdraw from, dominate or subordinate, be thoughtful or heedless, be task-focused or social, and the like. You sent those signals to one another without being fully aware of doing so. If you did not receive feedback—others showing or telling you that they have received your signals and were uncomfortable with the messages—then you automatically assumed that you were fine in what you were doing. Yet others might have been uncomfortable and did not say anything. They did not know you well enough to predict how you would react. Not wishing to cause trouble that might sweep them into conflict and possible rejection, they did not respond. You did the same with them. The problem, of course, is that these initial moments are precisely what begin to set in motion the patterns of behaviors and rules of engagement that powerfully shape at least the initial arcs of team functioning.

Choice points thus presented themselves from the first moments of your team's existence. A member interrupted another. Two members engaged in side conversations or passed notes. A member did not show up for the first two meetings. A member arrived late and left early. A member ignored e-mail from the team. A member talked far too much and listened far too little. A member said nothing. Each of these moments offered you the chance to call attention to how you worked together. The more often you took that chance, the more likely that you helped your team develop into an effective performing unit. When you avoided taking that chance, you inadvertently sanctioned others' behaviors.

Stuckness and Movement

Speaking openly is, of course, quite difficult. As we saw in the trip to Abilene, we are pressed toward silence by our desires to belong to groups. These desires were particularly strong in the beginning of your team. You did not really know one another. You did not have a sense of how others would respond if you raised concerns about how the team is working together. This created an almost impossible, paradoxical situation. It is at the beginning of the project team's life, precisely when it is most difficult to raise issues about how members are working together, that it is most important to do so. How you dealt with this paradoxical reality has shaped much of what has, to this point, occurred on your team.

Smith and Berg (1987) offer some useful language in their book about group dynamics to help you look at the implications of the choices that you have made thus far. They suggest that when you are able to raise issues—even when it is most difficult to do so—and speak about the patterns on your team, you are able to create new ones to try together. You and your teammates pay the tolls, and move along the path of development. If you are not able to do this, you get *stuck*. Teams that are stuck are unable to do anything other than what they already do, even as their members know how ineffective they are.

So how do you know if your team is stuck? There are some obvious signs. Members do not show up for meetings. Your team is split into subgroups that have little to do with one another. No one leads or is allowed to lead. You argue a lot, or never disagree at all. Your team makes the same mistakes over and over again. Your team does not achieve its desired results. Some signs are less obvious, and are located within your thoughts and feelings. You are bored in meetings, wishing they were over. You dread their meetings or interactions. You are disengaged, participating and caring little. You are often frustrated with one another. You resent the team and having to be on it. If these signs fit you and your team, you're stuck.

The difference between teams that are stuck and those that are not is clear, and by this point in the chapter, obvious: the extent to which you and your teammates raise issues and examine, learn about, and seek to change the ways in which you work together. All project teams get stuck at some point. Behaviors that were useful at one point are no longer as useful, as your tasks change or you require more of one another. The question is what occurs when those moments of stuckness occur. As Figure 6.1 depicts, there are two general possibilities. Your team can learn about its processes, change them, and perform. You will get stuck again, inevitably, as you do things that you have not done before, but like a wheel turning, you continue to move into new areas of learning, changing, and performing.

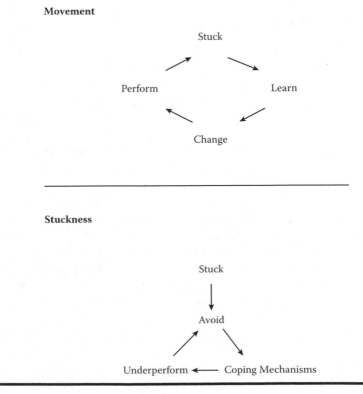

Figure 6.1. Movement and stuckness.

Or your team can get momentarily stuck and then remain there by avoiding discussing how you are going about your work together. Avoidance presents itself in different forms. You can act as if everything is fine. You can ignore the signals of stuckness—your own dread or frustration, the disconnections among team members, the poor outcomes—or explain them away by blaming one another. You can disengage, just waiting for the course to end. You can sustain such avoidance with various coping mechanisms. You split into subgroups. You put in minimal effort. You isolate other members. You blame the professor. Each of these responses allows you to continue to avoid looking directly at and speaking directly of the patterns you have allowed to occur. Each also leads to underperformance: The energy that you put into coping mechanisms is energy that you do not put into actually fixing what is wrong and then working together effectively on the project. The underperformance causes frustration that cannot be collectively addressed and is thus avoided. The cycle continues, unless interrupted in some fashion.

Principles of Movement

It is not too late to interrupt this cycle. It is not too late to inspect the patterns by which you work together, and improve them. Your team will get stuck. All do. The question that occurs throughout this chapter—indeed, throughout the existence of your team—is what you and the others will do when you find yourselves acting in ways that are repeatedly ineffective and self-limiting. Real stuckness only occurs over time, after teams have given up. You have lots of chances before that to look at the choices you have made and to make different choices before you get so stuck as to be immovable.

There are principles to follow to help you get unstuck and moving again as a team.

Recognize the Signs of Stuckness

Change cannot occur unless you and your team recognize that the team is stuck. I described the signs, which range from the easily observable (the team argues too much, or not at all; grades are poor; members do not show up for meetings) to what you experience (constant boredom, frustration, cynicism). The team will develop new patterns of behavior only if you see such signs and interpret them as having to do with the whole group and the choices that each of you have made. This requires you to move away from typical interpretations that place blame on other individuals (e.g., "We're not getting anywhere because she doesn't contribute anything," "Our team did badly on the last two assignments because the professor did a lousy grading job"). Instead, you need to look at how the whole team is stuck in patterns that you have created together by what each of you has or has not done thus far. In the second scenario given, for example, team members would need to understand that their own ongoing frustration with their patterns of participation—some members participating a lot, others not at all—is a sign that the team itself is stuck, rather than the easier but ultimately less helpful idea that certain individuals are just too dominating or too quiet. Identifying the issue as a *team* issue—the pattern of participation and contribution—forces everyone to look at what they could do to help the situation.

Raise the Issue in the Group

Recognizing that your team is stuck is necessary but not sufficient for getting unstuck. You must also speak of what you notice. You must call attention to how your team is operating less effectively than it might. You can give a very simple, powerful message: "I think we're stuck." You speak of your own experiences. In the second scenario, you might say, "I find myself dreading these meetings, which I think has to do with my frustration with how some of us speak a lot and others do not speak much at all." Raising issues in this way serves multiple purposes. You are describing rather than evaluating, which makes it less likely that others will get defensive. You are sharing your own experiences and observations rather than reporting what "many of us think," which makes people feel ganged up on. You are offering information rather than attacks. You are focusing on the team, not just on one person. Each of these makes it more likely that your teammates will hear rather than block out your message. There are no guarantees, of course. No matter what language you use, raising such issues is risky. Others might turn away, not wishing to address certain behaviors or issues, but at least you have tried and given the team a chance to get unstuck.

Use the Project Task or Team Mission as an Anchor

People are usually willing to look at their own and others' behaviors if they are not achieving outcomes about which they care. On your team, you and the others care, more or less, about doing well along the various dimensions by which you define success—grades, relationships, or learning. You can use this as a lever for change and movement. You must make the link clear and strong between the patterns that you notice and outcomes that matter. In several of the given scenarios, you could say something like, "It seems that by avoiding telling one another where we're not performing that well, we're shortchanging ourselves in doing well on this project." If, indeed, you and the others want to do well, those shared desires can become the anchors for potentially tricky, difficult conversations among team members. Similarly, if the desires are for you and the others to enjoy the experience, make friends, or learn a lot, these can also be anchors that enable you to talk about what is going well and not so well. These are important levers. They help get people's attention, pointing them toward changing behaviors and patterns that get in the way of what they say they want.

Be Positive About Signs of Progress

Change is difficult. It forces you to let go of familiar ways of doing things. It often takes a while to happen and to see. People need to feel that their efforts are paying off. You thus need to recognize the signs of movement. Perhaps your meetings are more efficient, or participation is more equitable, with more members engaged in real dialogue and learning together. It is really important to name such positive signs of progress. You and your teammates need to appreciate the ways in which you are moving toward healthier ways of interacting. You need to appreciate even small movements, for they can build momentum and get you unstuck. Appreciation goes a long way toward helping you stay with a process that can feel frustrating and impossible. In the given scenarios, for example, you would look closely for any positive signs of change—a dominant member stepping back, a quiet member stepping forward, the team dealing with a conflict directly—and reinforce them. You do this by speaking directly to one another—"I really appreciate your working harder on this project," for example, or "I'm really impressed that we are able to disagree with one another and come up with better ideas than we had before." It is far more effective to praise positive signs of movement than to sanction negative behaviors. Praise helps people feel good, and makes them want to repeat behaviors to re-create the experience.

Change the Rules by Which the Group Operates to Build in Progress

You are more likely to improve how you work together when you realize that small changes often imply larger ones. You might say to your team, for example, "I think we need to show up on time so we can all get started together." This relatively simple statement is a much larger one as well. You are speaking, really, to the more general principle of team members respecting one another: showing up on time, coming prepared to meetings, providing constructive criticism, following agendas, and taking mutual responsibility for the flow of meetings. Your relatively minor comment is, of course, an intervention. You are trying to change the rules by which your team functions. Interventions come in different sizes. We start small, often enough, and if these are ineffective, we move on to more encompassing interventions. In the fourth scenario, for example, the team used subgroups, which proved damaging to the team's ability to pull together and submit work that was well integrated. You might begin by suggesting that the subgroups share information before putting together their separate parts. If this does not help with the integration problem, you can move on to the larger issues: What is it that we need to do to make sure that we function as a team, rather than a set of small groups that don't really share ideas and work with one another effectively? You are attempting here to change the larger rules that govern much of your behaviors in relation to one another. You are thus revising the initial—and inevitably incomplete—contracts by which you work together.

Get Some Outside Help

There are, of course, moments in the life of your team when you are unable to raise or deal with difficult teamwork issues by yourselves. At those moments it can help a lot to draw on the outside perspectives of faculty, teaching assistants, and even students from other courses or teams. This is not easy to do. You might feel embarrassed to ask for help. It might seem to imply that you are somehow deficient, that you lack the insight, skill, or knowledge to figure things out yourself. If you get caught up in that belief, you allow yourself to stay stuck needlessly. You resign yourself. Asking for help does not imply that outsiders need to "fix" a problem. Rather, it indicates that your team needs an outside perspective— a relatively unbiased observer—to continue its own efforts to change certain patterns. Ideally, such an observer simply poses the right questions, and makes sure that you and the others stay on track in the conversations that you need to answer those questions. Most teams will, indeed, not ask for help, at least while it is still possible to change dysfunctional patterns into more functional ones. This is too bad. It robs you of the chance to create a more effective team, and to practice crucial skills of getting a team unstuck.

Keep at It

It is far easier to not change than to change. The status quo has its own lure, its own momentum. We often fall into familiar habits of thought and action, and stay there, unless the costs of doing so prove too high and we must create different habits with costs that we hope are lower. The process of creating new habits—new patterns of team behavior and new rules of engagement—is often painstakingly slow. A team tries to follow its agenda better. Dominant members try to control others less, and passive members try to contribute more often. Members try to come more prepared for constructive dialogue. Project leaders try to be better at communicating and disseminating information. Each of these efforts takes time and repetition. Keeping at it—truly engaging in continuous improvement—means that you have to decide that your team and its purposes are meaningful. You will need to care more about your work and your learning than about trying something new or difficult and failing, upsetting others, or not being liked.

These principles of movement work because they involve transparency—the making explicit of what is implicit in how you work together. The choice points in the life of your team, when you and the others get stuck, are inevitable, given that there are things that you have not done together before. The ongoing choice, really, is between acting reflexively (just doing what you've been doing) or reflectively (thinking and talking about what you've been doing). It is only when you pause to examine what you do together that you can actually make choices about whether you wish to continue or to change. Without such pauses, you tend to act based on whatever assumptions you have about what others are thinking or feeling and what drives their behaviors. Others do the same about you. When you act on the basis of those assumptions, you often get stuck in ineffective patterns. The principles of movement are an antidote to this process. They enable you to speak openly about your work together. They help you move through limiting assumptions and into the solving of issues that usually crop up in project teams.

Meeting One Another

Many of these choice points will show up in your team meetings. It is there that you become stuck. It is there that you give up on one another or figure out how to work more effectively together. Your team meetings are thus revelations. If you look closely enough, your meetings will show you exactly the places where you keep cycling through the same ineffective patterns. They will also reveal points of intervention—the places where you can change how you work together.

The question, then, is *how* you meet one another. There are different ways to understand the word itself. You can meet others simply by happening upon them, becoming acquainted with them, or congregating in the same place as they do. You also meet others by coming into their presence. You face them directly, without avoidance. You meet their gaze, without turning away. You engage them, and engage with them. This is a different, deeper sort of meeting. It is in this sort of meeting with others that you expose and solve problems related to how you work together as you take the project team journey together.

Too often, though, you might find yourself in the other type of meeting, with which most of us are painfully familiar. In these meetings you are not facing one another directly, metaphorically if not literally. You are turning away, in terms of speaking honestly of your experiences with one another. The results are ineffective, exhausting team meetings. These meetings are, inevitably, the product of *avoidance*. There is, often, much to avoid. Your project itself might be so ambiguous, difficult, upsetting, or frustrating that you avoid tackling it directly. Rather than stay focused on those tasks—and thus feel frustrated, anxious, or upset—you ignore, avoid, or digress. You might avoid difficult issues related to your process—how you make decisions, hold each another accountable, give feedback, or participate. Avoiding such conversations takes time and energy. It renders meetings unproductive, as you move around but not into and through the conversations you most need to have.

Avoidance can take different forms. You might address difficult issues, but outside the team, in subgroups, rather than with the team as a whole. This strengthens the subgroups, which often then morph into coalitions, but weakens the capacity of your team more generally to address and work through difficult issues. You might simply pretend difficult issues do not exist, or hope that if you ignore them they will disappear. Your meetings thus drag on, increasing your frustration. Some of you will withdraw and give up on the team. Others will explode, lashing out at one another in anger. In both cases your team fractures. The fractures are often strong enough to leave you unable to join together to reflect on your shared difficulties with the project itself or how you've organized yourselves to complete it.

These fractures show up in team meetings. The energy and enthusiasm with which you interact, the patterns of participation, the nonverbal gestures and body language, the extent to which you raise different issues and look for what their disagreements can teach—all that, and more, offers diagnostic clues about the extent to which your team is stuck or developing into a high-performing unit. Such clues abound in team meetings. If you look closely enough at your meetings, you can get a sense of the routines into which your team has settled in how members deal with one another. Your routines can be exactly right. They can ensure that you are truly meeting one another in ways that help you move through the project effectively. Your routines can also be very wrong. They can be defenses by which your team avoids examining issues and topics that make you and your teammates anxious or upset. Such defenses—for example, the unwavering pattern of overwhelming politeness and deference—protect you even as they limit your effectiveness.

Defensive routines can mark what happens between face-to-face meetings as well. Avoidance is often aided and abetted by e-mail and other electronic communications. It is relatively easy to ignore, avoid, or move away from certain topics with electronic communication. You can also raise contentious issues via e-mail but do so badly, given that it is a media for serial monologues rather than for real dialogues. Real dialogues are a function of truly meeting one another. You talk together, face-to-face or on the phone. You give clues to one another—through tones of voice, nonverbal gestures, silence, forcefulness and gentleness—that help steer conversations toward a joining together and away from misleading assumptions, hurt feelings, and hit-and-run attacks. You cannot do that in e-mail, even with emoticons inserted at the end of your sentences. Using e-mail as a way to "discuss" your team processes is a compelling sign that your team is, in fact, avoiding rather than engaging its issues.

Defensive routines have real costs. They waste time: The same conversations show up again and again, without resolution. They are frustrating because they get in the way of you achieving your goals. They create casualties: Some members usually get isolated from and blamed by others for the team's stuckness. They distort decision making: You will misinterpret information and develop limiting strategies simply because you wish to avoid addressing certain issues. These are real costs. You will feel them, and—unless interrupted—they will do real damage to how you work together.

Trust, Again

It is tempting to believe that it is too late to change the ways in which the team operates. This belief is also a defensive routine. It is an unconscious wish to avoid the anxiety related to potentially difficult conversations. It is true that you cannot change who others are, but you do have some influence over their behaviors, and hopefully, control over your own behaviors, so there is hope.

However, hope needs courage to be realized. It is not easy to act as if it is safe to say what you think and feel when you do not really know if that might be so. You will always face some degree of risk, in the form of others isolating or rejecting you because they do not wish to deal with the issues that you have raised. You might be secure enough personally to take that risk, figuring that you'll be okay regardless of what happens, or you might be so frustrated by the patterns of your team that you'd rather risk rejection than have the team remain stuck as it is. For most, however, there is a real weighing of the costs associated with raising issues against the unknown benefits of doing so. Here is where courage enters the picture. It takes courage to say things that feel uncomfortable, not really knowing how others will react. Each team needs members who display this courage. Someone needs to name the issues—the proverbial elephant in the room—and others need to join the conversation. If you can put yourself in play, your team can interrupt ineffective patterns and create new ones.

It is easier to be courageous, of course, when we trust that others will join us. We thus cycle back to the issue of trust on your team. Much of what enables you to move toward others—to meet them, in the deeper sense—is related to how much you trust them to meet you as well. Throughout your time together, you have been gauging others' abilities to meet you halfway. You have been examining their behaviors, looking for clues to help you figure out how much you can trust them and how safe it is for you to say what you think and feel. You have all been sending signals about your capacities to remain open to or defensive about looking at the team's process and your own individual contributions, useful and not, to that process. These signals are barely perceptible, fleeting, but they register. Each of you has taken those signals and woven stories about the team and about one another. These stories help you make sense of the team and they lead you toward or away from trust, hope, and action.

You need to be careful here. Each of us is susceptible to self-fulfilling prophecies: We make predictions of the future and then act to make those predictions come true. If you do not trust others to do what they say they will do, you will tend to believe that you do not really need them to get work done. You do most of the work yourself. Your teammates resent this but take the path of least resistance, letting you do the work. You are thus confirmed in your belief that you must do everything alone. You are exactly right in your prediction, and you are exactly wrong. Or you believe that others on your team are not going to do much work. You then take over the planning, dictating to others what they should do. The others feel disempowered, and their enthusiasm for the team dissipates. They lose interest and focus. You now feel affirmed in your initial belief that others will not work hard. In both examples, you have helped create the very realities that you feared—and, it must be said, for which you unconsciously wished, because it created situations that affirmed you and the story that you like to tell about yourself and others.

This chapter is an extended meditation on the importance of identifying and altering patterns of team behavior that you know to be dysfunctional. I end this meditation with one more crucial point: If you discuss the issue of trust, as a team, you help create trust on the team. A simple, powerful intervention for your team is to simply say it aloud: "I notice that we are not being as effective as we might be. I believe this might have something to do with some patterns that we tend to follow in how we work together. Can we trust one another enough to talk about these without taking it so personally that we end up attacking one another or defending ourselves?" This is clear and straightforward. It is the difference between a team that gets stuck and stays there, mired in ineffectiveness and frustration, and a team that gets stuck, looks at how and why, tries to do things differently, and moves on toward its goals. Say these things aloud, and you pay the toll. Keep them hidden, and you drive off the road. This is your choice.

Summary

Your team inevitably develops certain routines of work and interaction that, over time, settle into patterns that become woven into the fabric of its culture.

These patterns might be healthy or might not be. Teams that evolve into high-performing units are those whose members examine the patterns that they've created and make choices about whether to sustain or alter them. This is the work of process improvement. Teams that engage in such improvement become self-aware and self-correcting. They solve the problems that inevitably crop up in how they work together. Other teams remain stuck, struggling with the same issues over and over in meetings that result in little progress and movement. This chapter described the principles by which effective teams move through and past difficult issues. Two Team Development Exercises are useful here. The fourth exercise—"Team Effectiveness Pit Stop"—offers a reasonably simple way for your team to get a check on how effective its members believe it to be on various dimensions. The fifth exercise—"Choice Points"—offers a way to follow up on what you learn together. This exercise enables you to look at some of the critical moments in the life of your team thus far that shaped its effectiveness in various ways. Together, these two exercises offer a useful way to significantly improve your team process.

Chapter 7

Useful Conflict

Conflict is one of the main ingredients of a successful student project team. Conflict enables you to put together opposing forces—whether they are ideas about the project, beliefs about how to proceed, personal preferences about work products—and decide together what makes most sense, given your goals and objectives. Without conflict, you will agree too much and too easily, at least on the surface, and the best ideas and practices remain undiscovered. Without conflict, small annoyances take root and grow into larger frustrations, leaving you unable to work with and trust one another. Without conflict, reasonable and inevitable differences among team members harden and calcify, to the point that you become unreasonable with one another.

The toll here is clear: You must find ways to have good fights with one another. Good fights leave you stronger and wiser as a team. They create connections among you, not casualties. They keep you moving as a team, and enable you to respect and learn from your differences. Indeed, conflict helps manage differences. It enables differences to come into play, get looked at in relation to one another, and get reconciled. This is not, of course, how most people understand conflict. They think of conflict as battle. This image carries with it a number of not very useful associations. It suggests a certain amount of violence, people working against one another in angry, disrespectful ways that create winners and losers. It is no wonder that many people believe that conflict on teams is bad and best avoided.

You might find it tempting to believe that your team does not need conflict. You and the others always seem to agree. You all think alike. You compromise easily, willingly, well before conflicts arise. Other teams get mired in conflict,

137

their members fighting a lot, but not your team. You and your teammates are above that. This is, of course, a wish and an illusion. It is not possible for a group—of students, executives, baseball players, or consultants—to not have conflict and still be a healthy, successful team. It would mean that there are absolutely no differences among you, that you are precisely the same person. Because cloning is not yet a common occurrence, this is rather unlikely. The lack of any conflict—and the belief that your team has transcended the need for it—usually means that you and the others are not ready to test your differences with one another.

In the early stages of a relationship people usually highlight their similarities and suppress their differences. This buys them time to construct boundaries around them that separate them from others. It is at the point that they feel that they can trust that those boundaries—the connections between them— are strong enough to withstand testing that they begin to show differences to one another. These differences existed since the first moments of the relationship. They were just hidden. They emerge when people are at least somewhat confident that the relationships they have built up thus far could, like rubber bands, handle testing and stretching without breaking. The question is whether or not your team has enough built-up trust and goodwill to deal with real differences without breaking apart. If, thus far, the answer has been no, your team suppresses its differences and avoids reaching deeply for the contributions of its members.

Your team might have the opposite problem. You disagree a lot. Differences are asserted loudly and often. The team seems filled with devil's advocates. You know that meetings are going to be dragged out, as members argue over issues that often aren't worth disagreeing about. This is a different sort of problem than having too little conflict, but it, too, is rooted in some difficulty with trust. You argue a lot when you doubt others' intentions or capabilities. You hold onto control because you do not feel that others have the team's best interests at heart. On such a team, differences are far more prominent than similarities. This makes it difficult to put those differences into proper perspective. You use your differences as weapons, not as sources of insight and creativity. You get battle-weary. You fight a lot, but not well. Sooner or later, you or others withdraw from the battlefield, and from the team more generally.

What you are after, then, is just the right amount of conflict. Too little, and you do not get to use differences in perspectives and beliefs to test and sharpen your ideas. Nor do you draw out one another to get the best from each other. Too much conflict and you drive one another away. You diminish rather than build trust and respect. The most effective project teams exist somewhere in the middle. Their members are capable of expressing differences respectfully, with the intention of learning from one another. They do not pretend that differences do not exist, nor do they blow them out of proportion. They simply let the differences exist and try to figure out what they mean for the work they're trying to get done.

Truly successful teams thrive on the right amount of conflict. Their members look for differences. They understand, on the basis of past experiences or just their intuition, that little differences, unexpressed, grow into bigger and more dangerous ones. People need to express their ideas, beliefs, opinions, and perspectives. If they cannot do so directly, in dialogues marked by real participation, they will do so indirectly. Sidebar conversations, distracting e-mails, grimaces, eye rolling, interruptions, and sarcasm are, more than anything, signals that team members cannot find ways to express themselves productively. If your team cannot tolerate differences, people will act out in such ways. They express their disagreements in ways that are not particularly helpful for your team, and indeed, are likely to frustrate others. Unless this sort of process is interrupted, these indirect expressions of differences are likely to grow larger and more frequent. You see this with children who act out their frustrations by pushing and pushing—whining, throwing tantrums—until they are either taken seriously or punished. This occurs on teams as well, with slightly more sophistication.

Finding the right amount of conflict can be a difficult process. The difficulty is rooted in our own ambivalence about differences. We know that differences are crucial to success. If we all think alike, we have little chance to discover what we already do not know. It is when we push up against one another that we take into account new insights, directions, and ideas. At the same time, however, differences can make us anxious. If a teammate has a different approach to a problem or disagrees with your analysis, you might feel threatened. You might feel that you need to change your approach, or that they do, as if one of you must be right and the other wrong. Or the differences in how you and your teammate think—based on different cultures or backgrounds, for example—might seem so large that reconciling them seems painfully difficult, if not impossible. You are thus likely to have two differing impulses: You want to move toward differences, knowing that they are likely to be valuable for the team, and at the same time, want to move away from them, as they implicitly threaten your own understandings and preferences. This is a tricky place to be.

You are not alone with this difficulty. All the members of your team are trying to figure out how to handle differences at the same time. These differences can be small: how you like meetings to begin, the use of agendas, e-mail etiquette, or perhaps the formatting of slides. The differences can be large: whether you think aloud and talk through ideas or work on them alone, the importance of face-to-face meetings, your commitments to doing work well or getting projects done with minimal effort, the extent to which you want to control decisions, or expectations of personal support. Implicitly, without discussion, you have developed unwritten rules to govern how you deal with such differences. I call these *rules of engagement*. They reflect the choices that you have so far made together in navigating your twin desires to move toward and away from your differences. Such rules might be productive, helping you achieve your objectives, or they might not.

Rules of Engagement

Think about the word *engage* for a moment. It has various meanings. You can engage others in conversation. You can engage their attention and hold their interest. You can become interlocked with them, as gears engage or people become betrothed. You can engage them in combat. Any of these meanings could be relevant to how you engage one another on your team. The rules that you establish to regulate how you deal with your differences help you engage and interlock with one another, in conversation and in combat. The rules guide how you come forth to meet one another in all your differences. They position you to work productively, or not, with one another.

Unproductive Rules

Project teams can put into play certain unwritten rules that lead members to engage differences in particularly unproductive, even destructive ways. You should know something about these rules to identify and rewrite them before they do too much harm to your team.

Avoid, Ignore, Smooth Over, Suppress, Laugh Away, or in Other Ways Fail to Deal With Differences and Possible Conflicts

This is the *ostrich rule*: Bury your head in the sand and pretend that differences and conflict do not exist, in the hope that, if you pretend long enough or hard enough, they will go away. A teammate always seems to disagree with the others, which you and they ignore, hoping it will stop. Two members get into a momentarily heated argument about whether the research for the project is complete enough, a third member interrupts with a joke, and you use the moment to change the subject. In such cases your team tries to make the conflict go away. This pattern is driven by an unspoken fear that the differences on the team are too large and unwieldy, or intractable, and if confronted directly, would splinter and destroy the team. Team members sense that they do not have enough shared trust and respect to hold them together if they deal directly with the differences between them. The conflicts do not, of course, go away. They simply go underground, and like untreated wounds, do increasingly greater damage to the team's relationships.

Choose to Get Along Rather Than Productively Engage Differences and Potential Conflicts

This is the *laid-back rule*: Act as if your team is so relaxed, so easy with one another, that any differences are just not worth dealing with, as they might get in the way of the wonderful sense of "groupness" that you've created. There is some truth here: Some battles are just not worth fighting, as whatever might be gained in terms of the work itself is offset by the stickiness of the conflicts. However, there is also often a great deal of avoidance hidden within this rule. A member of your team hands in work that is well below par, which you end up spending a whole night rewriting and integrating into the rest of the report. You never mention this, not wanting to cause a conflict. Or two members present conflicting visions of what the project should be about. Wanting everyone to get along, you offer a relatively weak compromise that people half-heartedly accept just to end the discussion. In such cases your team has substituted the task of getting along with one another for its primary task of creating high-quality work together that would enhance learning. The substitution represents another sort of avoidance, in the guise of politeness and a seeming ease with one another.

Frame Differences in Terms of Right and Wrong

This is the *tournament rule*: Treat differences as if they are in constant competition with one another, anointing some as winners and some as losers, to lessen ambiguity and anxiety. You thus play off one idea against another. You favor one member who represents certain expectations over another. You give more attention to a cynical or positive member and less to her opposite. You let two members argue over and over, watching them get stuck in their positions, hoping that one of them will win and the other be silenced. In each case your team has set up a competition, pitting people against one another based on the differences that they represent. The competition can be quiet, held in the silences among you, or it can be loud, with teammates engaging in destructive argument. You engage in some form of overt or covert voting, choosing winners over losers. The problem here, of course, is that creating winners and losers undercuts the possibility of collaborative working relationships. The team also shuts down creativity. Framing differences as either–or situations undercuts the team's potential for those differences to become avenues to new insights and ideas.

Frame Conflicts in Terms of Individuals Rather Than in Terms of Issues They Represent

The *scapegoating rule* allows teams to act as if individual members cause problems rather than represent or embody them on behalf of their teams. The rule requires you to act as if certain members of your team are problematic, in that they raise problems with how members should work and relate together. You believe that if those members were just not on the team, the problems they raise would not exist. This is an illusion. A member demands that other team members pay more attention to the research for the project, saying that they are not doing a very good job. You tell her that her expectations are way too unreasonable; you think of her as too obsessive and controlling. Perhaps two members of your team argue over the right way to approach the assignment. This occurs several times, until you and the others tell them to resolve this on their own and not waste valuable meeting time. In both cases your team avoids dealing with important issues related to how you go about the project, which your teammates have unknowingly raised. Yet because these issues raise anxiety, the majority of the team decides, without really deciding, to treat the people who raise the issues as the problems. So you silence the member with high expectations, and expel the two arguing members, telling them to settle it elsewhere. Members get scapegoated, and then exiled.

Push Conflict Outside the Team

The *export rule* involves taking all potential differences and conflicts within the team and projecting them outside the team. You create external enemies that draw you together and allow you to ignore the differences among you. The enemy might be other project teams in the class, which you believe are, for example, too intense, too laid back, or too close to the instructor. Your team strives to become unlike them. Team members who might have some characteristics of those stereotypes suppress them, to the point that there are no longer any differences among you. Perhaps the enemy is the course instructor. Her assignments are too difficult or ambiguous; his grading is too unfair or subjective. These assertions make it seem as if the real differences are between the team and the instructor. This is a simple way for teams to avoid important internal conflicts. Blaming the instructor becomes the substitute for looking closely at how the members themselves might have let one another down. Although creating external enemies is a way to draw your own team together, it shuts down useful explorations of your own differences.

Productive Rules

The unwritten rules by which your team can handle its differences productively are, for the most part, the opposite of those just described. These rules encourage project teams to move toward rather than away from the differences among members. Following rules such as these is precisely the way in which your team can have good fights with one another and continue its journey.

Allow Differences to Surface and Breathe, and if Necessary, Develop Into Conflicts

The *surfacing rule* is the foundation for the productive engagement of differences. It supports your talking about rather than hiding from differences. Surfacing often does not take much effort. Differences have a way of signaling their existence. They lie just beneath the surface of your conversations, waiting to be brought out into the open where they can inform those conversations in helpful ways. You might be wary or shy about revealing differences, particularly if there have been signs that they might not be completely welcomed. Surfacing them thus means following the tiny signals that they emit—as from a weak radio station or low-level beacon—and making room for them. A member of your team looks down or away each time the discussion turns to whether a section of the report seems complete enough. Two members disagree with one another, using sarcastic humor, about the use of technology to manage the team's communications. A member suggests that voting about whether to include a certain set of data in the research report does not make sense, and pushes the group to discuss it more. Each of these is a different sort of signal that differences exist among team members. The surfacing rule guides you to focus on these moments as signals. It leads you to prod one another to say what you are thinking. It leads you to try and open up rather than close down conversations when they expose differences among you.

Embrace Differences as Opportunities for Learning and Creativity

The *embrace rule* follows closely on the surfacing rule. It requires you to view differences as the friend to the task, not an enemy to be vanquished. We embrace differences by seeking them out. Your team comes up with an approach to its project. There is no disagreement. Your choice here is to be pleased that everyone is on board so easily or to be suspicious. The first choice will most likely lead you to Abilene. The second leads to a search for differences that can make your approach smarter and better. Your ideas are improved only when they are challenged. You need each other to act as the "loyal opposition": people who share your desire to achieve a goal but disagree on the specifics about how to get there. In winning them over—and in their winning you over—you usually have to create solutions together that are mutually satisfying. You press one another to defend opinions and preferences. You argue, you protest, you teach, you differ, and then, finally, you agree, and in reaching that agreement, you find that you learned some things that you would not otherwise have learned. You also did more than that: You forged closer relationships, based on a mutual knowing of what each team member truly thinks and feels. You know how you are similar and different. Such knowing makes the team experience more engaging and more real.

Frame Conflicts Around Tasks, Not Individuals

The *framing rule* holds that conflicts need to be examined in terms of structural issues—how a team organizes and performs its work—rather than in terms of what seems on the surface personality or interpersonal issues. This rule pushes you to look at conflicts in terms of what they say about your team and how it approaches work rather than about the individuals who are raising issues. A teammate is constantly badgering the rest of you about turning in your report sections on time. You are getting angry with her. If you frame the issue in terms of the individual—she's uptight and controlling—then there is little that you can do, because fixing someone's personality is a bit beyond your reach. You could frame the issue more usefully, however. If you look more closely, you might see how the team has set no real limits around when assignments are due, with no sanctions for those who are late. Your teammate is responding to that structural issue. If you look for such team-level structural issues rather than assuming that it's just about individuals, you slow your tendency to scapegoat others for issues that the entire team has not adequately resolved.

Use Lots of Data for Evaluating Alternatives and Resolving Conflicts

The *data rule* helps you move conflicts from the abstract and the personal into the realm of fact. The cleanest way to resolve differences about team strategy and process is to find data that lend credence to various perspectives. Some members of your team want to adopt one strategy for the project—say, testing out a research design or a marketing approach in a particular setting—and others favor a different strategy. Exploring the differences should be a process of collecting and presenting as much relevant information as possible and sifting through it to see what light it sheds. Maybe the project manager on the team wants the others to follow a certain protocol in putting their pieces together, and another member strongly disagrees. Here, too, there are data—in the form of others' previous experiences with different ways to integrate members' work—that can be usefully examined to resolve differences. The use of data helps frame the conversation as more or less objective. It helps make differences relevant and discussable.

Hang Onto Shared Goals and Interests Rather Than Positions

The *interests rule* holds that differences are integrated and conflicts more easily resolved when you focus on underlying concerns and needs rather than specific solutions. The more tightly you hold onto your positions—your solutions to what you see as the problems—the more likely you are to inspire destructive, competitive wrangling over whose position is best. Instead, hold tightly to your interests—the principles that you really care about in any particular situation— and insist that your teammates name their underlying interests as well. Once you all do this, you are likely to discover and create solutions that satisfy your mutual interests. Your teammate states, for example, that each member needs to give part of the final presentation. Another protests, saying this will dilute the overall quality and put your team at a disadvantage. They argue back and forth. You interrupt, and ask each of them what it is they really care about on this issue. With some prodding, the first member admits her interest in making sure that the workload is distributed fairly. The second member talks of his desire to give the team the best chance to succeed on the presentation. Your team is now able to have the larger conversation about how to satisfy both interests—fairness and achievement—and develop a way to divide work accordingly. Your team has used the process of principled negotiation to focus on its shared interests and goals. It has moved from "us–them" to "we"—a crucial shift in resolving differences. Box 7-1 describes this approach in more detail.

Approach Differences With Respect, Concern About Process, and a Sense of Perspective (and Humor)

The *perspective rule* asks you to keep in mind the larger picture: Your project team is a place where you can get some good work done, learn in a way that you could not otherwise, and create good relationships with others. It is a setting that you should take seriously, in that is the training ground for the teams in which you are likely to spend a good portion of your working career. However, it is not a setting in which you should take yourself so seriously that you neglect to honor and respect what your teammates bring to the process. This is, in effect, the Golden Rule: Treat others as you wish to be treated in the world. Respect your

BOX 7-1   PRINCIPLED NEGOTIATION

Resolving differences and conflict is, in part, a matter of negotiation. Negotiation refers to the process by which people attempt to reach agreements about issues that matter to them. This process need not be competitive. In a classic book entitled *Getting to Yes*, Fisher and Ury (1991) present a model of "principled negotiation." Good agreements are wise and efficient, and improve the parties' relationship. Positional bargaining does not tend to produce good agreements, encourages stubbornness, and tends to harm relationships. Principled negotiation provides a better way of reaching good agreements. Fisher and Ury develop four principles of negotiation. Their process of principled negotiation can be used effectively on almost any type of dispute—including disagreements on project teams.

PRINCIPLE #1: SEPARATE PEOPLE AND ISSUES

Fisher and Ury's first principle is to separate the people from the issues. People tend to become personally involved with the issues and with their side's positions, so they tend to take responses to those issues and positions as personal attacks. Separating the people from the issues allows the parties to address the issues without damaging their relationship. It also helps them to get a clearer view of the substantive problem. This means, first, trying to put yourself in the other's place rather than blaming him or her for the problem. Second, acknowledge the fact that certain emotions are present, even when they don't see those feelings as reasonable, and allow the other side to express their emotions. Third, listen actively, giving others your full attention, occasionally summarizing their points, and staying focused on what they are trying to communicate—without blaming or attacking them.

PRINCIPLE #2: FOCUS ON INTERESTS

Good agreements focus on interests rather than positions. Defining a problem in terms of positions means someone has to "lose." Defining a problem in terms of underlying interests makes it possible to find a solution that satisfies everyone's interests. You first have to identify both sides' interests regarding the issue at hand. Ask why they hold the positions they do and why they don't hold some other possible position. Answer this for yourself as well. Each of you usually has a number of different interests underlying your own positions. You will also share certain basic interests or needs, such as the need for security and economic well-being. Once you have identified your interests, discuss them together. If you want the other side to take your interests into account, you must explain them clearly. The other side will be more motivated to take your interests into account if you are showing that you are taking theirs seriously as well. Your task here is to keep a clear focus on your interests but remain open to different proposals and positions.

PRINCIPLE #3: GENERATE OPTIONS

Fisher and Ury (1991) identify four obstacles to generating creative options for solving a problem. You might decide prematurely on an option and fail to consider alternatives. You might be intent on narrowing options to find the single answer. You might define the problem in win–lose terms, assuming that the only options are for one side to win and the other to lose. You might decide that it is up to the other side to come up with a solution to the problem. To overcome these obstacles, you need to separate invention from evaluation. Brainstorm all possible solutions to the problem. Think out of the box. Suggest partial solutions. Be creative. Evaluate your ideas together only after a variety of proposals have been made. Start with the most promising proposals, and try to refine and improve them. Keep focusing on shared interests. Look for ways to make proposals that are appealing to the other side, that they would find easy to agree to.

PRINCIPLE #4: USE OBJECTIVE CRITERIA

When interests are directly opposed, use objective criteria to resolve their differences. If you make decisions based on reasonable standards it is easier for you to agree and preserve your relationships. You thus need to develop objective criteria. Usually there are a number of different criteria that you could use, and you must agree which are best for the situation. Criteria should be both legitimate and practical, such as scientific findings, professional standards, or legal precedent. One way to test for objectivity is to ask if both sides would agree to be bound by those standards. You need to approach each issue as a shared search for objective criteria. Ask your teammate for the reasoning behind his or her suggestions. Use that reasoning to support your own ideas. Keep an open mind. Be reasonable, and be willing to reconsider your ideas when there is reason to. Yet never give in to pressure, threats, or bribes. If the other party stubbornly refuses to be reasonable, shift the discussion from a search for substantive criteria to the conversation of how you are going to discuss your differences in ways that help rather than destroy your relationship.

teammates, and seek to learn about how they see what you see. Remain focused on their strengths rather than their weaknesses. Honor the principle of fairness, such that each of you feels treated justly in the context of decision-making processes that give all members the chance to be heard and taken into account. Keep a sense of humor, which allows you to join with others in laughter. This is at once the simplest, and most difficult, of the rules.

No team is perfect. No team creates and lives out productive rules without fail. There will always be moments when you try to avoid or ignore differences and hope that they disappear. There will be moments when you scapegoat others, blaming them personally for issues that the entire team has been unable to effectively resolve. There will be moments when you act as if the team has no real differences to speak of, that all of you get along famously, even when this is not so. There will be moments when you take your frustrations with one another out on other teams or your instructors. There will also be moments when you act disrespectfully to teammates or behind their backs. You will be human in these ways, falling short of what you know to be the right way to engage one another. This will all occur. The question, then, is what you then do. Do you keep doing these things or not?

Styles of Conflict

This question is, of course, rhetorical. It is far better to interrupt and rewrite unproductive rules than to let them rule you, but we know that this is not easy to do. This is partly a matter of the habits into which we routinely fall. Your team began creating habits right at the start. Particular moments occurred: Differences were revealed, and you and your teammates reacted in certain ways that set in motion how you would continue to handle such differences. One teammate disagreed with another over how often and for how long your team would meet. They briefly argued. Your team reacted in some particular way: You made a sarcastic joke about the instructor, perhaps, and distracted them from the argument; or a teammate suggested that they resolve this matter later; or someone noted that this was an important issue that everyone needed to provide input on and the team developed some agreements about commitments and priorities. If the particular reaction seemed to "work" for your team, it set in motion a pattern for future such moments. You began creating your rules of engagement. If the rules worked the next time a difference showed up, and then again, they were reinforced and legitimized. They became the team's habits, for better or for worse.

Changing habits is, first, a matter of mindfulness. You have to be aware of your habits. You have to be aware of their strength and power, the extent to which they have you, more than you have them. You have to be aware of your own tendencies when it comes to conflict. Each person has styles that dictate how he or she instinctively responds in situations of conflict. You move toward or away from it; you meet it head on or deflect it. You get competitive or try and avoid it altogether. Your style is ingrained, well before you were conscious of such things. It is shaped by your gender, race, ethnicity, nationality, and religion, each of which frames how you manage differences and conflicts. Your style is also formed from your experiences within your family, which had its own rules of engagement, and with figures of authority on which you have modeled your behaviors. You forged them amidst situations in which you have found yourself, and amended or discarded them based on your successes or failures in those situations. These forces, in combination with the particulars of your own personality, shaped how you think and act when confronted with differences that are seemingly in conflict with one another. You have a certain style on which you tend, more often than not, to fall back.

The notion of conflict styles offers you a way to understand dimensions of yourself that you have probably sensed but not explored in much depth. You could, if you chose, learn about and change conflict styles, as you would any habit, for they are neither inscribed in stone nor on your DNA. They are simply choices that you have thus far made. They can be replaced by other choices that do a better job of helping you achieve your goals.

Thomas (1976) identifies five styles, or modes, of handling conflict. *Avoiders* duck conflict. *Accommodators* give in to others to resolve conflict. *Collaborators* try to create win–win solutions in conflict situations. *Compromisers* barter to resolve conflicts, engaging in give-and-take exchanges. *Competitors* approach conflicts as win–lose situations, and do their best to win rather than lose. Box 7-2 presents these styles in more depth.

Each of these five styles makes sense, in its own way, depending on your particular goals. Say, for example, that you care more about maintaining your relationship with someone else, like the person you're dating, than about what movie you see with him or her. In that situation, you should accommodate, which fits the situation exactly given what you care about. If you care a lot about the outcome and not at all about the relationship, like when you're buying or selling a car, you should compete. If you don't care much about the outcome or about the relationship—like when a fundraiser calls you at home to solicit money for a cause in which you do not believe—you should just avoid the situation. If you care a bit about both the outcome and the relationship, you should compromise, each of you getting some of what you want and then moving on. You should collaborate if you care more than a bit about both the outcome and the relationship. The difference between situations that pull you toward compromise and collaboration is a matter of degree. We collaborate with others when

BOX 7-2   CONFLICT STYLES

The Thomas–Kilmann (2002) Conflict Mode Instrument is designed to assess an individual's behavior in conflict situations in which people's concerns appear to be incompatible. In such situations, we can describe a person's behavior along two basic dimensions: assertiveness (the extent to which the individual attempts to satisfy his or her own concern), and cooperativeness (the extent to which the individual attempts to satisfy the other's concerns). These two basic dimensions can be used to define the five specific methods of dealing with conflicts.

AVOIDING (LOW ASSERTIVENESS/ LOW COOPERATIVENESS)

The avoider wants to stay out of conflicts. You avoid taking sides. You make others take responsibility for solving the conflict. You feel that a conflict is not worth the effort, that all conflict is wrong, or that a solution is not possible anyway, so you don't get involved. You are both unassertive and passive. You do not promote your own ideas and interests, nor help others to promote theirs. You do not cooperate in defining the conflict, in seeking a solution, or in carrying out the decisions made. Indeed, your first reaction is often to deny that any problem exists at all. If this fails you might withdraw, or stay on the sidelines as a silent nonparticipant. This is usually a negative and nonproductive strategy. You abdicate responsibility to others. Issues that are not dealt with grow and fester, leading to more serious conflict. You do not help create trust because issues have not been grappled with and resolved.

ACCOMMODATING (LOW ASSERTIVENESS/ HIGH COOPERATIVENESS)

The accommodator tries to preserve, at any cost, the relationships within the team. You do everything possible to reduce the risk of damaging relationships with the others involved. Issues, goals, and progress in the work are less important than relationships. You try to embrace everyone involved in the conflict. When confrontation cannot be avoided you go with the proposal or solution that results in the least strain on relationships. You seek solutions acceptable to others, and do not push your own ideas and solutions. You placate others by conceding your own interests and goals and by giving in to those of others. You sacrifice yourself and might even be willing to accept blame for the conflict if it will help to bring peace and harmony. This is, at best, a short-term strategy. Over time, you will come to feel taken advantage of by others. You might come to feel that it is your responsibility for maintaining good relations on your team. Your teammates might even begin to think that they and their ideas are superior. They will tend to become even more assertive and will expect you to give in to their goals and interests all the time.

COLLABORATING (HIGH ASSERTIVENESS/ HIGH COOPERATIVENESS)

The collaborator is always looking for the win–win solution for everyone. You care about the issues that the team is working on and about the relationships among team members. You believe that conflict is a positive, problem-solving process. You place equal emphasis on each party's ideas, interests, and goals, while seeking to maintain a good relationship among those involved. You are convinced that conflict can be managed in such a way that it will lead to positive growth for everyone on the team. You seek win–win decisions and promote mutual respect, open communication, and full participation by all team members in the process of managing a conflict. You are firm about what you believe is important, yet sensitive to people's feelings. You encourage full participation and communication, and look for all members to clarify issues and interests, share in decision making, and implement agreed on solutions. You thus look to build trust and stronger relationships, while still arriving at the best solutions for the team.

COMPROMISING (MEDIUM ASSERTIVENESS/ MEDIUM COOPERATIVENESS)

The compromiser likes the notion of give and take, of negotiating and bartering the interests and goals of each side in a team conflict. You do not believe that it is possible to satisfy everyone fully, so you try and make sure that everyone is at least partially satisfied and that relationships are not harmed in the process. You thus seek to take part of each proposal but not the whole of any of them. You use negotiation, bargaining, and trading, getting each side to give something up to find some reasonable middle ground in which no one is unhappy but no one is completely thrilled either. You focus on making sure that everyone gets something they want, and that everyone is making approximately the same kind of compromise as well. You spend time persuading others to get on board, even though they might not love the solution. Ideally, you find creative and effective compromises; often, you get solutions that simply represent the lowest common denominator and delay rather than resolve larger issues. In doing so—in sacrificing the "best" for the "good" solutions—you avoid stalemates over issues and relationships.

COMPETING (HIGH ASSERTIVENESS/ LOW COOPERATIVENESS)

The competitor thinks of conflict as a win–lose competition, and would rather win than lose. You feel that your own ideas, values, and goals are of supreme importance and you are willing to sacrifice relationships to achieve your goals. You might be quite assertive, to the point of domineering, or use smooth diplomacy, but your goal is the same: to win. You do not often cooperate in finding any solution other than your own. You are positional. You might try to intimidate others who disagree with you, or you might simply wear them down by stubbornly insisting on your own way. There is an arrogance here that undermines relationships on your team. You help polarize the team, creating an "us" and "them" competition in the face of differences that, without interruption, might leave lasting wounds that make further resolution of conflict almost impossible. The competing style also results in a lack of enthusiasm by the "losers" for carrying out solutions or goals that were forced through against their wishes. Defeated parties experience a growing sense of frustration with the way conflict has been handled and growing hostility toward the "winners."

we are fully aware that we have thrown in our lot with them, for better or for worse, and are committed to accomplishing our goals together. With that sort of commitment comes a belief that it is only when others are worked with (and cared about) as full partners that our goals will be fully realized.

If we were completely rational human beings we would precisely calculate the value of outcomes and relationships in each situation and, based on the results, access the appropriate conflict style and act accordingly. We would thus solve each conflict situation, as it should be solved. We are not always rational, however. Our tendencies and predilections compel us to choose certain styles over others, even when they do not fit our objectives. You might routinely accommodate others, giving in to their ideas even when you have good ideas of your own that you want heard. You might avoid conflict altogether at the expense of the project. You might take on every battle, competing with teammates at the expense of your relationships. You might seek to compromise, or to collaborate, with others, even though it might make more sense to simply give in and move on. In such cases you find that you act out of habit even though it does not make sense. You fight battles you should not fight or avoid battles that you should take on. You are, at such moments, less than rational. Your own tendencies take over. You are stuck in unproductive patterns of thought and action that leave differences and conflicts unsatisfactorily resolved.

This happens to teams, too. Teams also have conflict styles, and they can get stuck in them. Teams develop styles by allowing certain members to dominate initial conflict situations. In the first team meeting, a member of your team says that she believes a project manager should make all of the decisions regarding the direction of the project. A teammate tells her the idea is idiotic. Others nod. In that moment, a certain style (competitive) and rule of engagement (argumentative and disrespectful) has just been set in motion. Other choices could have been made. The teammate might have been asked about her reasoning, just so others could understand. Another member could have explained his own thinking, and then led the team in a conversation about issues of project direction and accountability. In that moment, another style (collaborative) and rule of engagement (shared interests and concern for process) would have been set in motion. Team styles of managing differences are born in such moments. If you and others let certain responses pass without remark, you have allowed one member with a certain style of managing conflict to superimpose that style on the team more generally. Your silence is your agreement with that style. The more that style gets used to handle subsequent differences on the team, the more firmly it takes hold, and the more certain become the rules of engagement that maintain it. Over time, it becomes increasingly difficult to dislodge that style and use other, more productive styles in situations that call for them.

It should be apparent that, on student project teams, most of the conflict situations that you face call for a collaborative style. Collaboration requires you to talk about the differences that you each bring to the team and figure out how to draw on them to make your work better. The collaborative approach assumes, of course, that you care about both making the project as good as you can and creating strong and healthy working relationships with one another. This is also the most difficult approach. It takes a great deal of time and effort. It requires you to work at creating trusting, open relationships in which feedback is given and received. There will, of course, be moments when you will avoid conflict, accommodate others, fashion compromises, or compete with one another. This is part of the nature of relationships. However, in a team marked largely by a collaborative style, such moments are relatively few, and understood as fleeting in nature.

Teams fall short of creating collaborative working relationships when members overemphasize doing really well on the project or getting along with one another. They then largely manage their differences through competition or accommodation. Those styles support their work on the dimension they care about even as they diminish the chances of success on the other dimension. However, members of these types of teams are not particularly content. They regret what they have let go. There is still some desire, even beneath layers of cynicism, to move toward more productive ways of managing differences. They just need to find ways to move from the habits they have fallen into and create new, more productive ways of managing differences.

The Stories We Tell

When you look closely at unproductive patterns of behavior, like conflicts that have gotten out of hand or people who have given up hope of working well with one another, you can see how they are held in place by stories that people tell themselves and others. Two teammates always seem to disagree with one another. The story that everyone accepts is that they just don't like each other and need to be kept as separate as possible. A teammate always seems to take a very long time to go through and edit reports and presentations. The team's story is that she is obsessive and controlling. The team is performing poorly, in spite of spending many hours working together. Their story is that the course instructor is ambiguous in his assignments and unfairly subjective in his grading.

You create and tell such stories all the time on your team. You might not be aware of doing so. You might believe that you are simply stating the obvious, but explanations for patterns of behavior are only "obvious" because you have created stories, told them again and again, adding to and elaborating them, to the point that they become the acceptable versions of truth. We create stories to make sense of situations that might otherwise be confusing. That is what stories do, and why we tell them incessantly: It is the way we create meaning out of a jumble of events and interactions. Stories are like the frames that we put around pictures: They narrow our attention, directing our focus and telling us to ignore that which is outside the frame.

Our stories are thus the ways in which we make choices about how to understand and act within situations. These choices can be quite flawed. Our stories are often biased in our favor in ways of which we are unaware. Consider the preceding situations. You tell a story about two teammates that do not like one another because it lets you avoid looking at how they are arguing an issue that all of you should be discussing, such as how honest members should be in giving feedback to one another or how much time to put into the project. The others are silent, letting them argue, letting them damage their relationship. Or you tell a story about the obsessive teammate because it is easier than looking at how the other members have gotten lazy in their work, knowing that she will do the work of editing, which you both appreciate and resent. Or you tell a story about the unfairness of the instructor to avoid looking at how you and your teammates have not held one another accountable for the quality of your work. It is easier to cast the blame elsewhere and avoid difficult conversations.

Even in such cases your stories are not completely wrong. There are often bits and pieces of truth within them. The two teammates do not particularly care for one another. The editor is more obsessive than the others. The course instructor is somewhat ambiguous. If you focus only on those aspects and weave your stories around them, however, you are unable to look at other possible angles as well. You lock yourself into certain perspectives. You and the team become stuck, as your explanations leave you with little to do in the way of making useful changes. If you believe that the problem is that two of your teammates simply don't like one another and cannot get along, your options are limited. You could try and keep them separate. You could tell them to go work out their problems with one another elsewhere. You could let them argue, hoping that one will give in to the other. Each of these options produces undesirable outcomes. Your team loses the combatants' energies and ideas, as their focus becomes moving against or away from one another. Similarly, if you believe that a teammate is just too obsessive—or mean, lazy, selfish, incompetent, controlling, or any other character flaw—there is little that you can do, given that you cannot alter another's personality. There is even less that you can do with an instructor who you believe to be unfair or incompetent. You have framed situations in ways that can only leave you helpless and frustrated.

You have also framed them in ways that support unproductive rules of engagement. When you act as if the problem is that two members don't get along, you are likely to invoke the tournament rule (setting them up against one another, in the hopes that one will win, thereby ridding the team of disturbing differences), the ostrich rule (ignoring, minimizing, or pretending that the differences do not exist), or the laid-back rule (insisting that differences are not important and unworthy of attention) of engagement. When you act as if the problem is the course instructor or his assignments, you are likely to follow the export rule of engagement (acting as if all differences and conflicts exist outside the team, and ignoring those that should be addressed within the team). When you act as if the problem is located with a particular team member, you are likely to invoke the scapegoating rule (blaming individuals for the differences that they raise and represent on behalf of the team). When you tell stories that are flawed and marked by half-truths, you invoke rules of engagement that are not only unproductive but also can be dangerous for individuals and undermining to the team.

The Lure of Scapegoating

Among these unproductive framings the most common (and insidious) is the scapegoating rule. It happens routinely on project teams. A member raises the issue of wanting to spend more time on team process, and is considered too "touchy-feely." A member is explicit about wanting to limit the time and energy he spends on the project, and is labeled "selfish." A member asks for lots of help from others, and is cast as "needy." These labels—these framings of the individuals—are key to the stories that people tell. They are often difficult to resist, due to a number of interesting dynamics.

Scapegoating is a process of simplifying and reducing others for our own purposes. We take an aspect of someone else—an ability to draw firm boundaries, for example, or a desire to spend a lot of time editing—and act as if that dimension defines him or her. In our minds we expand that dimension, making it larger, to the point that we ignore the other parts of who they are. We make them into one-dimensional characters. It's as if we were casting them in roles—the controlling character on stage left, the selfish one on stage right—in some play that we direct. This is a useful analogy. When we scapegoat others, we are casting them in roles, making them characters in a production of a story that we stage during the course of the project team.

Why would we do this? We want to populate stories that justify our team's failure in ways that leave us relatively blameless, so we pretend. We pretend that another member is only selfish, only lazy, or only incompetent. We pretend that we are none of those things. We act in ways based on that pretending. The story unfolds before our eyes. It is the other person who is the problem. If only he was different or if only she was gone from the team, all would be well. The team would be great. We pretend this is true and after enough pretending we come to believe it as the truth.

We are not consciously aware of this process. We just move toward it, driven by our desires to avoid looking at the parts of ourselves—our own laziness, selfishness, incompetence, and other imperfections. We take those parts and project them onto others. We simplify them, and we simplify ourselves, too. The plays that we stage, inevitably, are about good and bad, and star heroes and villains. They are simple morality plays. A teammate seeks to damage the team through her personal failings or intentions. We try to halt the process and minimize the damage. We struggle valiantly. If we fail—if the team fails—at least we tried as hard as we could. It is not our fault. We just could not stop "them" from disrupting the team. This is our story. It leaves us blameless, heroic, and stoic. When we hold fast to such stories, we create casualties. We harm those we scapegoat, for they are unable to participate as fully and openly as they might otherwise. We harm our teams, for we rob them of the chance to draw fully on all aspects of each member. We harm ourselves, for we no longer have the capacity to learn about and improve the parts of ourselves that we have projected onto others.

The scapegoating process also draws some of its power from the ways in which we cast others into their roles because of their *identity groups*—groups into which they are born that come to define how others see and react to them. Identity groups include, for example, gender (men and women), religion (e.g., Muslim, Christian, Jewish), race (e.g., Asian, White, African American), ethnicity (e.g., English, African, Irish), and sexuality (e.g., heterosexual, homosexual). People often unconsciously ascribe certain traits to members of particular identity groups (nurturing, athletic, shy, angry, uptight) and use those traits to help them stage and tell stories. You are more likely, whether you wish to admit it or not, to consider a white male as uncaring, a black woman as angry, or an Asian woman as submissive then you would consider others with those traits. We use such primitive labels to help us cast others into certain roles, the better to scapegoat them should the need arise.

One version of this dynamic occurs in project teams composed of students from different countries. There are real differences on these teams. The language barrier can loom large. People from different national cultures can also approach relationships with one another quite differently. Some cultures value personal friendships more than others, as a way into productive working relationships. Other cultures value a sustained focus on tasks and avoid conversations that require team members to discuss how they work with one another. Such differences can easily translate into people stereotyping and scapegoating one another. Those who do not speak English fluently are framed as holding the team back, not pulling their weight, or wasting the time of others. The native English speakers are framed as dominating, controlling, and impatient. The team splits into factions, formed around nationality and fluency, and disintegrates, each side blaming the other for their shared failure at cross-cultural communication.

The scapegoating dynamic is easy to fall into. It simplifies things greatly. When a teammate raises issues that have no easy answers—how much time and effort you put in, how much help you give one another in a quasi-competitive classroom situation—it is far simpler to act as if he or she is the problem than to get everyone to think about the underlying issue being raised. Scapegoating is a way to make others go away—if not physically, then in terms of how seriously others take them. If you don't look closely at them but instead dismiss them with a story that makes them the issue, you don't need to look closely at how you are implicated in the underlying issue. You simplify them, and you simplify yourself. This makes things less complicated. Working with and through differences requires patient talking and listening. Writing others off takes hardly any time at all.

The problem is that scapegoating, like other unproductive rules of engagement, does not accomplish much that is worth accomplishing. As long as you locate problems in "them," you are unable to help change or improve situations. The trick, then, is to not locate problems in one another. You must help yourself to stop creating and telling stories that blame others or in other ways lead to unproductive methods of engaging differences. You need to create more expansive, nuanced stories that open the possibility of change and improvement. This is the first step toward managing conflicts that show up on project teams. The second step is to practice and master the difficult conversations that actually help make a difference. In the final section of this chapter I examine those two steps more closely.

Fighting the Good Fight

There are a number of useful tools and frameworks to help you manage conflict. They help structure dialogues to enable people who disagree to discuss issues and create solutions. Invariably, they involve listening actively to others, validating their feelings, and moving positively toward mutually satisfying outcomes. These tools are unlikely to work, however, unless you really want them to work. Driving any significant change is a real desire for things to be different, coupled with an awareness that you yourself will have to be part of the change. Too often people want to resolve conflicts by having *others* change how they think and what they do. This is not a particularly effective strategy. It tends to create tournaments in which combatants joust against one another and damage relationships. Nor is this strategy ultimately desirable. If you resolve a conflict by one side just backing down, you have lost the capacity to learn from the differences that are presented. The conflict subsides but the differences remain. Those differences will present themselves, over and over, until they either are fully looked at and taken into account or end up fracturing your team.

If you do truly wish to work with disagreements in ways that enable you and others to learn, and leave your team the better for it, the work begins. It begins with you—or more precisely, with the stories that you frame about conflicts. As noted earlier, when you frame disagreements in terms of personality differences or interpersonal animosity, you drastically reduce the possibility of making your team better at what it does. Your best hope is to minimize the damage, by isolating or mollifying "difficult" members or by keeping them apart from one another. Actually making your team stronger happens only when you frame disagreements differently. With a different story comes the possibility that members who seem "difficult" are only so because they are representing—"representing"—an issue to and for the team. If you are willing to at least consider that possibility, it opens the door to the other possibility of making your team stronger and better. It makes possible the fighting of good fights.

Generating Alternative Hypotheses

So what does this mean, in practice? It means that you look not just at but also beneath interpersonal conflicts. When you look at conflicts, you tend to see people who don't get along. You personalize the conflicts, locating the problems within people or their relationships. When you look beneath the conflicts, you see what your teammates are representing on behalf of the team. If you look beneath rather than at the team member who wanted to spend more time on team process (the "touchy-feely one") you could see her raising a crucial issue for the team (the collective willingness to reflect on and attempt to change team processes). The team's response to the individual is, in fact, partly about members' reactions to (and anxieties about) facing the choices that they have made and having difficult conversations with one another about those choices. If you look beneath rather than at two teammates who argue about how long team meetings should be, you could see them as representing two sides of a larger team issue (the struggle to figure out the right levels of commitment and strike the right balance of excellence and effort).

Your stories about differences and disagreements on your team are, in fact, *hypotheses* that you have developed. Hypotheses describe the relationships among critical pieces of information. You've noticed, for example, that a teammate gets agitated whenever a deadline draws near for a project deliverable. You've also noticed that when this occurs, he sends multiple e-mails, pressing others to get their materials completed. Some members comply and others do not. Several times there have been arguments about this, which flare up and then go away. Your explanation is that your teammate is uptight and nervous and gets controlling. You monitor your teammate's anxiety and see the results. You have thus built and in your mind confirmed a hypothesis. Over time, you come to accept it not as hypothetical but as proven fact. It is now the way in which you see the conflict between the uptight, controlling teammate and the others on the team. Your diagnosis of the problem ("he's just too uptight") now frames how you handle it (wait for it to blow over).

Clayton Alderfer (1987), a prominent organizational psychologist, suggests that looking beneath rather than at such conflicts is a matter of developing alternative hypotheses to explain them. The habit of holding several alternative hypotheses increases the likelihood that you will be open to new data inconsistent with any one hypothesis. It is tempting to ignore or distort new data if they disconfirm your only explanation. You are likely to only see how your teammate is controlling as long as you believe that is the real issue causing the conflict on the team. You might thus ignore other sorts of data that call your explanation into question.

Alderfer teaches that creating alternative hypotheses requires you to deliberately try and change your level of explanation. The current explanation, like many that get created, focuses on the individual level: your teammate's personality or temperament. Change the level of explanation and focus on an aspect within the team itself. Look at the data: Deadlines draw closer, your teammate reminds others to get their work in on time, some teammates comply and others do not, resentment builds on all sides, arguments flare up and recede, and the process repeats itself. You could frame a hypothesis to explain these data that locates the conflict in the team's inability to hold members accountable for the timing and quality of their work. You would then look to see if the team is lax in enforcing agreed-on expectations for when work is due and its quality when it is given to others.

You can now test each hypothesis that you have developed to explain a conflict, to see which holds the most promise as an explanation. Hypotheses are tested by further observation. When other team members press one another to get their work done, does your teammate still get anxious and demanding? Does your teammate seek to control other parts of the team's work? Hypotheses are also tested by direct intervention. You could ask your teammate directly about when he gets upset, why he thinks that happens, and what might be done about it. You could raise the issue of accountability and expectations on the team, and see the extent to which the team is split about the matter. If you have used your alternative hypotheses to predict the likely responses to new situations, the new data should either support present hypotheses or help to generate new ones.

You are likely to find, as you develop and test various explanations, that there are multiple streams flowing into conflicts. Individuals can be problematic. Your teammate might have a tendency to be controlling. Indeed, you will all bring your own issues—with authority, power, trust, intimacy, control, and the like—into your teams. These issues will spur disagreement. People can also not like one another, and range from politely distant to hostile in their relations with one another. This, too, will cause discord on the team, and the team itself will develop habits, some good and others bad. Creating alternative hypotheses to explain conflicts and disagreements means looking at each of these streams and seeing which can be altered. The discipline here is to avoid the easy hypotheses that blame others, look only to confirm your story, and elevate it to the realm of fact. You need to force yourself to expand the universe of explanations, even if they happen to involve you as one of the contributors to the conflict on the team.

Managing Difficult Conversations

Once you are reasonably comfortable with your assessment about what lies beneath a conflict, you should address it constructively. To the extent that the conflict is significant and enduring, you will most likely need to engage in what we can safely call "difficult conversations." Difficult conversations are anything that you might not want to talk about, such as your teammate constantly interrupting you or the fact that half of your team is routinely late to meetings. We are often reluctant to open a difficult conversation for fear of the consequences. Yet unless we do—unless you do, on your team—real disagreements will remain and their influence will expand.

A useful framework for handling difficult conversations comes from a book entitled *Difficult Conversations: How to Discuss What Matters Most* (Stone, Patton, & Heen, 1999). The authors suggest that three particular conversations underlie every difficult conversation. The *"What happened?"* conversation involves disagreement over what happened, what should happen, and who is to blame. The *Feelings* conversation is about the parties' emotions and their validity. The *Identity* conversation is an internal conversation that each party has with herself, over what the situation tells her about who she is. The authors identify common errors that people make in these sorts of conversations. The key to having effective, productive conversations is to recognize the presence of these deeper conversations and avoid the common errors. Box 7-3 discusses this process in more depth.

This framework helps turn difficult conversations into learning conversations. Learning drives the resolution of interpersonal conflicts. The learning conversation involves working through each of the three conversations—the "What happened?" conversation, the Feelings conversation, and the Identity conversation. The authors suggest beginning as if you are an objective third party. Tell the story as if you were an observer from the outside, with no stake in the outcome. Tell the "third story"—not a story from your point of view, or from the other's point of view, but from the point of view of a narrator who witnessed events. Note the differences between the two stories that you and the other party would tell, without framing one story as right and the other as wrong. Your goal is to understand the other person's perspective better, to share your own perspective, and to talk about how to go forward together. As you pursue this goal, seek to truly understand events and what they mean for both of you. Acknowledge the feelings and identify issues that were triggered, in you and in them. Unless you are able to express these issues, they will become roadblocks, halting your progress.

Resolving differences and coming to good resolutions is primarily a matter of your own orientation. A competitive orientation, in which you seek to make yourself right and others wrong, is destined to fail. Even if you get them to back down, you've damaged relationships, perhaps irreparably, with teammates. You need to adopt a different stance marked by curiosity rather than certainty, exploration rather than debate, and complexity rather than simplicity. These internal shifts help make possible the shifts in your conflicts with others.

Communication—the process of listening and speaking—is the key to moving through difficult conversations and resolving conflicts. Listening is the more

BOX 7-3   DIFFICULT CONVERSATIONS

In their book *Difficult Conversations: How to Discuss What Matters Most*, Stone, Patton, and Heen (1999) suggest that underlying every difficult conversation are actually three deeper conversations. These conversations and their implications are summarized here.

THE "WHAT HAPPENED?" CONVERSATION

The challenge of the difficult conversation is that the situation is more complex than any one person in a conflict can see. There are three common mistakes that we make in struggling with this challenge.

■ *Mistake 1*: We assume we have all the relevant facts of a situation. We assume that our view of the matter is right. We might agree with others on the facts, but we often differ in our interpretations of what the facts mean, and of what is important. To have a conversation that helps us learn, we need to shift from our certainty about what is right to a curiosity about the others' views of the situation. We need to adopt a stance of "and" rather than "or," which helps us acknowledge both our own views and their (differing) views.

■ *Mistake 2*: We tend to assume that we know what others' intentions are, but we're often wrong. We base our assumptions on our own feelings: If I feel hurt then you must have meant to be hurtful. We also tend to think the worst of others and the best of ourselves. To counteract this tendency, we need to avoid making the leap from impact to intent. We must ask others what their intentions were. We need to remain open to their explanation, and we need to hold loosely rather than tightly to our own beliefs about their intentions. The authors also note that if others present their hurts to us, and we explain that we had no intentions to hurt them, we tend to believe that they have no reason to feel hurt. We can avoid this by acknowledging the other's feelings, and by considering the possibility of our own complex motives.

■ *Mistake 3*: We focus on assigning blame. This prevents us from learning what really lies beneath the problem. The more difficult, complex work is to map each party's contribution to the situation. Contribution emphasizes understanding causes, joint responsibility, and avoiding future problems. When we acknowledge our own contributions we help shift the other party away from blaming. Contributing to a situation does not imply being blameworthy for that situation. We contribute to problematic situations, for example, by having avoided dealing with issues in the past or just by the nature of our personality or temperament.

THE FEELINGS CONVERSATION

We consider conversations difficult because there are feelings involved. We are angry, frightened, vulnerable, or frustrated. Expressing these emotions is risky. We often frame difficult conversations in ways that ignore their emotional content, as if there are only facts to discuss and solutions to devise. The problem is that unexpressed feelings remain within us. They leak into conversation. We are aware of them even as we try to push them away. This makes it hard for us to be good listeners. We also translate our feelings into judgments, characterizations, and attributions about others. The need to blame often indicates unexpressed emotions. To avoid this, we need to identify and understand our feelings and share them clearly. We need to encourage others to do the same. We can only do this when we acknowledge that our emotions are an important part of the situation, regardless of how rational or justifiable they are. We need to take some time to convey—and be conveyed to—the full range and complexity of feelings, without rushing to evaluate them. We need to acknowledge one another's feelings.

THE IDENTITY CONVERSATION

Conversations are also difficult because they threaten or challenge our identities, our sense of who we are. Difficult conversations might call into question our sense of our own competence, our goodness, and our ability to contribute. Managing the internal identity conversation requires our learning which issues are most important to our identity. We also need to learn how to adapt our identity in healthy ways. Rather than think of ourselves as just this or just that—good or evil, strong or weak, smart or dumb—we need to think about all the different parts of who we are. In doing so—in rejecting all-or-nothing thinking—we are less likely to be upset by any particular conversation that might otherwise threaten our wish to see ourselves in certain idealized ways. This enables us to more easily admit to our own mistakes, mixed intentions, and contributions to the problem. It enables us to maintain a balanced sense of self in difficult conversations. It also enables us to prepare for rather than fear or attempt to control others' reactions. We are not so on edge, so threatened, or so vulnerable because our sense of self and worth is not so directly tied into the conversation itself.

important and difficult of the two. Listening well enables others to feel valued and heard, and reduces their need to attack and defend. Genuine listening cannot be forced. You have to *want* to hear others' stories and experiences. You need to inquire, to learn those stories more deeply, and ask open-ended questions rather than make statements or cross-examine others. Acknowledge others' feelings as valid and understandable, and do your best to imagine what it feels like to be them on the inside. This is the act of truly listening to others: taking them in, absorbing and digesting their experiences, to the point that you "get" them and see them not as the "other" but as "another" person, like you, trying to do their best in difficult or confusing situations. Speak in ways that help them see you in the same way. Tell your story clearly. Rather than presenting your conclusions as "truth," share how you arrived at them. Show how you derived your hypotheses. Tell them what really matters to you, in terms of your interests and your experiences. Say what you mean rather than making them guess. This sets the stage for problem solving, for developing and choosing options that meet each side's most important concerns and interests.

Notice that there is no place in this framework for electronic communication. As I have noted elsewhere, e-mail is useful for sharing information. It is deeply flawed as a method for building and strengthening relationships. Conflict resolution is, at its core, a relational process. It requires people to be together: to look at one another, to read and react to nonverbal cues, to have moments of silence and reflection, to laugh together, and even to be constructively angry at one another. E-mail makes it too easy to engage in hit-and-run attacks. It leaves too much room for misinterpretation. It is a medium in which messages cannot be softened or adapted in the midst of a conversation. It creates serial monologues under the illusion of dialogue. It leaves no room for tone or nuance, and too much room for recipients to imagine senders' intentions and motives in often inaccurate and damaging ways. Difficult conversations are made more so when you do not engage them directly in the presence of one another.

Risks and Rewards

It is easier to read a chapter on the benefits of conflict than actually engage in conflict itself. Difficult conversations are difficult for good reason. They are complicated and messy, particularly if you've avoided them and negative feelings have built up. You might not feel good when you're actually in them. You might find yourself angry and frustrated, moved to say damaging things to one another. You have to manage to not get defensive and take things too personally, or to go on the attack, all while listening to others and doing your best to get a full picture of their intentions, experiences, and perspectives. This is not a simple process, and not without risks. Teammates can draw apart, nursing real or imagined wounds. You can get distracted from work. The team can flounder as you try and change long-standing habits.

Yet the rewards are also high for resolving conflicts well. You can turn the differences among you into strengths. Rather than try and prove who is right and who is wrong, you can use your differences as ways to test and strengthen your ideas. You can learn to get the most from one another. No one has to become a casualty on the team, dismissed in some fashion because they represent differences or an unpopular stance. Trust is enhanced as members become increasingly comfortable with expressing what they think and feel, knowing that they will be taken seriously rather than shot down by others. You and your teammates feel accepted by one another even as you disagree. Your team becomes a safe place in which to discuss all manner of topics. Your team keeps moving along its journey, unlikely to remain stuck at any one place.

You and your teammates are constantly calculating the magnitude and likelihood of the risks and the rewards of conflict. You are constantly making your choices: Do I take this on? How important is it? What style should I adopt? What difference will it make? These are not simple choices. You might arrive at a different conclusion than do others and have to act alone, which shifts the ratio of risks and rewards. None of this is simple, but we do know one immutable truth: Real differences never go away. They insist on being taken into account. They will grow louder, more obvious, and more threatening. Like a tropical storm that heads out to sea, differences that do not get their due get upgraded to disagreements, and later, to full-blown conflicts that can get destructive. We know this, even as we like to pretend otherwise.

You can intervene. You can effectively acknowledge, respect, integrate, and learn from differences on your team. This might require a shift within you: To not make the differences personal, get anxious and threatened by them, and tell stories that leave you blameless and others culpable. The toll that you and your team have to pay here is to drive right into the storm—into its middle, which can be surprisingly calm—and do the right work together to make sense of how you got there and what you can do together to make it right. The road that you travel as a team will keep leading you back to this place. This toll has a habit of reappearing, sitting there immovable in the road, demanding payment. You only get it to go away by paying it, driving through it, leaving it behind you, and in the process, leaving your team wiser and stronger.

Summary

Conflict is a necessary dimension of your project team. Handled well, conflict enables you to develop the best ideas, most creative solutions, and constructive improvements in how you work together. There are teams with too little conflict, with members agreeing too easily, and others with too much conflict, their members unable to let one another exert influence. Your team needs to develop the right amount and types of conflict: enough to express and learn from differences, yet not so much that members cannot remain joined in their work. This chapter focused on ways to find and maintain that balance. Various unspoken "rules of engagement" were described by which teams regulate differences among their members; some of these rules lead to productive conflict, whereas others do not. These rules partly reflect the various conflict styles of you and your teammates. Five conflict styles were described, along with implications for the style of your team more generally. Your team's style of conflict is partially locked in place by the stories that you and others tell about what happens on your team. This chapter discussed how teams develop stories in ways that help or hinder their abilities to handle differences and conflict in useful ways. Developing useful stories inevitably involves difficult conversations. The sixth Team Development Exercise—"Managing Differences"—provides a structured way for you to engage such conversations, in the context of examining the "rules" by which your team has thus far managed important differences.

Chapter 8

Full Engagement

Imagine the following scenario. Your project team is doing reasonably well, or at least, well enough. You have a sense of your goals and are heading in their general direction, with some experience of success. There have been some difficult moments, with some members doing a lot more work than others or struggling over influence and control, but the team is generally doing fine. You and the others have figured out what works, in terms of how to coordinate your efforts and do the work necessary to meet your obligations. You've made some efforts in the direction of giving and receiving feedback. You've ventured a bit into difficult conversations, trying to resolve differences that posed problems for the team. Relationships among you have settled into place, for better or for worse. You know which conversations to have and which to avoid. You like some teammates more than others. You're frustrated with some more than others, and some are probably even frustrated with you, but it's fine. You could continue like this through the end of the project.

This is a relatively familiar scenario. It describes quite a few student project teams. It's not a bad scenario. This sort of team is quite workable. The team has become a vehicle built for the purpose of getting from one place to another place—from the beginning of the project to its completion. The team is simply the means of transportation. It is what it is and it need not be more.

Imagine a different scenario. You look forward to team meetings. The project has had its ups and downs, and there been difficult moments as you and the others sorted out differences in how you wanted to work on the project. You feel as if you are learning a lot, however—much more than you would have expected—not just about the course material but about your teammates and yourself. You find the experience engaging, not boring. Your teammates are a source of interest and challenge, even amidst your occasional frustration with them. There is ease among the team members. You take issues and ideas, and one another, seriously. You make a good deal of room for each member to say what he or she wants to say, even if it seems kooky or intense. There is good humor and laughter. You trust one another. You believe that members have good intentions. You see commitment. You forgive one another inevitable lapses of attention or slights inflicted as you work through your differences. You are glad to be part of your team.

This scenario is also familiar, although for fewer teams. The difference between the two scenarios is in the level of joy and ease members experience on their teams. The experience of being a member of the team in the second scenario is one of delight rather than duty. You are delighted to be part of a team whose members like one another, and more important, bring out the best in one another. There is a level of connection that somehow moves beyond that you would expect for students who have been assigned to work together. The connections are real, and hard-won, not superficial. You do not pretend with one another. You have found a way to push against one another, to fight well, and you and your relationships and your work are better for it. You have allowed yourselves to be real with one another. You have found some delight in this. It is fun to be on this team.

This is partly a matter of luck. You have to be fortunate enough to have a team of individuals who allow themselves to be at ease while also caring about the team and its work. They have the capacity to trust rather than defend themselves against others. They are secure enough to say what they think and feel, and to give and receive feedback. Their differences with one another are meaningful but not so large and gaping that they are essentially unbridgeable. They are willing to make the team more than just the vehicle for getting the project done. They have the capacity to invest themselves more deeply into the team, in the belief or the hope that the experience will mean something more than just the completion of a course project.

However, the second scenario comes about not just because a team is filled with people who can work well with others. It comes about because its members choose to fully engage. They do not just go through the required motions of becoming a project team. They choose to take their journey seriously—to make it a voyage that will mean something to them personally, to their own learning and growth. They choose to truly create a team, even after the instructor has, seemingly, already formed it for them. They understand that formation is not the same as creation, for the latter does not stop, as members search for continuous learning and improvement. Team members choose to search for ways to get better at their work. Indeed, they choose to think of the team as work, in the sense of being useful and important, rather than "just school." They make their team part of their real lives; they treat it as part of their real worlds. They thus become available to learn something real for themselves.

Not everyone makes the choice to try and create this sort of team. The first scenario requires your physical presence at team meetings and presentations. It requires you to do a certain amount of work, in the form of preparation and deliverables. It requires you to engage in discussions, to contribute ideas, and to help the team identify and solve problems that would otherwise get in the way of the team completing its work. It does not, however, require you to find joy and meaning in your work on the team. It does not require you to dig deeply into your experiences on the team—your frustrations, challenges, insights, and relationships—and take them up with your teammates. You are required, mostly, to get with and then through the team experience.

The second scenario requires more of you, not necessarily in terms of the time that you spend but in how much intensity you bring to your interactions. The difference is one of depth. You must engage more deeply, make yourself more present in the context of your team. What does this mean, exactly? It means that you act in ways that enable your teammates to know you more fully. They know what you think and how you feel about what is happening on the team. They know how you are similar to and different than others. They know what you are good at and not so good at. They know almost as well as you do your hot buttons, the places where you get unreasonable and the triggers that make you lose focus. They know about your previous experiences on teams, and what you think about why they were good or bad. They know these things because you told them. You did this because your teammates were doing this and you wanted to keep company with them. You did this because you wanted to have a real experience with others, even though you knew that you could stay relatively superficial with one another and it would be good enough. The superficial can be fun, yes, but it cannot be deeply affecting. You wanted the team to be better than that. You wanted more.

The difference between the two types of teams is that between good and outstanding. Good teams get the work done, and it's more or less fine. Outstanding teams transform their members. They are vehicles not simply for getting work done but for taking their members from one place to the next, leaving them far wiser about teams and about themselves. Of course, these teams have to pay a toll. They must create patterns of interaction that enable their members to fully engage in their work together. This is difficult. It happens when teams are able to overcome an obstacle: members' unwillingness to openly acknowledge and change perceptions of one another that shut down their abilities and willingness to fully engage on their team. In this chapter I explore more carefully the relation between fully engaging, the creation of outstanding teams, and the obstacles and strategies that people create for themselves.

The Self Presented

The thesis of this chapter is psychological, which some of you will gravitate toward and others of you will not. It's this: The more comfortable you and your teammates are in revealing the different parts of yourself, the more able you are to fully engage in your work together and achieve the sorts of outcomes that you wish. Throughout this book I have emphasized the notion of "engagement"— the extent to which you bring yourself into the work and into your relations with others on the team. This is a psychological concept, and an important one. It refers to how *absent* or *present* you are as a team member.

Absence and presence can be understood literally, in terms of the extent to which you show up for and remain at team meetings. However, they are also understood cognitively, in terms of how much you are really thinking about what the team is doing and working on. We are absent cognitively when we do our tasks—research, developing reports and presentations—more or less automatically, more eager to finish them than to get deeply drawn into them. There is, of course, a difference. Think of an activity that you had to do but did not care that much about, like learning statistics. You dutifully put your time into it, studying the concepts, learning them well enough to pass tests. Now think of an activity that you really wanted to do, like learning an exciting sport. You thought about it a lot, analyzed its principles and movements, and found others to talk about it with and help you figure out how to get better at it. You were cognitively engaged and intellectually present: Others could see your focus, your intent, and your absorption in what you were learning. You were also emotionally present as well. You cared about what you were doing. You felt great when you were doing well and improving and not so great when you were stuck. Your feelings were right there on the surface, not hidden, and they mattered.

The idea that you can be more absent or present as a team member is reasonably intuitive. You know when someone else on the team is there but not there. You know this about yourself, when you observe yourself with some objectivity. You know that when you are absent you go through the motions but not much more. You participate but don't take the lead in or get excited about conversations. You allow yourself to get distracted, answering your cellular phone or surfing the Internet or playing with your electronic devices. You think about the project as much as you need to or are pushed to but not eagerly or deeply. The team exists, to some degree, apart from you, and you apart from the team, the two intersecting briefly when you do the work that you need to do. If you look closely enough, you can see this in yourself and in others.

This is not an all-or-nothing proposition. It is more accurate to say that at any moment in time—assuming that you show up for meetings—you are a combination of presence and absence. This sounds esoteric or philosophical but it doesn't have to be. A useful analogy is that of the phases of the moon. At different points in the moon's cycle, parts are visible and other parts are shadowed and cannot be glimpsed. So, too, are you on your project team. At different moments parts of you are visible and other parts hidden. You make some parts visible by exposing them to the light, by bringing them out of the shadows and into play during team interactions in which you are truly engaged. You keep other parts hidden, through tactics of disengagement. Consider these illustrations.

Scenario 1

A member of your team, Tim, is pushing the team to do more than just complete the research on the company that you were assigned and hand in the report. He says that, because the company's headquarters are local, the team should interview several of its executives and incorporate their perspectives into the report. He argues that it will make the report much better and more interesting. Joan tells him that it's an interesting idea but not very practical. She looks at her calendar as she talks and begins listing all of the tasks that she needs to get done in the next few weeks before the report is due. Ramon, another teammate, jokes that Tim is just looking for a way to get a good job after graduation. Tim looks at Ramon and asks him what he really thinks about the idea. Ramon laughs and makes another joke about graduation. Tim lets the idea drop. You notice over the next week or so that Tim, while doing his part of the project, keeps his comments briefer. He seems to you less excited about the report.

Scenario 2

Gillian and Matt, two members of your team, are doing much of the work. You remember when the team first discussed the project. No one had wanted to volunteer to serve as the project manager. Mike nominated Gillian on the grounds that she had a lot of operational experience outside of school. She had not volunteered, as she wanted to get away from managing projects and let someone else have that experience. But she agreed, telling the others that she would organize the team for the first deliverable and that someone else would have to take over after that. Gillian does a great job as project manager. She assigns roles, creates timetables, makes sure that team members are sharing their work, and keeps the team going. The problem is that, with the exception of Matt, the other members do not do much at all. The rest of you show up to brainstorming meetings without ideas to share. You wait for Gillian to remind you to do what you agreed to do. You contribute little. Gillian and Matt are frustrated. They thought they would be able to learn from you and the others but find that they are the ones who have to guide, teach, and direct. They had not signed up for this.

Scenario 3

Your team is working on its final presentation. Isabella is waiting for Jamal to finish creating the presentation slides. She is an excellent presenter, articulate and comfortable in front of others, and up to this point, has shown little interest in what the project is really about. Jamal is technically good at making the slides but hasn't added much in terms of the content of the presentation. Will, another team member, is hovering in the background as you and the others work with Jamal to get the wording right on the slides. Will's primary contribution is to question your decisions, casting doubt not just on the wording of the slides but on some of the content more generally, much of which had been agreed on for several weeks. You think that his comments are useless, and that as a devil's advocate, he is more destructive than constructive.

You've been the project manager, and are fed up with him. You do not say these things, but you do manage to ask him, civilly, what alternatives he suggests. He avoids this by just asking another question. At that point you tune him out and help the others get ready for the presentation.

These scenarios reveal the nature of what it means for team members to be present and absent with one another. In the first scenario Tim was thinking a lot about the project and how to make it better. He put himself into it, cared about it enough to press ahead on an unpopular idea. His teammate, Joan, was focused on the logistics and the timing, and determined that Tim's idea was unfeasible. Staring at her calendar, focused on the tasks that she needed to complete, she was unable or unwilling to explore possibilities inherent in Tim's suggestion. She was helped in this regard by Ramon, who played the role of the joker, using humor to move Tim and the others away from his idea. Joan and Ramon were both caricatures. They were one-dimensional: Joan as the taskmaster, Ramon as the joker. They were present, but only in the context of those limited roles. Tim displayed more of himself. He allowed himself to be passionate, opinionated, and intent. He was not joined in this by his teammates. He later withdrew his intellectual curiosity and engagement.

In the second scenario a different but similar process unfolds. Gillian, and to some extent, Matt are working hard on behalf of the team. They develop strategy, come up with ideas, think a lot about the project and how to get it done, and drive it. Their teammates are followers. They show up to meetings. They do their assigned tasks but do not stretch themselves. Their combination of presence and absence is not simply a matter of how much work they do but how much they expose and express themselves on behalf of that work. They do this very little. Like students following their teachers, they complete assignments that they feel are required and do little else. The analogy is instructive. Unless students have some fire that is lit within them—a subject that excites them, arouses their curiosity, and drives them to become passionate about learning and doing—they remain in the passive role of "student" and express only what they believe that role requires. They do not really engage the material. They only engage in the role itself: They do their assignments and hand them in on time or not, they complain about their teachers, they wait for the project to be over. Gillian and Matt are left to care about the work itself, to their great dissatisfaction and frustration. They, too, have to take up a role—as teacher—which leaves their own desires to learn and explore with others unmet.

The third scenario illustrates how team members can be both partly visible and partly hidden. Each of the central members—Isabella, Jamal, and Will—plays a particular role, and only that role, on the team. One knows the technology for producing slides and adds little else; a second is the presenter, with little interest in the content; and the third just questions what others are doing while adding little himself. None of these team members has ventured far from these roles. They have shown little else of themselves. Isabella has participated little in designing the project. Jamal has shown little in the way of what or how he thinks about the project. Will has been unable to add material that has been useful to the project. It's as if each has been cast into a role that dictates precisely who they are and are not on the team. More to the point, each reveals part of who they are—the parts that get expressed through the roles that they play—while keeping the other parts that don't fit into those one-dimensional roles in the shadows. Their identities within the group are thus tightly connected to their roles even as they themselves—who they really are—remain relatively unknown. The team suffers because it does not really have complete access to all of its members, who might otherwise strengthen the project with their ideas and passions.

A certain picture emerges from these scenarios. The extent to which you are present is a function of how many parts of yourselves can be expressed in the context of your team. You are only slightly present when you take on a certain aspect—say, joker, devil's advocate, taskmaster, or passive student—and stay there. You present only the part of yourself that gets revealed through the tight constraints of that role. You only become more present when you present more parts of yourself, that is, when you take on different and multiple aspects, such as teacher, learner, driver, joker, presenter, and idea generator. Over time, as you cycle through different roles, each offering a vantage point from which to contribute something of yourself, more of your self becomes visible.

This is important, but not just because you might believe in "self-actualization" or in living freely and fully in each and every moment, as delightful as that might be. It is important because of the difference it makes in the quality and effectiveness of the team that you create. The self presented matters. Teams are truly outstanding only when their members can be fully present for much of the time. If you want to create outstanding teams you have to figure out how to become—and help others on your team become—three-dimensional people whose intellect and emotions are on tap and ready to be released and employed on behalf of the team and its work. Ordinary teams are marked by one-dimensionality. Members split off parts of their selves and leave them outside their team experiences. They have decided, usually without deciding, that they cannot bring in who they really are. This has real implications for their—for your—work, relationships, and experiences on the team.

Casting Calls

To understand this dynamic more—and the choices that you make about the extent to which you are present and absent—we need to look at the early moments of your formation. In Chapter 3 I described that process of formation, noting the importance of developing missions, distributing tasks, and forming boundaries that enabled you to join together and create a unit. During that process another subtle psychological dynamic was occurring as well. Each of you was also presenting a particular version of yourself. You made a choice, mostly if not completely unconsciously, about the identity that you would put forth and construct in the minds of others. You simplified your self, showing some dimensions and letting others remain in the shadows. You did this in brief moments, verbally and nonverbally, by what you did and how you reacted to others. You signaled to your new teammates a relatively simple way to categorize and understand you.

These categories are quick sketches. They are instantly recognizable. You might have been the comic or the serious one, the good one or the rebel, the quiet one or the loud one, the devil's advocate, the strong hero or heroine, the laid-back one or the intently competent one, the fighter or the peacemaker. You put forth this quick identity, this brief sketch of yourself, and stayed with it for a bit. Why? First, it enabled you to create a specific way to be known by others. You had an immediate place on the team. Second, you adopted a certain stance that helped you manage the anxiety that you inevitably had when joining a new team. Such anxiety is natural. It reflects concerns about whether we are going to be accepted by others and yet also maintain an identity of our own so we do not feel lost within the team.

The quick sketch that you put forth during team formation was, typically, one that you've found helped manage anxiety in other new situations. It's a familiar identity that has proven useful and adaptive in other unfamiliar settings. It offers a way of being known that works for you. Some of this can be traced to your family of origin. We often end up playing certain roles in our families. You might have been the "good one," making sure never to make waves. Perhaps you were the "rebellious one." These roles change as we grow but they never quite go away. We often instinctively turn to them. We are familiar with what they say about us and thus have some sense of how we will be perceived by others. We're probably relatively good at them as well. They make us acceptable, in some fashion, as long as they seem to serve a purpose for the team.

For their part, your teammates look for cues as to your identity during team formation to "understand" you quickly and easily. Such understanding (which is really just a quick labeling of you, and you of them) helps reduce for all of you a sense of anxiety and uncertainty about who everyone on the team is. You now "get" one another, and can fill in a picture of the team. Even if the picture is incomplete, at least it's something. It offers a way to make the unfamiliar familiar. It settles each of you into the team, and creates a foundation, after a fashion, for your next wave of interactions.

Your team then starts to build on that foundation as if it were whole and complete. The quick sketches of identity that you offer to one another take hold and tend to get fixed in one another's minds. It's as if you auditioned for and won a certain part. Others now look to you to play the part into which you were cast, just as you look to them to play their parts. You look for the comic or the soother to defuse tension; to the dramatic one to shake things up; to the hero or heroine to come to the rescue; to the skeptic to chastise the group; and to the cynic to make light of the project. The identities that you each initially offered thus get used in the service of the team. In particular, they were used at first—what we might call Act I of your team—to help you manage the inevitable anxiety that you and your teammates felt in the beginning of the life of your team.

These identities are maintained because you reinforce one another for playing your parts when the team needs it. The attention that you give to one another signals that you should keep showing one another the identity that you initially put forth and into which you were then cast. The joker makes a joke to defuse tension. You smile at him or say something to him later about how funny he was or how there had almost been a bad argument. You are giving him attention, positive reinforcement, for his joking. You affirm him as a joker. This sort of affirmation is the way in which you tell one another to stay in the roles into which you were cast. If the team did not wish a member to play a certain role, members would simply withdraw their attention, not offering positive reinforcement. The member would pick up on the signs, and like a plant maneuvering toward the sun and rain, would find another dimension of his or her self to display that will be positively received. You have that sort of power over one another, whether you realize it or not.

The intriguing part of this process is the way in which various identities get distributed around the team, such that there is no real competition among you in the formation process. Because each of you is unconsciously looking to carve out your own place on the team, you quickly stake out an identity, with a joke, a cynical remark, concern about the first assignment, or looking bored. If a teammate has already staked out an identity that you usually prefer, you might jockey for a bit (who can be more cynical, funnier, better organized) until one of you gets more positive reinforcement from the rest of the team and the other then selects a different sort of identity. In taking on different identities, or roles, you are emphasizing one part of yourself and not other, equally legitimate parts. You suppress the parts of yourself that others are playing up; you emphasize the parts that you are playing. It is as if your team handed out different roles—complete with scripts, demeanors, and stage directions—to each of you. Your team formation process was marked in part by each of you settling into the distinct roles for which you had auditioned and into which you were cast.

Act II

This psychological piece of the formation process is the genesis of the extent to which you are absent and present on your team. You were present when expressing the dimensions of your self that fit with the initial role that you took up during formation. When the team needed a joker, say, or someone to be cynical about the team or its project, and that was your role, others would look at you and smile, waiting, or they would easily yield the conversation to your interruption. At such moments you were stage front, spotlight on. That part of yourself was clear and present, in the light. When the team needed to look seriously at whether it had completed the given assignment, and that was not your role, others would look away from you and attend to another whose role was more relevant. You were stage rear, spotlight elsewhere. Even though you might well have had something to offer there, it was not your role to do so. You were partly absent, in the shadows.

Act I was thus marked by the creation of relatively one-dimensional identities. Each of you revealed some parts of yourselves, which others grabbed onto as a way to "understand" who you are and what you were likely to bring to the team. You obliged one another by continuing to act in ways that fit with those initial impressions and by not showing other parts of yourselves that might be confounding in one way or another. This is not a matter of deliberate play-acting, in which you were pretending to be something or someone you were not. Rather, it was a matter of you unconsciously playing up some parts of yourself to be readily, if incompletely, known by others, and playing down other parts that were more complicated, threatening, or redundant with the identities that others were establishing around you.

This dynamic is pretty typical of the team formation process. At the time it served necessary functions, enabling you to create a stage for Act I—the movement from the unknown to the possibly known. It was not a complicated structure, based as it was on single planks—quick sketches and caricatures of who you "are"—rather than on more heavily layered beams of nuanced understandings of one another, but it worked well enough. The initial identities got you going, enabled you to know a bit about one another, and eased those first conversations in which you needed to make some initial decisions. That structure was meant only as a temporary stage, however. It was built quickly, slapped together to move you quickly from your initial uncertainty and anxiety to a somewhat more certain place. That structure is flawed, though. It is not sturdy enough to serve as a stage on which you can move from simply good to outstanding—from Act I to Act II.

What does this mean, exactly? Imagine that you are a member of one of the teams illustrated in the scenarios described earlier. On each of those teams members were locked into certain roles. There was the taskmaster, focused only on schedules and logistics, who didn't even engage in brainstorming an interesting angle for the project. There was the joker, always trying to get a laugh, even when there was a useful difference of opinion between members that might have led to a really good solution. There was the follower, who got so used to just letting others drive the project that she did not bother to share her quite good ideas about how to make the project better. There was the technology geek who knew how to put together presentations but not how to really look at them and make them better. When people are locked into such roles—by themselves and by others—they do not contribute as much as they could. The team loses them, to some degree, and cannot function as well as it might, like an arm that does not have a full range of motion. The team can perform certain limited movements—meet, divide work, get it done, and move on—but no more. As members get locked into certain limited patterns, so too does the team.

These limited movements can be relatively benign. It doesn't hurt much to be seen as the taskmaster, the joker, the teacher, the follower, or the technology geek. These are roles that do not make us feel too badly about ourselves. The costumes might not be all that flattering, all the time, but they're not that bad. However, there are other, more dangerous roles. In the previous chapter I described the process of scapegoating, in which individuals get blamed for causing the team's problems. The scapegoat is the malignant version of individuals getting locked into roles or identities that simplify who they really are. This process wounds people. Their costumes are not simply unflattering or ill-fitting clothes, but straitjackets into which they are painfully bound.

Whether benign or malignant, the identities that you each assume in Act I can, if unchanged, cause great frustration. You get frustrated with others for not contributing more and you get frustrated when you are treated as if you only have certain things to contribute, as if you really are just one-dimensional. You resent the fact that even though you might show flair for organizing or for defusing tension with a joke the others act as if that is all you have to offer. Such frustration brings anger and resentment. You might act out, skirmishing with others, creating cliques, or sabotaging the team. You might check out, withdrawing from the team and doing only the minimum. This lessens your ability to contribute, of course, and also your ability to fully connect with your teammates. If the quick sketches of identity that you and the others created at the beginning of the life of your team are not eased in some fashion—held loosely rather than fixed tightly in your minds, such that each of you is seen as more than just one-dimensional—this frustration and alienation will lead directly to stuckness, for you and for the team itself.

Another metaphor might be useful here. Like the first stage of a rocket, the initial identities that you created during the team formation process launched you into the orbit of your new team. And, like that part of the ship that contained the booster rockets, it will need to fall away to make possible the rest of the journey. This is easy enough to write and difficult to engineer. You must do more than simply push a button and watch your initial construction fall away. Your task is more difficult. You have to redesign your ship even as it hurtles forward. You have to drag along the initial construction of identities that you created even as you try and make them more complete. This is not simple work, as the next section illustrates; some project teams will not or cannot do this work, and remain in Act I throughout their journey. The work involves disclosing more and more aspects of your self, to the point that you are as fully present as possible. It is that presence that enables you and your team to be not simply good, but outstanding.

Disclosing the Self

Disclosing yourself is not as esoteric as it sounds. It simply means saying what you are really thinking and feeling, within the bounds of good taste and civil discourse. This might involve something like, "It's hard for me to participate because I don't think that we're really listening to one another"; "I thought that we just did a really nice job of solving that problem"; "I think that I ought to lead this next part of the project, since I've had a lot of experience with that industry"; "I'm frustrated with how slowly we're working"; or "I'm really confused about this part of the project and just don't know what to do next." None of these statements is particularly earth shattering. Yet each has the potential to reveal something truthful about the speaker, in terms of what he or she is really thinking or feeling in the present moment. The speaker is disclosing some part of himself or herself. Such disclosures—particularly when they go against what one would expect from the initial identities that you assumed when you first joined your team—provide the team with real information on which to make choices about how to move ahead.

To understand this process more fully, you need to know something about both why you would want to disclose more of yourself and what tends to get in the way of you doing so. So why disclose? One reason is that it helps you be more effective on your team. As long as you only show the parts of yourselves that fit with the initial role that you adopted, you limit your contributions to the specific moments in which that role is useful. The taskmaster is useful when it comes to driving the schedule but not so useful when it comes to brainstorming; the out-of-the-box thinker is useful when it comes to being wildly creative and less so when the team has to drive toward completion; and the joker is useful for defusing tension but not so useful when it comes to fully resolving an important conflict. In each case, the student lessens his or her effectiveness by adhering to a particular identity or role on the team. He or she would be more effective by staying focused on the task at hand—brainstorming, finishing details, engaging in difficult conversations—and contribute to that task as best he or she can, saying what he or she thinks and feels in useful and relevant ways.

Another reason to self-disclose is to become less lonely on a team. Loneliness is the feeling of being isolated, unknown, and alone. It is directly related to the sense of being stuck in a role, in which some parts of you are seen and many other parts remain hidden and unknown. When you do not show others who you really are, by saying what you think and feel, they cannot and therefore do not know you. They will know a part of you—the part that you show them—but not much more. This can make you lonely. We each have a basic human need for intimacy. It is part of the individual psyche, a basic motivating force of life. The desire for real connection—to be known, to connect fully with others—drives behavior. Intimacy gives meaning to our lives. It involves, at its core, authenticity: the sharing of real thoughts and feelings, giving and receiving real feedback, empathy, and caring about others as separate individuals. Intimacy is not the same as easy friendship, sexuality, or other substitutes. It involves the depth, the core, of who you are. It involves the spontaneous expression of your self.

Obstacles to Disclosure

The desire to be effective and useful, and to join with others rather than be lonely, drives self-disclosure. What gets in the way? The first set of obstacles has to do with you as an individual. The second set of obstacles has to do with the team and the dynamics it has thus far set in motion.

Internal Obstacles

Self-disclosure involves disabling the internal "editor" that might prevent you from saying what you really think and feel, particularly when you might reveal not just the good parts of who you are, but also those you see as bad. Disabling the internal editor is difficult. You might wish to appear, to yourself and to others, in certain ways, and self-disclosures can get in the way of such self-preservation. You might not want to seem imperfect, in ways that you fear might lead to rejection. You might feel a sense of competition with others, and self-disclosure might make you feel that you're giving up something to others.

To the extent that you feel these things, it makes it more difficult to be fully yourself in the team.

You might also not be sure that you want or can really handle the conflict that might occur if you say what you think and feel. Self-disclosure is the vehicle by which your individual differences become apparent on the team. There are always individual differences among team members, in values, beliefs, and morals; types of intelligence; ability to feel and express feelings; interpersonal skills; maturity; courage; and needs. It is difficult to acknowledge individual differences. This difficulty reflects the ways in which people tend to react to differences with evaluations, of good or bad or better or worse, rather than with an acceptance of differences for what they are. Surfacing differences—they are always there, beneath the surface of the team—thus seems divisive, and bursts the sense (the wish) that "we're all alike." Showing real differences, by speaking your mind, thus opens you and the team up to the possibility of conflict. You might not like that. You might prefer to protect the team, and yourself, from that possibility.

Another set of internal obstacles has to do with the implications of intimacy. Intimacy with others—which occurs only in the context of revealing who we really are—can be messy. Superficiality is reasonably clean. You pretty much know the script, like cocktail party conversations that remain easy, if a bit routine. Intimacy is more complicated. There is no script, as you discover things about others on your team, and they about you, that lead to conversations and interactions that you cannot easily predict. This takes time and energy, and stirs up emotions. You might not want to invest yourself in such ways. You might not want to get close to another set of people, only to see those relationships end, in some fashion, with the conclusion of the project or the course. It often does not feel good to open up to others, to get close to them, and then have those relationships end. You might prefer, unconsciously if not consciously, the relative loneliness of the superficial to the messiness and potential pain of the more intimate, self-disclosed relationship.

Finally—and at a deeper psychological level—you might find that you prefer to keep some parts of yourself hidden, not just from others, but also from yourself. There are aspects of ourselves that we might not like. We might not like to seem foolish by asking questions or needy by asking for help. We might not like to appear smart or serious. We might not like to show that we are insensitive, focused on success. We might not like our own intensity or our own playfulness. This dislike of particular aspects of who we are is, more often than not, based on messages that we received from others—parents, teachers, siblings, authority figures—earlier in our lives. We took those messages to heart and in some ways banished or suppressed parts of ourselves that seemed "bad." This makes it more difficult to be authentic when situations call for us to express parts of ourselves that we have hidden away. We are often not particularly good at showing them, as we haven't had much practice. And because we believe that they are bad, we are not very willing to bring them to the surface, expose them to the light, and learn about them. This becomes a serious, self-imposed barrier for self-disclosure.

External Obstacles

The team itself—or more accurately, the group dynamics that play out beneath the surface of the team—provides its own set of obstacles as well. The obstacles are related to how much room there is to safely express the various aspects of who we are. Consider your various interpersonal relationships. With some people, you feel that you can say pretty much whatever you want, within reason, and it will be okay. These people cut you a lot of slack, and you probably do the same for them. You can be funny or serious, confused or certain, needy or rebellious, intense or playful. You know that they can hold an image of you that is complex enough to contain all of those dimensions, and that over time, as that image grows more and more expansive, they will come to know you well and deeply. With other people, you feel more constrained. There are limits and rules that implicitly guide who you can and cannot be with them. You limit yourself to acting in certain ways that fit within acceptable guidelines, and you do not stray far from a certain script and character. Their image of you is specific and particular; they will always know you only in certain limited ways.

You have relationships with teams as well, and like interpersonal relationships, you can be more or less yourself with those teams. Project teams differ in how much of you is sought after and welcomed. They offer more or less space for you to display the various dimensions of your self. The dynamics are much the same as they are in your interpersonal relationships. In your relationships, other individuals have more or less need to want to see you in certain ways. This might be because they are used to seeing you in those ways and do not want to have to change those images. Typically, though, it is because they have some investment in seeing you in certain ways because it allows them to set themselves apart from you in ways that they like. Your brother might see you as lazy and confused because it allows him to feel relatively hard-working and smart. Your friend might see you as serious and intense because it allows her to see herself as playful and creative. As long as others wish to see themselves in certain ways, they use you to help them sustain those images. They take the parts of themselves that don't fit with how they wish to see themselves and put them elsewhere, onto you and others, so they are able to say "I'm not like that, and you are." (Chances are quite good that you are doing the same with them.) As a result, people will want to see you in certain ways, and will do their best to ignore information that says that you are *not* like that. To allow you to be other than how they wish to see you would burst their illusions about you, and thus about themselves. You have less room with these people to disclose the different dimensions of who you really are.

This same process occurs in project teams, although in a slightly more complicated way. The complications are a function of the group dynamics discussed earlier, set in motion during the formation of your team. Each of you staked out certain identities at the beginning. You emphasized some parts of yourself and deemphasized others. You each became used to seeing yourselves, and others, in ways that made sense, and that you more or less liked. The question is how *much* you like those identities. How much do you want—or need—to keep seeing one another in certain ways, to see yourself in other ways? The answer to this question determines the extent to which your team is a real obstacle that prevents its members from self-disclosure.

Consider this question in the context of the brief scenarios presented earlier in this chapter. In one scenario, we have a team member (Joan) who focuses tightly on logistics, and another (Ramon) who mostly jokes and keeps matters light. They had these roles early, and they've stayed within them, even though that might not best serve the team or them personally. How much do the others want or need them to stay in those roles to make themselves seem more relaxed than Joan or more serious than Ramon? How deeply wedded is the whole team, including Joan and Ramon, to the patterns of identities that they have all created? How willing and able are they to act in other ways, to become real people rather than characters with one another, and in doing so, have real interactions—intense, ambiguous, messy, passionate, fun—with one another? We can ask the same questions about Gillian and Matt in the second scenario, who became the ultracompetent teachers on the team, and their teammates, who adopted the roles of the passive students. We can ask these questions about Isabella (the presenter), Jamal (the techno-geek), and Will (the cynic) in the third scenario. You can, and should, ask the same questions about your team. How much is your team an obstacle to self-disclosure?

Using Your Curiosity

Overcoming internal and external obstacles to self-disclosure is primarily a matter of doing your best to stay as curious as you can about yourself and others. This notion is at once simple and profound. Curiosity is a stance of openness. When you're curious about someone or something, you simply want to understand more. You are not judging. You are not attacking. You are not defending yourself. When you're curious, you suspend your own disbelief, your own assumptions. You are willing to invite in others' experiences and information. There is no need to do something—at least yet—with what you learn. You are just taking it in. You are a learner, trying to create richer, fuller, more complex images for yourself. Indeed, you can be curious about yourself as well, trying to learn as much as you can about who you are and what your own capacities and limits are. This enables you to create a complex rather than simple self-portrait.

To be curious is an implicit acknowledgment that one does not already know all that there is to know about someone else, or about oneself. Curiosity enables you to avoid being "pathologically certain," which is to reduce the world to terms that may be manageable and allow you to reduce uncertainty in ways that are misleadingly simplistic. Unhealthy relationships—with friends, family members, and in groups—are marked by the lack of curiosity. People are often remarkably certain that they know, understand, and can speak for others without further discussion. Curiosity allows you to suspend, even temporarily, your convictions that you are completely right in how you view others or yourself. It allows you to explore, to collect information that is open rather than closed to interpretation. If you are sincerely curious, you open yourself up to the possibility that others' experiences, interpretations, and perspectives will challenge how you wish to see events in ways that often serve your own needs.

You might not want that particular challenge, at least in some instances or with some people. You might prefer to hold onto a relatively simple story that you like to tell yourself—a story that, inevitably, tends to leave you feeling justified about whatever you are or aren't doing on your team. To the extent that you lock yourself into those stories, you choose a narrow certainty over a more expansive reality. You are unwilling to openly acknowledge and alter or expand your perceptions of others and of yourself as well. (Your teammates are probably doing much the same.) You thus do not allow information about others to inform your perceptions. You remain locked into seeing what you wish to see about others, and about yourself. It is as if you are looking at a single piece of a jigsaw puzzle and convincing yourself that it is the whole picture. Unless you use your curiosity to seek out other puzzle pieces, your image of others (and of yourself) will remain incomplete. It will be misleading as well, leaving you and the team operating on scattered pieces of information.

Say, on the other hand, you do wish to create a more complete puzzle and are willing to take on the challenge that will be posed to how you'd like to see yourself and others. There are several steps to this process. First, there is your own self-disclosure. To the extent that you put out more and more of your own jigsaw pieces, the more you and others are able to put together the larger picture. As we have seen, there are plenty of obstacles to self-disclosure. To take the risk, you must either be pretty self-assured (knowing that others will not really reject you and leave you alone) or have a fair amount of faith or confidence in yourself (knowing that you will be okay, regardless of what happens when you show different sides of who you are). Still, it takes courage.

The second step involves insisting that others pay attention to the pieces that you disclose that do not fit with how they would like to see you. Through the team formation process, and beyond, you each created identities in the minds of others. You got used to them, and so did your teammates. Now you are asking them to change and expand those identities. This will not be easy, as I described earlier in terms of obstacles to self-disclosure. Once you do show different parts of yourself, you might need to point those pieces out. "I can act in this way, too," you might need to say, or "Listen, I have an idea and not just a joke here." Such comments are markers, like flares that you send up, that signal new pieces that need to be fitted into the larger picture of you, and of the team itself.

These two steps—putting out some of your own pieces, and nudging others to pay attention to them—not only help you join the team more fully, but they help your teammates do so as well. When they see you step away from your initial roles, it makes it safer for them to try and do so as well. Because you're not forcing yourself to act in certain ways, you have less need for them to do so as well. This makes it easier for them to take the risk of stepping away from their initial roles. You can help them with this simply by showing how curious you are about them.

The third step, then, is using your curiosity. What does that mean, exactly? When your teammates show the slightest hints of being something other than what you expect them to be, you show interest. You ask questions that pull them out even more. You follow up on the signals that they send that they are not simply who they initially presented themselves to be. You do not react with judgment or evaluation. You accept what they have to say. You are thus creating a space for others to bring themselves—that is, the different aspects of their selves—into the open. In this space, they don't have to defend or attack or justify. They can just be, as they feel inquired into and welcomed by others who are sincerely wishing to learn and understand them as completely as possible. That is what your curiosity helps create for them.

What it really creates, of course, is a sense of safety. Throughout this book I have emphasized the importance of psychological safety: the sense that you have that it is okay to express yourself, that you won't be harmed or penalized in some way by your teammates. I described earlier the paradox of safety, noted by Smith and Berg (1987) in their book *Paradoxes of Group Life*, which holds that you cannot know whether a situation is safe unless you act as if it already is, and take a risk—and in doing so and surviving intact, actually create a greater sense of safety, as you can now trust the situation a bit more. Your curiosity helps lessen the risk for your teammates. You are sending signals that it is safer than they might fear. They will still test this out, and it is important what you do when they do. They will show you slight glimmers of others beneath the surfaces of who they seemed to be, and look carefully at how well you receive them. Will you ignore, turn away from, or in other ways dismiss them? Or will you handle them with care, staying interested and pulling for more, such that they feel valued and seen, and disclose more? It is the extent to which you are genuinely and sincerely curious that separates the two choices.

Play or Watch?

A group of people stands alongside a newly frozen pond. They draw their jackets tightly around them, their breaths visible in the cold air. They look out at the pond. They know that it is more fun to be out there, slipping and sliding around, kicking a ball or a puck, laughing, and arguing. However, they don't know how safe the ice really is. They wait for a while, trying to figure out what to do. Perhaps they see others out there on another part of the pond, which might embolden them. One member of the group finally dares to step onto the ice. She begins with a foot, then a leg, and then, finally, feeling that the ice might hold, both feet. She smiles hesitantly, ventures a bit farther. She strains to hear any cracking noises beneath the surface that would warn her that it isn't safe. No cracking. She goes farther out, still careful, and then starts to slide. She turns and gestures to the others to come join her.

This image captures what it means for project team members to self-disclose. The safest thing to do is stand on the shore. Members stay in the initial roles that they carved out for themselves. They walk around the edges, on solid ground. They do not get that close to one another, keeping an appropriate distance. This is fine; it is good enough, but it is not extraordinary. The most extraordinary teams are those in which all members are out on the ice, sliding, laughing, arguing, engaging, falling into and against one another, and having fun. They are not on the shore, trying to be as careful as possible. This is the choice that you must make, as your teammate gestures to you to come on out. What, then, do you do at that point? Do you join her or stay on shore and watch?

What you do at that point—at all the points in the life of your team in which you could come forth and say what you truly think and feel—matters a lot. It matters in terms of how much you can fully contribute to the team's work and to the growth of your teammates. It matters in terms of how you contribute to creating a place that is safe enough for you and others to express your differences and insisting that they are taken into account. It is only when individual differences are affirmed that people can really connect with others in a group. It matters in terms of how much your team offers a setting in which you are each free to be curious— to explore experiences, learn about yourselves, and develop understandings that do not have to conform to how you wish to see yourselves and others.

It is more fun to be out there on the ice, even if it is more risky. You could get hurt, sliding into each other. The ice might not be so thick in some places. It can be exhausting. But the fun shouldn't be discounted. Your team should be fun, not predictable and boring. You should laugh together. You should fight some. Good fights, based on your real reactions, lead to stronger relationships. They release your passion and get you energized. They also lead to lots of learning, mostly about yourself. You should learn something about yourselves, which can only happen when you expose those selves to others and see what happens as a result. You only learn about the aspects of yourself that you bring into the open. The project team is a great—and relatively risk-free—laboratory in which to learn about your self. Use it that way. Try showing your real self to others across different situations. Try openly acknowledging how you see one another, and how those perceptions might shut down your abilities and willingness to fully engage on your team. Try to speak as much truth as you can. Then look and see what happens—perhaps not right away, as you sift through the conversations, but later—to your levels of engagement on the team.

Summary

The difference between good project teams and outstanding ones is a matter of how fully their members engage themselves in their work together. Your team is great when you and the others do not simply go through the motions of a project team; rather, you choose to take your team seriously, making it part of your real life. This chapter focused on what full engagement looks like, where it comes from, and its effects on individuals and teams. You create such engagements when you choose to be fully present on your team—showing up, investing time and thought, responding truthfully, and caring about what happens and how you work together. If you are only partially present, you are less able to display what you have to offer; you are unidimensional on the team, a caricature that others only know from the surface. You move toward full engagement through self-disclosure. You reveal what you think and feel at important moments. There are internal and external obstacles to such disclosure. And there are ways in which you can overcome these obstacles, should you choose. Two Team Development Exercises can help with this process. The seventh exercise—"Informal Roles"—offers a process for identifying the typical roles into which you and the others fall, and the implications thereof. The eighth exercise—"Team Feedback"—is a more intensive process for sharing with one another your accumulated perceptions and providing useful feedback. Students have found that providing and receiving such feedback is instrumental in enabling them to become fully engaged in their teams—and for their teams to become truly outstanding.

Chapter 9

Final Examinations

Congratulations. You've handed in the final report, given the concluding presentation, and finished the project. You've arrived at the end of your journey. It's time to disembark from your team. Typically this is a pretty simple process. You pack up your things and go off. You might smile more, or more sincerely, at some members than others. You might make plans to get together with some new friends. You might even figure out how to be on a team with some of them again. You might be relieved that the experience is over, sad about ending some relationships, happy to have worked with the team, frustrated that you didn't get as much from the experience as you would have liked, angry about being taken advantage of by others, glad that you will not have to work with some members any more. You'll feel some of these, at first keenly and later, as time passes, they will fade and become part of your memory of the team.

You can also end the team differently. You can choose to take a final opportunity to learn as much as you can about how and why your team functioned as it did. Endings represent moments of reflection. The experience is still fresh enough for memories and emotions to be accessible; over time, both will recede, until what it left is mostly the story of what the team was. That story is typically incomplete: It is the one that you choose to tell based on a partial (and biased) understanding of events and interactions. You know something of what happened on the team, and you know your own motives, reactions, and experiences. But you most likely do not know of others' motives, reactions, and experiences. You will fill in that missing information with assumptions. This is like filling in the missing blanks of a crossword puzzle with words that you make fit with the clues that you have. The completed puzzle might look finished but it won't be right. Similarly, any story that you tell about your team based on only your own perceptions or beliefs will be incomplete and flawed. This can be problematic, and very much so. That story is a source of insights and lessons on which you will draw to guide what you do on future teams at school and at work.

So how do you avoid falling into the same traps in the future? How do you make sure that you re-create what you liked about your team? How do you not wind up having the same bad experiences on future teams that you had on this one? You *learn*—about yourself, the roles that you assume and avoid, team dynamics, and how to move through difficult periods and into more productive ones. Avoiding problems in the future is a matter of learning from the past. Ironically, those of you who are most likely to make use of this notion often have the least need for it, as you are usually the team members who have been seeking to learn throughout the team process. It is the others among you—who have not really taken up opportunities to explore and learn about your team's processes, or seek and truly receive feedback from others—who most need to learn what you have not yet learned. You might remain incompletely aware or unaware of your effects on your team, like a driver whose erratic or careless driving leaves accidents in his wake, yet he drives on, clueless of the havoc he has caused in spite of the onlookers waving frantically to get him to stop.

It is not too late, however. There is the chance for final examinations—to get clued in and learn from this project team before it recedes into the distant past. This will involve reflecting, together with your teammates, about what the team was and was not, and why that was so. For some teams this will be anticlimatic. You've taken advantage of opportunities throughout the project to talk together about how you're working. You've learned how to work together more effectively. You've changed some behaviors based on feedback. Your team developed some useful structures and processes to keep communication flowing and get work done effectively. You've gotten stuck and then unstuck, and arrived at a good place together. These final conversations are a way to identify the lessons that you can bring to your next team experiences. There will be few surprises, few challenges to the story of the team that you've constructed.

For other teams, these final conversations—if you have them and take them seriously—have a different quality and tone. These teams have not been able to go through the tolls that have marked their journey. They got off course somewhere along the way and never fully recovered. Much has not been discussed on these teams. Assumptions, stereotypes, and misperceptions exist in place of mutual understandings of one another's motives, behaviors, and experiences. The work here is to reverse the equation: Substitute understanding for assumption, reality for illusion, and insight for ignorance. This is not an easy process. It is more difficult when you have gotten used to avoiding the honesty of these conversations. You have little practice. You have few successes on which to build.

So why should you discuss your processes now, when the team is over and you can just turn away and leave?

There are several answers to this question. First, what do you have to lose? The project is over and it is unlikely that you will be with these teammates again. Why not try and see what you can learn from this experience, about who you are as a teammate and your effects on the team? It is quite likely that, unless told otherwise, you will continue to act in ways that you did on this team. Why not take the chance and see if you can learn something that will enable you to be better on the next team? Second, a student project team, particularly one that is ending, is a relatively safe place to give and receive feedback. It is a trickier process to do this in the workplace, where the stakes are higher and where others can exploit your vulnerabilities more easily. Students have little power over one another, which makes it easier—not easy, but easier—to try and learn about yourself. Third, closure is important. Closure involves developing as complete an understanding as possible about an experience. It involves getting the story right, and then feeling settled about what happened. This can occur only when your team comes together, with each member contributing his or her understanding. It is only then that each of you can put the jigsaw pieces together and see the picture of the team that emerges.

This chapter has two aims. The first aim is to discuss how the ending of your team can lead toward useful closure. The final toll of your team journey is to close the team experience in ways that enable you to learn about the team and yourself. The obstacles here are your desires to avoid that learning—or more precisely, to avoid the difficult conversations and the complicated emotions involved in that learning. The second aim of this chapter is to note the important lessons that your team experience offers as you move into other projects and other teams.

Ways to End

Endings are never easy. The ending of your team means closing the door on an experience that you shared with others. It means ending a set of relationships. If the relationships were good, there is some sadness in ending them. If they were not so good, there is some lingering resentment, frustration, and perhaps guilt. None of these emotions is pleasant to feel. Some of you will choose to end your teams in ways that let you avoid emotions that you would rather not feel.

Avoidance

The following are some of the classic ways of avoiding the experience of ending a team.

Denial

You've just finished the final team paper, and turned it in during the last class of the semester. You liked your team, mostly, and got along with the other members. It's the end of the first semester and you're ready for a break until classes begin again. The final class ends. You walk out with some of your teammates. You talk about the classes that you still have to go to, and an upcoming exam. You stop at the corner, about to head off in a different direction. "See you later," you say, and walk away.

Postponement

The presentation to the rest of the class went well. Your team worked well and really came together at the end, meeting late the evening before to finish and rehearse the presentation. You've liked some of the team members a lot. It was probably the best project team that you've been on and you hate to see it end. You agree with some of the others that you'll try and take some classes together and form a team together again. You're also planning to get-together—a team reunion—after the break.

Flight

The project is finally over. It was not the easiest experience for you. In fact, you're hoping to never have to work with any of these people again. You were stuck with too much of the work. Several of your teammates helped out but you still did too much work. The team turned in the research report during the final class. When the class was over, you quickly gathered your belongings and hurried out of the building, avoiding eye contact with other members of the team.

Fight (Version 1)

The final presentation is in just a few hours. Your team has been working hard for the last 2 days after having procrastinated for weeks. You're exhausted. You just want the slides done and no longer care how good they are. The presentation is almost done. The team just needs to figure out some last-minute graphics. Two teammates disagree over the color of the slides. You explode: "What the hell does it matter? It's just a background. This is ridiculous." They turn and look at you. Another member tells you, roughly, to be quiet. The next 20 minutes involve arguing and raised voices. You turn away and let the others finish. The presentation gets done, the project is over, and so is the team.

Fight (Version 2)

The team experience was great. You really felt connected to the other members. It was more than just a group of people working on a project. The conversations that you had—about the class, your lives, and the careers that you wanted—had been wonderful. You learned about yourself in ways that you had not expected. The work was good, too. The final report is solid and you hoped to get a good grade. You had been disturbed by one small event that had occurred. You thought that the team had agreed to have several members look at the final draft before handing it in. Yet the project manager took it upon herself to hand it in because she was pressed for time. You ask her about it. The conversation did not go well, and she became defensive. She raised her voice, causing another member to intervene. That was the team's last interaction.

Simplification

The project is finally over. You are relieved. You liked some team members, and were frustrated with others. It is the frustration that you feel the most. You worked hard on the final research report, as did a few of the others, but by the final draft you didn't much care about it anymore. You just wanted it over. Another teammate—who had become a friend during the course—called you on your attitude. He cared a lot more than you did at the end, and indeed, was sad that the team was over, saying that he learned a lot on this team, even though there were some members who did not carry their weight. You laugh sarcastically, telling him that it's one thing for others not to carry their weight, and another for you to have to carry them when all you really want to do is dump them over the side of the ship. You say that you feel sorry for whoever has to have them on their teams in the future.

Each of these represents a particular form of avoidance. In the first scenario, you simply deny that the team is ending. "See you later" is widely used to avoid more honest, and more difficult, parting words: "We'll never be on this team, in this course, ever again. I wanted to tell you what this experience was like for me." You will never have to say those words—or engage in the conversation that would likely follow—as long as you pretend that the team is not really ending. "See you later" is a well-understood code for "I might or might not run into you again, but either way, we don't have to talk about the ending of this team or our relationship." Denying that experiences or relationships are ending lets you act as if they are simply paused rather than halted. It lets you avoid potentially difficult emotions or conversations from which you might well learn a lot.

The avoidance of difficulty, and of learning, occurs in other forms as well. In the second scenario you postpone the team's ending by acting as if it will continue even when it cannot. You might well gather again with members of your team but it will not be a reunion: The team cannot again exist, given the absence of the particular reason, time, and context that gave its existence purpose and meaning. It might well re-form, in some configuration, but it will have to create itself anew. The notion of a reunion thus simply puts off (often forever) coming to terms with the ending of an experience or relationships that you found mostly positive and would rather not see end. Similarly, you might avoid endings of experiences or relationships that you found mostly negative, not with promises of reunions, but by simply fleeing. In the third scenario, you leave without comment. The class ends, you pack up and go, as if leaving the scene of a crime. Leaving in such ways is an attempt to close the door on an experience or relationship, turn the key in the lock, and go away. Such flight makes impossible the resolution of and learning from bad experiences.

The fourth and fifth scenarios offer variations on another defensive maneuver: picking a fight to avoid meaningful dialogues. In the fourth scenario, the team struggles with and argues over the final presentation. The final explosion was over a relatively minor issue—the color of the slides—but represented pent-up issues and emotions that had not been resolved earlier. The explosion threw members away from one another, as they withdrew or got angry. This helped avoid real conversations about how members were and had been working together. In the fifth scenario, as a member of a more functional team, you also engineered an argument, for different reasons but with similar results. Like a couple that argues just before parting for a lengthy separation, you pick a fight to avoid feeling the impending loss. It is easier for some of us to feel angry than sad. Fighting mobilizes us to leave, fueled by anger that masks sadness. In both cases we create reasons for anger that propel us away from others.

The sixth scenario shows a more complicated form of avoidance. On this team you and the other member split your emotional reactions to the ending of the team. You just felt frustrated and annoyed with others who you were glad to be rid of. Your friend was sad that the team was ending because he had mostly enjoyed the experience and learned a lot, in spite of dealing with others who did relatively little. You could understand these different reactions in terms of personality—one person is more negative and drawn to anger, and the other is more upbeat and positive. But you could also look at these reactions as a response to the team ending. Such endings typically invoke multiple reactions. You are sad that you won't be working with some members or that some parts of the project are over; you are relieved that the project is finally done; you are frustrated and angry with some members who never really stepped up and did good work; and you are glad to have learned what you did on this team. It is not easy to feel all of these emotions simultaneously, particularly when some are contradictory. You therefore end the team by choosing a primary emotion to hang onto. Others do the same. You thus avoid the difficult work of reconciling the different facets of your experience. You tell yourself a simplified version of the story of the team and leave it at that.

Each of these scenarios shows a way to avoid the complexity of ending your team experience. Each is grounded in the desire not to have potentially difficult conversations, in which people would admit to and feel emotions that they would rather not feel, such as sadness, anger, guilt, shame, or frustration. These emotions are very much a part of the story of a team, and of its ending. Each form of avoidance thus limits your abilities to come to terms with the experience of being on the team—to figure out what happened, and what did not, and move on unencumbered by what was not resolved or understood. When you end in such ways, you do not end; you simply leave. The difference is that between leaving your house and closing the front door so firmly that you are not distracted by the possibility of having left it open versus leaving it ajar and being preoccupied by having done so. It is the difference between closure and nagging uncertainty.

Closure

The better ways to end your team leave you with a sense of closure. Psychologists speak of the importance of closure, and with good reason. Closure resolves tension. Without a sense of closure an experience remains unresolved; it remains open, like an unsolved crime, and takes up space within you. You're thinking about it even when you're not; you're reacting to it even when you're in the midst of a different situation entirely; you're replaying its main events even when you're trying to work on something else. You're in a state of tension, waiting, even when you're not waiting, for resolution. Events happened on your team that were confusing or upsetting. They will remain that way, even as they recede into the past, unless you come to some deeper understanding of those events that enables you to let them go, to stop puzzling over them or let them continue to upset you.

Imagine, for example, that you were on a team like that in the flight scenario given earlier. The team did not work together well. You did not like many of the members, who were cliquish and not very interested in working hard on the project. You were frustrated much of the time, and at times, plain angry. You left the room after the final class without speaking to the other members, even the one or two who had worked with you. The team is over, as far as you're concerned, and you have no desire to think about the experience again. Then you're on another project team in another course. You're more careful now; you don't want to get taken advantage of again. You hold back. You volunteer for little. You watch and wait to see who else will step forward. You do not try and make friends on this team. You try not to care as much.

The problem here is that the first team experience is not really over for you. You keep reacting to it even though you are on a new team. Your frustration and anger, held over from before, shape your current behaviors. You are trapped in a story that should have already ended. The story running within you is of being on a team with others who value you only for your efforts on the project, treat you as an outsider, and exploit your desires to do well academically. This story is flawed and incomplete, even as it contains some truth. It does not take into account the others' experiences, perceptions, and interpretations. Your story holds you at the center, as hero or victim or protagonist. It is biased toward how you *wish* to see yourself. As long as you hold onto that story—indeed, as long as that story holds onto you—you will be unable to learn more completely how others perceived you and what you did to earn those perceptions. You will act in ways on your new team (and on the teams after that) that will make your story once again come true: As you hold yourself apart from new teammates, they will see you as an outsider and treat you accordingly. You've created a self-fulfilling prophecy. You trap yourself into reliving your earlier team experiences.

Closure is the process of assigning the proper meaning to the past, to the point that you are able to mentally and emotionally close the door on events that you now understand and accept. You are no longer preoccupied with what was or what might have been. Closure has both cognitive and emotional dimensions. The cognitive dimension involves developing a useful understanding of an experience that helps you resolve lingering questions or concerns. It's like going to a play or a movie in which there is some mystery—why certain events happened, what people's motives were, or who did what—that you finally come to understand. With understanding comes resolution: You don't have to think about it anymore because the story is complete. The emotional dimension of closure involves letting go of the feelings that you carry away from an experience. The emotions that you do not express—anger, resentment, sadness, gladness, guilt, and appreciation—swirl around within you even as you resolve to push them away. They take up residence within you. Expressing them, to your teammates or elsewhere, enables you to let them go. They no longer have you so tightly in their grip.

Closure is thus about relief. It involves the ending of a state of suspension— of not knowing, not understanding, not letting go—and getting on with your next set of experiences. This is important, but it is not easy. You might will yourself to believe that you have finished with your team, even though the experience of that team has not really finished in you. Aspects of that experience are still rattling around inside you. To stop and look carefully at those aspects is in many ways an act of courage, particularly when others are in midflight. It takes courage to push for conversations that others—and you, too—would rather avoid. These are challenging conversations, literally: They force you and your teammates to challenge the simplicity and bias of the stories that you wish to tell and believe about the team experience.

Goodbyes

So what does getting closure mean, in practice? It means saying goodbye. Not just the word, of course, but the conversation involved in a satisfying process of bidding others farewell. When you truly wish to say goodbye to others, you don't just wave to them and say "See you later." You sit with them, over coffee or a meal, and have a real conversation. You tell stories. You laugh. You tell them what you think they should know and might not. You listen to what they have to say about you. You talk about what did happen, and what did not, and how you felt about that. You review what went well. You talk about what might have gone better, and what you each might have done to make that happen. You express sadness or lingering frustration, when that is what you feel. You express gladness for what you were glad for. That is a proper goodbye, infused with meaning. It is a leave-taking process marked by respect for the process of learning with and from others.

There are two sets of goodbyes to give and receive. There is closure with the team as a whole. When everyone is present it becomes possible to complete the picture, as each member adds a piece to the jigsaw puzzle of what happened on the team. You cannot complete the story of your team by yourself or with just a few of your teammates, so you need to get together and tell the story of the team. You all talk about how you began. You talk about how the work went, revisiting the critical events. You talk about how and why the team was successful in some ways and not in others. You talk about what it felt like to be on the team, and how those feelings changed over the course of the project. You clear up mysteries, explaining as best as you can why you were as you were on the team, and asking others why they did what they did. You try to learn as much as you can about how you were perceived by others. You thank one another. You forgive one another, openly or silently. Then you say goodbye to the team.

There is also closure with particular members of the team, with whom there is unresolved tension. You argued with one teammate early in the project, after which you avoided her as much as you could. You resented another teammate for undermining you in front of the others and never addressed it with him. You really appreciated the support of another at a difficult time and never told her. You felt a real connection with a teammate and were in the process of becoming friends but never told him that the relationship was important to you. In each case there is something unresolved, a loose end left hanging. Closure means tying up that loose end. These are face-to-face conversations, ideally, in which you find ways to speak truthfully to others of your thoughts and feelings.

These are dialogues, not monologues. You should leave your conversations with a deeper understanding of others' motives and experiences. You should leave with an expanded sense of your own contribution to events and interactions. You should leave relieved of the burden of carrying emotions that should be expressed and let go. You cannot control how they will be received or where the conversations might lead, but you can control the extent to which you leave your team carrying experiences that should be left behind.

These are useful endings. They help complete what needs to be completed. They clear up confusion and misunderstanding. They let you leave situations behind even as you carry their lessons and meanings with you. They offer final opportunities for learning what you can about teams and about yourself. They present the final toll on the journey that you began some time ago. Paying that toll—moving into and through these ending conversations—enables you, finally, to arrive at a destination of learning.

Final Lessons: The Inner World of Project Teams

This book has focused on the inner world of your project team: on the dynamics of relationships, on struggles and conflicts, and on the emotions that shape your actions and reactions. The inner world exists just below the surface of the project itself, influencing the conversations and decisions regarding what you work on and how you do so. Unless you pay attention to what occurs there, your journey will be difficult, if not halted. If you do not attend to relationships, they fray and then tear. If you do not pursue difficult conversations, they will pursue you, reappearing when you are least suspecting and least prepared. If you do not acknowledge emotions, they will grow in scope and power, driving individuals to act them out in ways that are counterproductive, often destructive. The inner world demands attention. You ignore it at your own peril.

There are four themes related to the inner world of project teams that have traversed the chapters of this book. I offer these themes by way of conclusion. Each has direct relevance to future project teams of which you will be a member.

The Anxiety of Learning

One theme throughout the book has been the tension that most of us experience between wanting and not wanting to learn what we do not know. We are often ambivalent about learning. We understand intellectually that we do not know as much as we need to, about any particular subject, about teams, and about ourselves. We therefore believe that we should want to learn as much as we can. Yet learning provokes anxiety. This anxiety can be located in our insecurity that we should already know all that we need to. Learning might unsettle our sense of what we already know. We might feel shame in needing help. Our anxiety might reflect the difficulty of letting go of our habitual ways of doing certain things or understanding certain situations. Or it is located in the threat that new knowledge poses to the ways in which we like to see ourselves. We might learn information—such as how we are perceived by others, or the true effects of our behaviors on others—that upsets our sense of ourselves, the identities that we like to have for ourselves. The anxiety of learning stands in counterpoint to our desires to learn.

You have seen this tension play out in the course of your project teams. You have seen yourself and your teammates approach and avoid learning how to work together more effectively. You have seen teammates ask for feedback but not really take it in. You have seen your team try and reflect on certain events but avoid the real issues beneath the surface of those events. You knew that there was learning that needed to occur, but the team backed away from certain areas, as members signaled their inabilities or unwillingness to go to places that were too threatening. Your team both had and did not have the conversations that would have produced real learning and change. This simultaneous movement toward and away from difficult areas shows us the anxiety and ambivalence surrounding learning. The usual result is lessons that are half-learned and shrugged off when they conflict with what individuals would like to believe about themselves and their experiences.

The problem is that you need to learn as much as you can if you are to grow as a person and get better at what you do and how you work with others. You've struggled with this throughout the project team experience, even when you were not aware of doing so. These struggles are made more complicated by the nature of personalities, yours and those of your teammates. Learning is not easy if you are insecure and try to protect yourself from feeling stupid or vulnerable. It is not easy if you are uneasy with intimacy, in that learning about yourself involves being truly known and seen by others for who you really are. Nor is learning easy if you have difficulty trusting others to help rather than harm you. Learning requires you to open yourself up to others on whom you are dependent for expertise, information, perceptions, resources, and support. If you have had bad experiences in the past with others on whom you were similarly dependent, it makes it more difficult to trust others who do so in the present.

So what do you do, given the anxiety and the personal baggage around learning? You do your best to remain as present with the task of learning as you possibly can. You strive to pay as much attention as you can to information, about yourself or your circumstances, that comes your way. A lot came your way on your team. It started in the very beginning, when you discussed the mission of your team and how to accomplish that mission. There was an opportunity there to learn about what you and others really wanted, and did not want, from the team experience. There followed more and more opportunities to learn about yourself, as a leader and a follower, and the conditions under which you were most and least effective in those roles. There were situations in which you might have learned how teams get stuck, and then figure out how to make progress, and your own effects on those processes. There were times when others were communicating, overtly or covertly, how they perceived you, and why, and to what effects. If you were present at any of these moments—truly and deeply engaged in trying to figure out what lessons they have to offer you, individually and as a member of your team—then you learned, in spite of the pulls not to do so.

Such presence makes itself clear. When you're present you try to understand others' experiences and points of view rather than automatically dismissing or arguing against them. You seek information that will help you understand how the team can improve its effectiveness rather than blame others and give up on change. You say what you think and feel rather than remain silent or agree just to avoid conflict. You remain open to weighing arguments and facts rather than stay closed to any position other than your own. You are open to difficult conversations that might lead to difficult emotions rather than avoid the possibility of discomfort. You offer constructive, useful feedback to others in ways that show respect rather than avoid potentially difficult truths or act destructively. You seek feedback from others and value their perceptions and experiences as a source of learning rather than defend against and dismiss what you would rather not hear. You are, finally, curious about the team and yourself rather than overly certain about why events occur as they do. It is when you are present in such ways that learning best occurs.

Such learning flourishes in settings designed for that purpose. The team development exercises presented in this book were guides to help you create those settings. They provided ways for you to set aside time to address the process of your team—its inner world—and temporarily suspend your focus on content per se. They were meant to provide the structure, process, and conditions for minimizing your individual and collective anxiety about learning. When your anxiety is lessened, you are more likely to become present for the task of learning. You can let yourself learn and help others learn as well. The desire to continue learning grows, and strengthens in resolve to all that keeps you from doing so.

The Usefulness of Emotions

The central place of emotions has appeared as another theme throughout this book. The feelings that you have during the journey you took with your team are an important dimension of that experience. You might not have been completely aware of this. There is the unspoken but powerful belief that our emotional lives should be kept away from our work lives, as if the former might somehow disturb and weaken the latter. The underlying notion is that the world of work—and of project teams—is highly rational, organized by data and facts that are marshaled into clear argument and precise decision making. This is, of course, an illusion, sustained by a wish to control all that we cannot control. Your emotions are central to your life, at work as elsewhere. They inform your experiences. The more clearly you understand how they shape your thoughts and actions, the better off you are. Much of this book has focused on helping you with precisely that sort of understanding as you tried to create an effective team.

You might have experienced any number of emotions throughout your experiences on the team. You felt pleasure at a job well done or how well your team worked together. You resented the inequity of how the workload was distributed. You were angry at the inability of a teammate to communicate effectively, which meant more work for others. You were frustrated with how much time it always seemed to take for the team to make simple decisions. You were relieved when several teammates did most of the work on some aspect of the project by themselves. You felt guilty when you did not show up to help the team pull together a presentation the night before it was due. You were sad when a teammate messed up a part of a presentation for which she had not been prepared. You felt satisfied with how your team went about resolving a disagreement and arrived at a good decision together.

Such emotions are inevitable, given that you are a human being equipped with emotional apparatus that gets triggered in certain ways by certain events. These emotions are inordinately useful. They are powerful signals—sent by you, to be received by you—about whether you and your team need to change or remain the same. The positive emotions that you feel at any particular point in time tell you that whatever is happening should keep happening. The negative emotions that you feel give you the opposite signal: Whatever is happening should stop happening, and you or the team should do things differently. Your emotions are thus a sophisticated system for diagnosing areas for stasis and change. If you followed the paths to which your emotions are pointing they would lead toward continuous learning and process improvements.

So what might that look like? You would not only have your emotions but also reflect on them, examining their origins, possible meanings, and interpretations. You would try and figure out the messages embedded within your emotions, what they signal about what needs to change. You would thus act as if emotional experiences—yours and those of your teammates—are useful, valid sources of information. Indeed, you would behave as if the emotions that you experience on the team are, in part, triggered in you by the team: You contain them on behalf of the team, which needs them expressed and understood. Your anger at a teammate who agrees to a task and then shirks her work contains a larger message that the team needs to hear and work with: Its systems of equity, communication, and accountability are weak. Your guilt about remaining silent during a difficult decision-making process contains a larger message about the team's way of handling conflict and disagreement. Your emotions are your own, of course, but they also imply important aspects of the context in which they are triggered.

Taking this notion seriously means becoming an observer and interpreter of your emotions as a member of a team. You would thus reflect on your feelings, naming them to yourself, believing that they matter not just to you but for others, voicing them to others, and working to figure out what they might mean for you and for your teams. You might feel perfectly comfortable with this sort of process, having done this before, or you might feel less comfortable. It is not an easy process. It leaves you vulnerable. You might express a feeling that makes others uncomfortable, causing them to push you away ("That's about you, not us") to push away that feeling. You are then left to figure out yourself how much that feeling is, indeed, reflective of you ("that's your problem") and how much it is a signal that you picked up and to which the team needs to pay attention. It is neither simple nor effective to do that work alone. It is always risky to express your feelings, in that it might leave you being pushed away by others.

But consider the alternatives. You sit on your feelings, hoping that if you ignore them they will lessen or go away. The problem, of course, is that they usually do not. The more that you try and push your feelings away, the stronger they get. They might go underground, but they'll reappear somewhere else, in ways you might not be able to control. You'll then act out your anger or disappointment or frustration. Or you might withdraw: With no way to express your emotions, they sit there, blocking your ability to feel better about and contribute more effectively to the team. You can suppress emotions only at a cost to yourself and to your team. The team needs the information that your emotions provide, even if members would rather not hear and try to understand them.

This theme has been constant through the book. It is far better to interpret and try to work with your feelings during your team's journey than to be held captive by them. The team development exercises gave you various chances to name and work with emotions, in the service of identifying and resolving places where you got stuck. Ideally, you used those exercises to help your team, and at the same time, develop the skills necessary to move through difficult situations. These skills are transferable, but they require repetition. You cannot wait for formal team exercises to express your feelings and use them to inform team change. You need to create those interruptions yourself, as strong emotions emerge. Emotions provide the momentum for real change, but only if you let them. If you do not, and turn away from them, they become corrosive.

The Nature of Complicity

A third theme in the book has been how easily teams fall into patterns of behavior and how difficult it is to break free of those patterns. Your team argued in certain ways or avoided doing so. Your decisions came too quickly or too slowly. You created an efficient way to divide and conquer the project, which created barriers that you were or were not able to overcome. You let certain people lead, and not others, or you avoided any leadership at all. Your team created these patterns for reasons good and bad. The team followed its course and, like a train making its way along a track, would not be easily derailed.

It is not likely that you would have had a lot of success in changing the course of your team unless you had become aware of how you and your teammates were collectively responsible for its patterns. The premise here is that no repeated behavior occurred on your team unless you *allowed* it to do so. Any pattern of behavior—of leadership and followership, decision making, managing disagreements, subgroups and cliques, overly polite or rude discourse, and so on—could only remain if you were complicit with it. Otherwise, it would disappear, over time or suddenly. Teams have a great deal of power to encourage or extinguish behaviors. The power is that of attention: The more you attend to others for what they do, the more you reward them and their behaviors. You literally "pay" attention, as if compensating them for what they do on your behalf. Liking the payment, they continue the performance. Conversely, the less that you attend to others for what they do (the less that you "pay" them) the less you reward their efforts. They will withdraw their services and either seek to provide them elsewhere (i.e., withdraw) or find another way to have attention paid to them (i.e., change). The simple act of rewarding others with your attention or punishing them with the lack thereof is an inordinately powerful tool by which to shape team behaviors.

So what does this mean, in practice? You gave some team members more influence than others, attending more to what they did and said. You participated, actively or passively, in ways of making decisions or handling disagreements. You kept with a culture of inequity, politeness, cliquishness, or healthy feedback by acting in such ways or not opposing those who did. You were complicit, an accomplice. If asked, you might not have agreed with such patterns. You might believe them antithetical to what you are, what you stand for, and what you believe. Yet there you are, part of a team in which certain patterns hold true. It is difficult to acknowledge complicity. It might have been active, as you pushed for certain ways of working and interacting, or it might have been passive, as you remained silent or protested little while others acted in certain ways. There is little difference, really: By commission or omission, the team reflected you as much as it did any other member.

This might not sit well with you. You might not wish to admit that, consciously or unconsciously, you *wanted* the team to create the patterns that it did, even as those patterns distressed you. Teammates were rude or disrespectful to one another. They ostracized one member who was different. They wasted time, procrastinated, did a poor job. They dumped all the work on one or two people. When these behaviors occurred (or something like them) you were there, as actor or audience. If you did not help stop them, they had your tacit permission. But why would they? Probably because ongoing patterns, even those you disliked, served some of your needs as well, enough so that you were not willing to try hard enough to alter them. Those needs were there, somewhere under the surface, driving your complicity. They lay beneath your conscious thought that "it just wasn't worth dealing with" or that "there was nothing that you could do about it."

This is not an easy message to absorb. It holds you responsible for patterns and events on your team even when you feel that you're not. The message is rooted in what we know about group dynamics. We know that issues arise as people figure out how to work together. We know that certain individuals step forward to take the lead on those issues, based on how stirred up they get, and that others step back and let them do so. They are the lightning rods, attracting and absorbing the heat and light of striking issues and sparing those around them from direct attack. Specific members, for example, get worked up about control and leadership, equity of workload, or quality issues. The rest of the team lets them do so, waiting for some sort of resolution to emerge. We also know, however, that as a "bystander," you are complicit rather than innocent in the resolutions that emerge; you provide or withdraw support in ways that shape outcomes. You do this based on your own reactions to the issues. You let others waste time, for example, because you too are frustrated with the ambiguity or meaninglessness of the project. You let the team fall into rudeness because you too are angry with members who do not show up to meetings. When you take the lead on certain issues, others become complicit in their silence, their lack of real protestation and engagement.

There were lots of opportunities during your project team journey to learn about the nature of complicity. There were moments in which you chose silence, and in doing so, implicitly affirmed what was happening on your team. There were moments in which you used your voice and tried to alter patterns. That takes courage, given that others are invested in the status quo and will not lightly give it up, as it serves their needs. They resist you then, pushing you away or trying to convince you, trying to protect set patterns. Many of the interventions described in this book were designed to help you find and use your voice as the instrument by which to name and alter patterns in which your team was stuck. It was your willingness and ability to engage your voice that mattered the most.

To do so, you had to find your way past simple stories that kept you complicit. The team was not getting anywhere not because members were lazy or incompetent, a member had taken over, or two members did not like one another and were constantly arguing. It was stuck because of more complicated issues—an overly ambiguous assignment, cultural differences regarding the importance of work relationships, conflicting views about desirable outcomes. These more complicated issues require more complex understandings. You can develop such understandings by looking for explanations for ongoing patterns other than the simple ones related to individual personalities, agendas, and relationships. This moves you away from mere complicity and into conscious awareness of the choices that you and others have made.

The Inevitability of Choices

This leads directly to the final theme. Throughout this book I point to the many places in which you had choices to make as a member of your team. These choices varied. You chose how much of your time and energy to commit to the team. You chose how much to care about others on the team and how well the team performed. You chose how much you learned about the course material, about team dynamics, and about yourself as a team member and contributor. You chose what to say and not say to others, how much feedback you gave, and how much input you provided to the team. You chose how to move toward or away from others when situations got tricky and conflicts appeared. You chose how much to share of yourself with others. You chose how much you asked for and took in feedback from others. You chose how hard to try to change things. What happened on your team—to you and to the team and its work—was a direct function of these choices.

The choices that you made reflect any number of factors. There are the habits that you've formed over a lifetime of playing and working in teams. There are the tendencies that you have, shaped by personality and predisposition. There are the strategies that you've developed to deal with anxiety or confusion. There are your own desires for closer or more distant relationships with others. There are the particular circumstances in which you found yourself during your time with this team. Such factors swirled together and led you to make choices that, in essence, were about how much of yourself you would put forth. This is the real choice that you have, on your team and elsewhere in your life. It is a choice that you kept making, over and again, as your team began and continued its journey.

My insistence throughout this book on pointing out the places where you had choices to make was to help you make those choices consciously rather than simply drift into or rush toward them. Too often people make choices without being aware that they are doing so. They simply do what they do. If asked they might give seemingly reasonable explanations, or they might say that they had no choice, it's what they had to do, obviously. But that's not the case. A course of action becomes obvious to you only after you've dismissed all other options. That's fine, as long as you've gone through a rational process of weighing those options on the basis of looking clearly at relative costs and benefits in the light of useful data. It is not so fine when you've dismissed all other courses of action out of hand, without thinking them through. You have then moved from rational to irrational thinking. There's something else going on to propel you—anxiety, discomfort, fear, avoidance—that constrains your thinking. Like a horse with blinders, you see just one path stretching out before you, and you run.

So how do you avoid this? You force yourself not to run. You pause, slow down. You consider options. You become aware that you can make a number of choices on how to act and react. You take opportunities to reflect on the choices that you're about to make or just made. The team development exercises gave you such opportunities. They let you stop and reflect and make clear choices about how to work together. Such opportunities push you to make transparent—to yourself at the very least, and hopefully to others—the choices that you are making and why you are doing so. It is, of course, your choice about what you do with those opportunities. Do you rush through them, refusing to be halted as you race toward the only options that you wish to see? Or do you use them well, allowing yourself to look curiously at yourself and your team and explore what you have done and might still do?

Of these two options, the first is the path of least resistance. It is easier to act without reflection even if the results are less than optimal. It is simpler to act as if you are not making any choices, even when you really are. Reflecting on those choices complicates matters greatly. You become aware of the fact that you are an actor, delivering lines, and a director, helping to stage the play of your team. You are not helpless. You are not an innocent victim. You are responsible, in part, for what occurred on your team. This seems obvious. Yet many of us remain unaware of our responsibility, simply because we remain unaware of the choices we made. We do not understand that choices are inevitable and that we confront them constantly, in ways big and small. It is part of being human, of having free will. It is part of adulthood. The more conscious that you are of making choices, the more clearly you will understand your own capacities to help create healthy, vibrant, and effective teams in the world.

Conclusion

Your team is finished with its work. There was a project, and you were asked to organize around completing that project. You did that, for better and for worse. There were moments during which you felt good about the team and its work, and liked its results. There were moments during which you felt quite the opposite. There were moments when you felt little at all, just doing what you needed to do and then moving to other things on your list.

Yet your team had another purpose as well. It was a chance for you to learn valuable lessons about yourself. You were faced with a number of situations, some of which you handled easily and others with more difficulty. There were moments in which you were unclear about what to do. You were faced with situations, and with teammates, that you found disconcerting or frustrating. You acted then, in ways that were probably familiar, and ways that led to results with which you were or were not pleased. The question—posed throughout this book in lots of different ways—is whether or not you used those situations as opportunities to understand that, in fact, you were faced with nothing so much as your own self.

This point is important enough to use to end this book. You have a larger hand than you might realize in creating the types of situations you faced on your team. Teammates who do too little, decisions that take too long to resolve, conflicts that never seem to get resolved, or work that is not quite good enough: Such situations are surely rooted in many factors, but just as surely you are implicated as well, through what you do and what you do not do. If you take this notion seriously, a world of learning—about yourself, about teams, and about relationships—opens before you. You need to move toward that learning. Life will keep presenting you with opportunities to learn what you most need to learn. The issues that appeared in your team have and will appear elsewhere, in other forms and settings. They are like puzzles that keep showing up until you have figured out how to solve them. You can solve them, with resolve and curiosity and support. In doing so, you will move toward solving the puzzle that is you. Your team was just another chance in a long line of chances to do that very thing.

Summary

The ending of your team presents you with some final choices to make about how to end—and more to the point, about whether to learn some final lessons about teams and how to contribute to them in the future. Although this team is ending you are likely to have many more team experiences in the future—the majority of which are likely to matter quite a bit to your life. It makes sense to learn as much as possible to carry those lessons into those experiences. This chapter focused on how you might embrace or avoid such learning—these final examinations of your team experience—and the implications of your ability to get closure on your project team experience. The ninth and final Team Development Exercise—"Team Closure"—offers a process by which you can end your team constructively and leave with a set of insights that matter.

Project Team Development Exercises

Team Development Exercise 1: Contracting

Team contracts record your initial agreements about how you will work together. The agreements are living documents, to be revisited and revised as the team progresses. The language of the contract suggests that your agreements about how to work together are, in fact, about responsibilities. Each of you is responsible for how the team functions. Each of you must thus be clear about what you are willing to do, on behalf of the team, and about what you expect to receive from participating on the team. The contracting process thus serves multiple functions. It enables you to create shared expectations for how the team will function, given a certain set of goals; begin constructing boundaries that separate your team from others; and have a voice in creating the kind of team that you wish to have.

The contracting exercise is divided into three parts.

Part I: Mission Statement

Begin with your statements of principles: what each of you cares about, in terms of what you really value and want from the team experience. Discuss the costs and benefits of your principles, and the trade-offs that you are willing to make to satisfy the team as a whole. Work together to craft a mission statement that reflects consensus about what you each want from the team experience—the prioritized outcomes for which you are willing to collectively strive.

Part II: Initial Structures

Discuss and make initial decisions about dividing and integrating your work. This involves answering, as a team, the following questions.

1. What roles do we need to get our work done?
2. How should we be led?
3. How should we divide up the work?

Discuss and make initial decisions about coordinating efforts and communicating information. This involves answering, as a team, the following questions.

1. How often do we meet as a full team?
2. What should happen at our meetings?
3. What should happen between meetings?
4. How should we use available technology?

Discuss how you will make decisions that will affect the team. This involves identifying, as a team, when to use consensus, majority rule, or other decision-making processes.

Part III: Drafting the Contract

Your initial agreements need to be recorded and distributed to all team members, with a copy to the course instructor as well. These agreements will be used—looked at and modified—throughout the life of the team.

Team Development Exercise 2: Clarifying and Improving Roles

The project team must create roles that allow for all aspects of teamwork to be performed fairly, equitably, and competently. This exercise is designed to help your teams do this. The exercise has four parts.

Part I: Meeting Organization

Each member considers the three roles that enable productive team meetings, as listed in Grid 1. Select a role that you would feel relatively comfortable performing at some point on behalf of your team. Select another role that you might not feel comfortable playing but would be good for you to get better at performing. Then mark your preferences on the grid, publicly displayed on newsprint or whiteboard.

Grid 1: Meeting Organization

	Team Member A	Team Member B	Team Member C	Team Member D	Team Member E
Leader/ facilitator					
Scribe					
Process facilitator					

Look at the completed grid as a team. Develop a collective assessment or agreement of which roles specific team members should perform. You will, of course, need to distribute your members across all roles such that each is being performed and that none have too many people trying to perform them. There are various ways to do this. You can agree that each member will perform a role with which he or she has experience and expertise, and assist in another role with which he or she feels less comfortable. You can agree on a particular rotation through which members will cycle for specified periods of time. This will require some discussion, as you and the others search for agreement on the principles by which you will decide.

Finally, develop a definition for each of the roles. Because the members of your team might have different understandings of what the roles entail, it is important to develop a common understanding of the aims and behaviors that correspond to each role. The member who is designated as the first performer of that role drives this conversation; he or she makes sure to summarize the team's consensus. If you do not find this consensus, you are setting in motion a series of disappointments. These members are responsible for recording and distributing the team's consensus on the behaviors that correspond to each role.

Part II: Project Work Organization

Repeat this process for the six roles that are relevant to organizing and completing the work of projects.

Grid 2: Project Work

	Team Member A	Team Member B	Team Member C	Team Member D	Team Member E
Project manager					
Resource					
Researcher					
Writer/ presenter					
Finisher					
Quality inspector					

Part III: Initial Feedback Process

After several weeks of meetings or project work, do an initial check on the extent to which your team members are performing their roles in ways that meet definitions and expectations. Considering each team member in turn, write down brief feedback comments on blank, unsigned index cards. Comments need to focus on the behaviors that others perform as they participate on the team. Focusing on behaviors is useful for both the giver and receiver of feedback because it spotlights specific actions that are amenable to change (rather than general personality traits and the like). Your comments should be in the following format: What should the other person: *Start* doing; *Stop* doing; *Continue* doing. Make your comments constructive. Write them with the intent to help others, not to hurt them.

Assign individuals to serve as feedback givers for one another. Each team member is thus assigned to collect the index cards that were written about another team member. The assigned giver then sets up a time to meet with the assigned receiver. Givers prepare for those meetings by reading through the cards and synthesizing them, in terms of possible themes that emerge. In the meetings themselves, the giver reads each card aloud, and then discusses the general themes. The giver and receiver work together to understand those themes, and changes in behavior that the receiver might wish to try.

Part IV: Articulating the Lessons

At your next team meeting, discuss your experiences of and reactions to the process of analyzing roles, and of giving and receiving feedback to one another. What did you learn about the team from that exercise? Each member summarizes what he or she concluded from the feedback, in terms of what behaviors he or she would work on improving. Other team members agree to provide ongoing feedback when requested to do so.

Team Development Exercise 3: Decision Rules

Team members must figure out how they will influence one another in ways that allow for shared responsibility and effective decision-making processes. This exercise is designed to help your team look at the choices that you and others have made in relation to influence and decision making. The exercise has four parts.

Part I: Sample Generation

In this first part of the exercise, you and the others identify the various decisions that your team has made thus far. Choose examples from two categories: *strategic decisions,* related to choosing courses of action; and *tactical decisions,* related to selecting how those courses will be implemented. Record the list of decisions publicly so all members can see them.

Part II: Examples of Healthy and Unhealthy Processes

Using index cards, each of you writes down items from the list typifying examples of healthy and unhealthy decision-making processes. Each member writes four index cards: two representing healthy and unhealthy strategic decisions, and two representing healthy and unhealthy tactical decisions. Mark the cards clearly so you know the categories into which they fall.

In making judgments of the health of a decision-making process, make sure that you separate *process* and *decision outcomes.* Although good processes usually produce better decisions, there are factors outside of a team's control that shape outcomes. Focus on how you experienced the process itself. Healthy decision-making processes typically involve the following: all members are able to contribute and feel listened to and heard; members base decisions on data rather than assumptions; the costs and benefits are weighed; alternatives have been closely examined; and all members are satisfied, to some extent, with the decision.

The recorder for the team gathers the index cards and, using the public list, marks the items according to how frequently they were nominated in their particular categories. Based on the frequencies, identify as a team two examples from each of the strategic and tactical decision lists—one healthy, one unhealthy—for the team to discuss in more depth.

Part III: Decision Rules

Discuss each decision-making example, beginning with the healthy and unhealthy strategic decisions and concluding with the tactical decisions. For each example, create a collective list of the healthy and unhealthy aspects of the process by which each decision was made. Describe what occurred. Seek to *understand* the processes and not give in to the urge to ignore, deny, attack, or defend what occurred.

Then identify the explicit and implicit decision rules that guided the decision-making processes. The explicit rules are relatively obvious: the use of certain leadership or facilitator roles, for example, or a majority-rules vote. The implicit rules are more difficult to decipher but crucial to uncover. These rules guided how decisions were really made: who had the most influence, the use of various tactics (humor, guilt, sarcasm), subgroups and coalitions, and the like. Describe these, without blame or recrimination.

Describe the differences between the decision rules that occurred in the healthy and unhealthy examples of strategic and tactical decisions. The purpose here is to identify the types of rules that enable healthy decision-making processes, as distinct from those that do not.

Part IV: Commitments

In the last part of the exercise, discuss why the relatively less healthy rules were followed. Talk about—and learn about—the reasons your team allowed certain patterns to occur even though you knew that those behaviors were not the healthiest for the team and that the resulting decisions were not likely to draw on the ideas and commitments of all members. If you can speak openly about why you acted as you did, you are more likely to arrive at a place of shared understanding.

Each of you then makes commitments about what you are willing to do to ensure the use of the healthy decision-making rules on the team. Focus on your own behaviors, not the behaviors of others. Frame your commitments in terms of what you are willing *to start, to stop,* and *to continue* in future decision-making processes.

Finally, discuss what you will do to ensure that members keep their commitments. Discuss the structures and interventions necessary for healthy decision-making processes. These might include authorizing certain roles (decision-making facilitator, devil's advocate) and using certain techniques (brainstorming, nominal process). They might also include using "process checks" during important decision-making situations (calling time-outs to check in with each member about the fairness of the process) and after-action reviews in which members discuss how they made strategic and tactical decisions after finishing project segments. The team commits to implementing such procedures.

Team Development Exercise 4: Team Effectiveness Pit Stop

This exercise offers a relatively simple way for your team to check how effective its processes are. Like a pit stop in a car race, your team uses this exercise to temporarily stop running so fast and check the status of the vehicle that is your team. The exercise thus offers midstream data you can use to improve particular aspects. The depth and intensity of this exercise lies somewhere between brief process checks that happen at the end of meetings and after-action reviews that enable teams to reflect on what they learned after completing significant portions of their projects (see Chapter 8 for descriptions of those exercises). This exercise has three parts.

Part I: Individual Assessments

Use the scale printed at the end of this exercise to assess particular dimensions of the team's performance. For each of the nine categories listed, circle the number that reflects your own assessment of the team's performance to this point. You should also make notes, where appropriate, of specific examples of behavior or interaction that serve as the basis for your assessments.

Part II: Analyzing Team Patterns

Your team then meets to analyze the pattern of individual ratings and see what that pattern suggests about areas of improvement. You will create, as a team, a grid to array the scores. The grid looks like the following, with individual scores filled in by each of you. Publicly display the grid so your team can look at the scores together.

	Team Member A	Team Member B	Team Member C	Team Member D	Team Member E
Learning					
Goal clarity					
Informal leadership					
Decisions					
Feedback					
Conflict					

	Team Member A	Team Member B	Team Member C	Team Member D	Team Member E
Listening					
Trust					
Innovation					

The resulting array of scores depicts the patterns of members' perceptions about your team processes thus far. The exercise involves you learning as much about those patterns as possible, and in particular, exploring the areas where a number of members believe that the team could be doing better than it is. You will need to resist trying to convince members who gave low ratings in certain areas that the team really is quite good in those areas, and it is the team members' perceptions that need to change. If this occurs, you will have missed the opportunity to learn about team patterns and how to improve them. You will have only sanctioned or isolated members who took the risk to try and improve the team's processes. If others try to convince you that your perceptions are misguided or misinformed, you need, for the sake of the team (and your own sanity), to stay true to your ratings, and insist that they matter.

Part III: Individual Commitments

The analysis of the patterns of perceptions about team processes is useful only when it leads directly to changes in members' behaviors. In this third part you need to identify strategies that will improve the team in areas you have defined as deficient. These strategies might be structural (e.g., using agendas, decision processes that require everyone's input). They might relate to how the team defines the duties of certain roles, such as the facilitator or project manager. Or they might focus on the processes by which members communicate and provide feedback to one another. Once your team identifies these strategies, each of you need to make personal commitments, clearly and concretely, about what you are willing to do more or less of to improve team processes. Unless you make these more specific commitments, the lessons are likely to remain abstract and general and not get translated into new and better team processes.

PIT STOP FORM

For each of the nine categories listed below, please circle the number that reflects your assessment of your team's performance to this point. Make notes, where appropriate, of specific examples of behavior or interaction that serve as the basis for your assessment.

1. LEARNING AND DEVELOPMENT

POOR		FAIR		GOOD		EXCELLENT
1	2	3	4	5	6	7

This team actively encourages the learning and development of its members. We make good use of the different abilities, knowledge, and experience that each of us brings to it.

This team pays little attention to the learning and development of its member. We do not make good use of the abilities each member brings to the group.

Notes:

2. GOAL CLARITY AND AGREEMENT

POOR		FAIR		GOOD		EXCELLENT
1	2	3	4	5	6	7

Our goals are unstated, confused, conflicting, and/or ambiguous.

Our goals are clear to all and shared by all. We all care about our team goals and are committed.

Notes:

3. INFORMAL LEADERSHIP AND CONTROL

POOR		FAIR		GOOD		EXCELLENT
1	2	3	4	5	6	7

Control rests with just a few. They call all the shots and the rest of us just follow. One or two people tend to dominate all our discussions, regardless of the task at hand.

Control tends to be shared within our group. Influence is based on skill and performance. Initiatives shift from one person to another, depending upon the tasks at hand.

Notes:

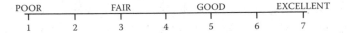

Figure 10.1

4. DECISIONS AND COMMITMENT

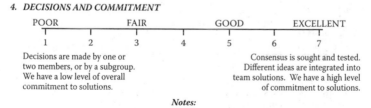

POOR   FAIR   GOOD   EXCELLENT

1   2   3   4   5   6   7

Decisions are made by one or two members, or by a subgroup. We have a low level of overall commitment to solutions.

Consensus is sought and tested. Different ideas are integrated into team solutions. We have a high level of commitment to solutions.

Notes:

5. FEEDBACK

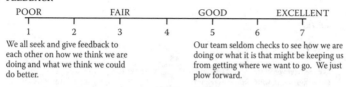

POOR   FAIR   GOOD   EXCELLENT

1   2   3   4   5   6   7

We all seek and give feedback to each other on how we think we are doing and what we think we could do better.

Our team seldom checks to see how we are doing or what it is that might be keeping us from getting where we want to go. We just plow forward.

Notes:

6. CONFLICT

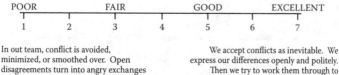

POOR   FAIR   GOOD   EXCELLENT

1   2   3   4   5   6   7

In out team, conflict is avoided, minimized, or smoothed over. Open disagreements turn into angry exchanges that are usually left unresolved.

We accept conflicts as inevitable. We express our differences openly and politely. Then we try to work them through to mutually satisfactory solutions.

Notes:

Figure 10.1   Continued

7. LISTENING

POOR		FAIR		GOOD		EXCELLENT
1	2	3	4	5	6	7

We do not listen to each other. We tend to push our own agenda. Some of us compete fiercely to be heard; others just give up. Ideas must be repeated to be heard.

We work hard at listening to each other. We listen with focused attention. We ask for clarification or elaboration of ideas. We understand and are understood.

Notes:

8. TRUST

POOR		FAIR		GOOD		EXCELLENT
1	2	3	4	5	6	7

We are relatively distrustful of one another. Communication with our group tends to be guarded and cautious. We are afraid to be frank with each other.

We have learned that we can trust one another. We encourage candor and take risks with sensitive information. We openly express our likes and dislikes about how we function.

Notes:

9. INNOVATION

POOR		FAIR		GOOD		EXCELLENT
1	2	3	4	5	6	7

We are in a rut. We operate on autopilot, exerting a lot of pressure toward conformity within the group. We have become rigid in our roles, without new ideas or new approaches.

We are flexible and value diversity. We seek new and better ways to operate. We encourage innovation and experimentation. We actively try new ideas and approaches.

Notes:

Figure 10.1   Continued

Team Development Exercise 5: Choice Points

It is important to examine the key moments that occur in the life of project teams. The underlying premise of the exercise is that the choices that you make at important moments shape the way in which your team functions. Unless those moments are looked at—put on "pause," like still pictures of a video, and examined for what they contain—they pass by unnoticed and have lasting influence. In this exercise you are asked to notice those moments. You are asked to notice the choices that you made during those moments. You have the chance to change the course set by those early choices.

The exercise involves two parts. You will need blank index cards as materials for the initial exercise.

Part I: Key Moments

Begin by recording on a blank index card what you thought were two or three key moments thus far in your team. These moments could involve anything that you found remarkable—that is, worth remarking on at the time, even if you did not do so. Such moments might include, for example, key decisions, patterns of participation, feedback given or withheld, and any interesting interactions among members.

Place your index cards on the table, shuffle them along with those from everyone, and then distribute them, one per member. Take turns reading the cards. This process ensures anonymity, enabling you to discuss the key moments without concern as to who called attention to them. Read the card you are given as though it was your own, regardless of whether that is indeed the case.

Discuss each moment, assuming that each moment that someone recorded was important in some fashion. Do not diminish or dismiss the meaningfulness of the moments. Your job is to learn as much as possible about each moment. This involves three components.

1. Look at the moments themselves: How was that moment important? How was the moment resolved?
2. Discuss your own actions and experiences during and after each moment, and the choices you made. What choice did I make at that instant, and why did I do so?
3. Look at the impact of each moment on team process: What pattern(s) of behavior did that moment set in place? How have we continued to follow those patterns?

Part II: Choosing Our Patterns

After your team discusses all the key moments written on the cards, look at the "rules" that you have implicitly been following. Formulate statements that describe those rules. For example, your statements might look like "Treat the first idea that seems reasonable as the answer and not try and come up with other possible directions and strategies," "Show up late to meetings," or "Create an agenda and then ignore it." Or statements might look like "Listen closely to others and build on their ideas," "Follow through on your commitments," or "Come prepared to meetings." Again, these statements should describe what your team really does, not what it wishes it did. Your team should formulate five to eight statements.

Discuss those operating rules in terms of the extent to which each helps and hinders the team doing its work and achieving success, however you had defined "success." For each statement, list the positive and the negative consequences. For the statement "Treat the first idea that seems reasonable as the answer," for example, the team would list efficiency as the positive, and the lack of creativity and constructive argument that leads to good decisions as the negatives.

Look at the results of the exercise and discuss which rules should be amended. Amend those rules, describing the behaviors that you would like to see. Also discuss the obstacles that might prevent you from acting according to the newly amended rules, and what the team can do to diminish those obstacles. Finally, commit to trying the new behaviors.

Team Development Exercise 6: Managing Differences

This exercise offers your team the opportunity to look closely at the ways in which it manages differences among members. Every project team develops certain "rules" by which to manage differences. These rules can be functional or dysfunctional. They are also habitual: Once created, they are difficult to revise, particularly if you are not consciously aware of using them. This exercise enables you to become aware of them, and to choose when and when not to follow them as your team progresses.

The exercise has three parts.

Part I: Individual Reflections

The first part of the exercise involves you thinking carefully about specific examples during the life of your team thus far in which differences arose and were handled in particular ways. These examples will probably involve differences in perspectives and beliefs, ideas and strategies, commitments and efforts, or styles of work and communication.

You will need to identify two types of examples. For the first example, think of a situation in which a difference was handled *well* by your team. What happened? What were the productive rules that your team seemed to be following? For the second example, think of a situation in which a difference was *not* handled so well by your team. What happened? What were the unproductive rules that your team seemed to be following? (In answering this second part of the question, refer to the list at the end of the exercise of productive and unproductive rules for managing differences, as discussed in Chapter 6.)

Part II: Team Reflection

Your team then meets to compare notes. This conversation has several components. First, each member shares his or her example of a situation in which a difference was handled well by the team, and what productive rules seemed to be in effect at the time. Second, your team should look carefully at these situations and try and figure out why they were handled well. What were the conditions that helped you and the others? What conflict styles (i.e., avoiding, compromising, competing, accommodating, collaborating) did members use during the situation?

The next conversation follows much the same path, with a focus on the situations that members felt that their team did not handle well. Each member shares his or her example of a situation in which a difference was not handled so well by the team, and what unproductive rules seemed to be in effect at the time. Again, look carefully at these situations and try and figure out why they were not handled well. What were the conditions that seemed to get in the way? What conflict styles (i.e., avoiding, compromising, competing, accommodating, collaborating) did members use during the situation? The point here, of course, is to learn as much as you can about what your team did, and why, and not seek to blame specific members.

Part III: Lessons and Commitments

The final part of the exercise involves drawing lessons from your conversations that will guide how your team acts productively while managing important differences in the future. Working together, your team needs to identify the conditions that make it more rather than less likely that you will invoke productive rules for managing differences. Then each of you needs to make specific commitments about what you need to do to help create and sustain those conditions. Your team should create a written record of the lessons, conditions, and individual commitments. This record should be distributed to each member, and placed as an addendum to your team contract.

Productive Rules for Managing Differences

- The *surfacing rule:* Allow differences to surface and breathe, and if necessary, develop into conflicts.
- The *embrace rule:* Embrace differences as opportunities for learning and creativity.
- The *framing rule:* Frame conflicts around tasks, not individuals.
- The *data rule:* Use lots of data for evaluating alternatives and resolving conflicts.
- The *interests rule:* Hang onto shared goals and interests rather than positions.
- The *perspective rule:* Approach differences with respect, concern about process, and a sense of perspective (and humor).

Unproductive Rules for Managing Differences

- The *ostrich rule:* Avoid, ignore, smooth over, suppress, laugh away, or in other ways fail to deal with differences and possible conflicts.
- The *laid-back rule:* Choose to get along rather than productively engage differences and potential conflicts.
- The *tournament rule:* Frame differences in terms of right and wrong.

- The *scapegoating rule:* Frame conflicts in terms of individuals rather than in terms of the issues they represent.
- The *export rule:* Push conflict outside the team.

Team Development Exercise 7: Informal Roles

This exercise focuses on the informal roles that you tend to take on in groups and teams. *Informal roles* are those that you assume routinely, almost instinctually. They are not assigned to you, nor do they serve an obvious purpose for the team, such as a project manager or researcher. They are simply patterns of behaviors into which you fall. They serve certain purposes for you (otherwise you would not adopt them so often), and for your team as well. These purposes might be useful, and they might not be. In this exercise you have the opportunity to look more closely at the informal role(s) that you take on and the effects on your project team. This exercise is in three parts. It should take between 60 and 90 minutes.

Part I: Naming the Roles

The first part of the exercise involves you identifying for yourself the informal roles that you have thus far played on your team. The following list contains some of the more common ones that tend to occur on project teams. Select the one that most clearly describes the type of role that you tend to play. If you play a different role than one on this list, label and choose that one instead. If you tend to play more than one role, you may select another as well. For the purposes of this exercise, do not select more than two informal roles.

The comic	The hero/heroine
The serious one	The control freak
The good one	The devil's advocate
The quiet one	The rebel
The loud one	The rude one
The soother/peacemaker	The anxious one

Part II: Checking Perceptions

Your teammates might or might not agree with your perceptions of the informal role(s) that you tend to play. You might wish to see yourself in certain ways but in fact are perceived quite differently by others. The extent to which they see you in the ways that you see yourself is a useful learning tool in itself. In the second part of this exercise you share with one another the roles that you have identified for yourselves. Each of you responds to the other, agreeing or disagreeing with the roles that were selected. There should be some consensus about the informal roles that each of you tends to assume.

Part III: Explorations

Naming the informal roles is a useful step toward understanding them in more depth. These roles serve important functions, for you and for the team, but the functions might not always be good ones. It is difficult to look at these functions by yourself. In the final part of this exercise, each of you takes a few minutes to record your answers to the following questions. Then share your answers and ask others what they think.

1. Why have you taken on your role? Is it a familiar one for you?
2. In what kinds of situations is that role triggered?
3. What are the costs and benefits of that role for you?
4. What does your role do *for* the group? What does it *cost* the group?

Conclude the exercise by talking about strategies that you can use to minimize the costs of the informal roles that each of you assume. If you are the "quiet one," for example, this might mean recognizing when you are falling into that role and forcing yourself to speak up; and it might mean others recognizing that as well, and inviting you into the conversation. Similar interventions can be designed for each informal role.

Team Development Exercise 8: Team Feedback

This exercise is designed to enable you to provide and to receive feedback from one another. At this point in the journey of your team, you have had enough experiences together to have formed some definite perceptions about one another as teammates. These perceptions shape how you treat others, and how they act toward you. More important, they are a source of information that each of you very much needs if you are to become a more effective contributor, to this team and to others that you later join. If you can find ways to share those perceptions with others, you can provide them with the opportunity to improve, now and in the future. If you can find ways to receive others' perceptions, you can provide the same opportunity for yourself. Either way, the feedback process gives your team the best possible chance to create itself into a highly performing unit.

The team feedback exercise occurs in three parts.

Part I: Preparations

You are more likely to receive and make use of feedback when you have asked for it. Preparing for the team feedback exercise thus involves each member figuring out what he or she would like to receive feedback about. The other members of your team have a certain set of particular experiences with you. This means that they have information for you that might be difficult to get from others. What might that information be? Your task in preparing for the feedback session is to frame a question that others can answer that will elicit information about yourself as a member of this team. You might ask, for example, how others perceive your leadership qualities, your ability to be creative, or how collaborative you are with others. Frame a question with an answer that you care about, and that others on your team are uniquely positioned to address.

Your team needs to distribute members' questions in advance of the feedback meeting, via e-mail or in person. Each member then takes time to make notes in response to each member's question. These notes form the basis of the feedback you will provide during the session. In framing your responses to others' questions, it is important to focus on the *behaviors* that others perform, and their effects on the team's interactions and work. This helps you stay away from more abstract (and often misleading) notions of personality traits. Prepare specific examples of the behaviors that you noticed.

Part II: Feedback

Your team should set aside approximately 90 minutes for the feedback exercise. Divide the time equally among group members. Each member will have the opportunity to be the recipient of the feedback from others on the team. Your team should identify two roles through which members can rotate during the exercise: a *timekeeper*, who keeps others aware of the time; and a *facilitator*, who helps restate questions, asks members to provide specific examples if the feedback is too general or ambiguous, and reminds members to identify both areas of strength and areas for improvement.

Team members provide feedback, based on their preparations. This is a constructive process, meant to give you and your teammates the opportunity to gather information that might lead to real improvements. It is important during this process to follow the basic principles of providing feedback to others, as discussed in Chapter 3. Make sure that when you are providing feedback, you are *describing* rather than evaluating. Describe others' behaviors and their effects, or your own experiences of situations and events that are relevant to the feedback. Your evaluations are likely to be less constructive; even if they are positive, they will offer little useful information or cause others to be defensive. It is also important when providing feedback that you do not simply agree with what others have said before you; pay attention to the notes that you made prior to the session, even if they lead you to disagree with others or make the feedback more complicated for your teammate to assimilate.

The effectiveness of this exercise also depends on how well you receive feedback. Do so without defensiveness. Take notes, writing down what others say. Do not argue or disagree. Ask for clarifications. Ask for examples, but not to explain away, only to understand others' perceptions. Make sure that you understand how others perceive you. Press your teammates for examples of areas where you can improve. Resist the urge to dismiss what they say when you don't like what you're hearing. At those moments you need to resist the desire to tell yourself a story—about how others are biased, wrong, envious, or misinformed, or about how you're not really yourself on the team, how you haven't been trying and so they don't really know the real you. These are simply ways for you not to look at the possible truth of what they're saying about you. Assume for the moment that their perceptions are valid. If so, what lessons might you take from what they're saying? If they're right, what does that mean about you? There is time later to convince yourself that they're wrong. For the short period during which the focus is on you, learn about how others might be right and what that suggests about you as a team member.

Part III: Reflections

After each member has had a chance to hear others' feedback, take a few minutes and reflect on the exercise. Talk about what it was like to give the feedback to others. Talk about what it was like to receive feedback from others. Talk, finally, about how you and the others might make it possible to give and receive feedback as you go about working together. This is important. High-performing project teams routinely find ways for members to give feedback to one another without necessarily halting their work to do so. They create mechanisms to help them do this—brief check-ins at the beginning, middle, or end of meetings or deliverables. They create patterns of communication that enable signals to be sent and received, without engendering bad feelings or defensive reactions. Spend a few minutes at the end of this exercise talking with one another about how to ensure that necessary feedback occurs as a matter of course, to avoid letting small issues of miscommunication or misalignment mushroom into larger, more destructive ones.

Team Development Exercise 9: Team Closure

The ending of your team offers a final opportunity to learn important lessons about yourself and the evolving dynamics of a project team. This final exercise focuses on closure: the thoughtful ending of your team in ways that leave you the wiser for having been on its journey. The exercise occurs in three parts, and can be completed in about 30 minutes.

Part I: Critical Incidents

One way to achieve closure is to revisit the story of your team—its high points and low points—from members' distinct points of view. Each of you should identify what you believed were the critical incidents that marked your team's journey. These were incidents that shaped the course of the team, for better or for worse; they were moments that got the team stuck or got it moving. After you've each thought of these, share them with one another. As a team, create a timeline that shows when those incidents occurred, relative to one another. Then talk briefly about the more important ones, using the following questions as guides:

1. Why did the incident occur as it did?
2. How did the team handle the situation? Then what happened?
3. Why did each member do what he or she did during the incident?
4. How might they have handled the situation more effectively?

This conversation is important. It allows your team to tell its story through the voices of all of its members. It enables your team to step back and look at its evolution—how far it has come—and the places where the journey was rougher or smoother. It enables you and your teammates to clear up some lingering mysteries, about why you and they did what they did. It also enables you, if you choose, to ask others their perceptions of you and your effects on the team.

Part II: Key Lessons

The second part of the exercise gives you the chance to articulate the lessons that you learned at the end of the team experience. Articulating for yourself concluding lessons helps you crystallize your learning; articulating those lessons for others helps them look at the experience through different eyes, and gain perspective from doing so.

Each of you should thus take a few minutes and write down answers to the following two questions: What was the key lesson that you learned about *yourself* during the project? What was the key lesson that you learned about *project teams,* in terms of why they are and are not successful, during the project? Share these lessons with one another.

Part III: Goodbyes

Finally, thank one another for whatever you can thank them for. Appreciate others for what they did, small or large. Forgive them for what they did not do, as much as you can, openly or silently. Say goodbye without recrimination or avoidance.

References

Alderfer, C. P. (1987). An intergroup perspective on group dynamics. In J. W. Lorsch (Ed.), *Handbook of organizational behavior*. Englewood Cliffs, NJ: Prentice-Hall, Inc.

Berg, D. N. (1998). Resurrecting the muse: Followership in organizations. In E. Klein, F. Gabelnick, & P. Herr (Eds.), *The psychodynamics of leadership*, 27–52. Madison, CT: Psychosocial Press.

Fisher, R., & Ury, W. (1991). *Getting to yes*. New York: Penguin.

Freud, S. (1989). *Introductory lectures on psycho-analysis*. New York: Norton.

Hackman, J. R. (1989). *Groups that work*. San Francisco: Jossey-Bass.

Harvey, J. (1989). *The Abilene paradox and other reflections on management*. New York: Lexington Books.

Janis, I. (1971). *Victims of groupthink*. New York: Houghton-Mifflin.

Kaplan, R. S., & Norton, D. P. (1996). *The balanced scorecard: Translating strategy into action*. Cambridge, MA: Harvard Business School Press.

Katzenbach, J., & Smith, D. (1993). *The wisdom of teams*. Boston: Harvard Business School Press.

Kegan, R., & Lahey, L. (2001). *How the way we talk can change the way we work*. San Francisco: Jossey-Bass.

Kolb, D. (1984). *Experiential learning*. New York: Prentice-Hall.

Schein, E. H. (1999). *Organizational culture and leadership* (2nd ed). San Francisco: Jossey-Bass.

Smith, K. K., & Berg, D. N. (1987). *Paradoxes of group life*. San Francisco: Jossey-Bass.

Stone, D., Patton, B., & Heen, S. (1999). *Difficult conversations: How to discuss what matters most*. New York: Penguin.

Thomas, K. (1976). Conflict and conflict management. In M. Dunnette (Ed.), *The handbook of industrial and organizational psychology*, 889–935. Chicago: Rand McNally.

Thomas, K., & Kilmann, R. (2002). *Thomas–Kilmann conflict mode instrument*. Palo Alto, CA: Xicom.

Training circular 25-2D (1993). Leader's guide to after-action reviews. Washington, DC: Department of the Army.

Tuckman, B. W. (1965). Developmental sequences in small groups. *Psychological Bulletin, 54,* 229–249.

Subject Index

A

Abilene Paradox, 118; *See also* Decision making
After action reviews, 27–29

B

Balanced scorecard, 9–10

C

Choices
    and consequences, 3, 117, 205–206
    choice points, 119–125, 154–166
    choice points exercise, 221–222
Conflict

    importance of, 137–140, 164–166
    managing differences exercise, 223–225
    principled negotiation, 146–147
    styles of, 148–154

D

Decision making
    biases, 154–158
    consensus, 109–110
    decision rules, 108–112

    decision rules exercise, 214–215
    tactics and techniques, 104–106, 111–112
Difficult conversations, 160–164; *See also* Conflict
Disclosure, 179–183
Division of labor
    importance of, 47–50
    inequity, 64
    roles and role clarifications, 64–72

E

Emotion, 200–203
Engagement, 170–179

F

Feedback
    feedback exercise, 228–230
    guiding assumptions of, 72–76
    informal roles exercise, 226–227
    initial feedback exercise, 212–213
    techniques, 76–78

G

Grades, the problem of, 31–37
Groupthink, 105–106; *See also* Decision making

I

Influence and authority
    authorizing processes, 92–94
    shared influence, 100–103
    stances toward authority, 96–98

L

Leadership and followership, 98–103
Learning
    and anxiety, 198–200
    and curiosity, 183–186
    avoidance of, 37, 131–133
    conditions for, 25
    nature and importance of, 13–18, 23–25
Learning teams, 26–31

M

Meetings, 65–67
meeting organization exercise, 211–212
underlying dynamics of, 131–133
Missions and purposes, 128–129
    mission statement exercise, 209–210
    mission statements, 44–46

P

Paradox of safety, 61; *See also* Team Formation
Participation, 79, 170–174
Pit-stop exercise, 216–220
Principles of movement, 127–131
Process checks, 30
Process losses and gains, 104–107; *See also*
    Decision making

R

Rules of engagement, 140–145

S

Scapegoating, 156–158; *See also* Team
    dysfunctions
Self-fulfilling prophecy, 117
Stuckness, 2, 78–81, 125–127
Success, 7–11
    and grades, 7
    and learning, 7–8
    and team interactions, 8

T

Team contribution scoring system 85–86
Team culture, 116; *See also* Team
    formation
Team development
    changing patterns of interaction, 117
    project team journey, 19–20
    stages of, 11
    tolls, 11–13
Team dysfunctions
    and accountability, 84–85
    and complicity, 203–205
    diagnosing problems, 38–40
    framing problems, 79–81, 154–158
Team endings
    avoidance of, 191–195
    closure, 195–198
    closure exercise, 231–232
Team formation, 53–59
    contracting exercise, 209–210
    communication structures, 50–52
    missions, 44–46
    role development, 47–50, 175–176
Team projects
    project roles exercise, 212
    quality standards, 82–83
    useful roles for, 67–70
Team warning and termination process,
    87
Trust
    creating, 88–89
    importance of, 86–89
    and safety, 133–134

Author Index

A

Alderfer, C., 159

B

Berg, D., 61, 100, 125, 185

D

Deacon, S., 87

F

Fisher, R., 146–147
Freud, S., 96

H

Hackman, J. R., 8
Harvey, J., 118
Heen, S., 161

J

Janis, I., 105

K

Kaplan, R., 10
Katzenbach, J., 48
Kegan, R., 37–38, 40
Kilmann, R., 150
Kolb, D., 24

L

Lahey, L., 37–38, 40

N

Norton, D., 10

P

Patton, B., 161

S

Schein, E., 116
Smith, D., 48
Smith, K., 61, 125, 185
Stone, D., 161

T

Thomas, K., 149, 150
Tuckman, B., 11

U

Ury, W., 146–147